D1117910

LAND OF THE FEE

LAND OF
THE FEE

Hidden Costs and the Decline of the
American Middle Class

DEVIN FERGUS

OXFORD
UNIVERSITY PRESS

OXFORD
UNIVERSITY PRESS

Oxford University Press is a department of the University of Oxford. It furthers
the University's objective of excellence in research, scholarship, and education
by publishing worldwide. Oxford is a registered trade mark of Oxford University
Press in the UK and certain other countries.

Published in the United States of America by Oxford University Press
198 Madison Avenue, New York, NY 10016, United States of America.

© Oxford University Press 2018

All rights reserved. No part of this publication may be reproduced, stored in
a retrieval system, or transmitted, in any form or by any means, without the
prior permission in writing of Oxford University Press, or as expressly permitted
by law, by license, or under terms agreed with the appropriate reproduction
rights organization. Inquiries concerning reproduction outside the scope of the
above should be sent to the Rights Department, Oxford University Press, at the
address above.

You must not circulate this work in any other form
and you must impose this same condition on any acquirer.

CIP data is on file at the Library of Congress
ISBN 978-0-19-997016-2

1 3 5 7 9 8 6 4 2
Printed by Sheridan Books, Inc, United States of America

CONTENTS

FIGURES

———◆———

ACKNOWLEDGMENTS

This book benefited greatly from the generous input and insights of so many people. Given that this is a book about hidden costs, it's only fitting that I make at least some of the countless debts I owe public.

I've gained perspective by standing on the shoulders of individuals, colleagues, critics, mentors, and scholarly communities. In particular, Manning Marable and Alan Brinkley early on encouraged me to embark on this journey into the crisis of consumer finance, governance, and inequality at a time when access to credit seemed limitless. Elizabeth Blackmar, Fredrick Harris, Ira Katznelson, Kenneth Jackson, and Samuel Roberts all asked important questions during the nascent stages of this work. In addition, Carol Anderson, Anthony Badger, Sheldon Garon and family, Tyrone Forman and Amanda Lewis, John L. Jackson and Deborah A. Thomas, Gail O'Brien and Anthony LaVopa, Thomas Schwartz, Daryl M. Scott, and Earl Lewis offered valuable advice on research and scholarship at key moments throughout the penning of this book. George Lipsitz, whose work has always been an intellectual guidepost, provided an early venue and platform to think about the sociohistorical forces informing the topics discussed in this text and how the built and imagined environments matter to social mobility. My fellowships at the Woodrow Wilson International

Center for Scholars and the then James Weldon Johnson Institute for Advanced Study at Emory University provided generous time, place, and resources to think, exchange ideas, and write and a constellation of scholars willing to exchange their work with mine as the project was still in its conceptual stages.

Working with my book series colleagues Louis Hyman, Bethany Moreton, Julia Ott, and press editor Bridget Flannery-McCoy at Columbia University Press has been not only one of my most intellectually enriching experiences, but also great writing therapy, teaching me to trust the book development process. Their insights into book publishing could not have been replicated elsewhere.

Travel abroad provided the critical distance that is often needed when one is writing on a contemporary and fraught subject. In particular, I'm grateful for the University of Edinburgh, Northumbria University, Salzburg Global Seminars, the American Council of Germany, the Friedrich-Schiller University, and Cambridge University mates Marc Bennett, Andrew Preston, Lauren Winner, Simon Hall, Nathaniel Millett, Dominick Sandbrook, and Adam IP Smith, where my ideas about following the money—and the fees—originally took root.

I've been privileged to present or discuss various parts of my work at a wide range of venues. Some of the most informative and memorable included the Assets@21 Workshop, the Seminar on Racial Inequality at the University of Virginia, the Washington History Center, the Gilder Lehrman Institute on the American Presidency, the UIC Institute for Research in Race and Public Policy, Vanderbilt's Robert Penn Warren Humanities Center, the University of Minnesota's Crisis Economics Workshop, and the Department of City and Regional Planning Colloquium at the University of California–Berkeley.

I was also incredibly fortunate to stumble upon and be welcomed into several useful networks, working groups, and other sustained dialogues in the course of researching and writing that have sharpened my methodology and helped me make connections beyond my home discipline of history. At the University of Southern California's Dworak-Peck School of Social Work's Race Symposium, I am grateful for the contributions of Deans Marilynn Flynn, Cherrie Short, Jody Armour, Gabriel Crenshaw, Terrence Fitzgerald, Arline Geronimus, Erick Guerero, Lauren Silver, Flannery Stevens, and David C. Wilson.

From the Russell Sage Foundation Beyond Discrimination Workshop, thank you to Fredrick C. Harris, Robert Lieberman, Anthony Chen, Richard Eibach, Phillip Goff, Rodney Hero, Desmond King, Morris Levy, Devah Pager, Benjamin Radcliffe, Lisa Stulberg, Valerie Purdie Vaughans, Vesla Weaver, and Dorian Warren. The expertise of the members of the Critical Tax Perspectives Workshop—Dorothy Brown, Samuel Brunson, Bridget Crawford, Karie Davis-Nozemack, David Herzig, Anthony Infanti, Carolyn Jones, Nancy Knauer, Marjorie Kornhauser, Lynn Lu, Reginald Mombrun, Lisa Phillips, John Calvin Scott, Andre Smith, Palma J. Strand, Camille Walsh, and Sarah Webber—proved critical to my research, as did that of the Race, Debt, and Property Collective started at the University of Wisconsin's Institute for Research in the Humanities (organized by Vincent Lloyd and Amaryah Armstrong) and the Deconstructing Ferguson Working Group (Benjamin Justice, Tracey Meares, Vesla Weaver, Bennett Capers, Deirdre Dougherty, Colin Gordon, Elizabeth Hinton, Clarissa Hayward, Issa Kohler-Hausmann, Meira Levinson, Lisa Miller, Donna Murch, Melissa Nobles, Josh Page, Andrew Papachristo, Manuel Pastor, Megan Quattlebaum, Daria Roithmayr, David Schleicher, Rogers Smith, Joe Soss, Forrest Stuart, Tom Sugrue, Gerald Torres, Tom Tyler, and Bruce Western). In addition, I am grateful for my relationships with the Closing the Racial Wealth Gap Initiative, Experts of Color Network, and Asset Building Network.

Dialogues with think tanks, consumer advocates, and policy research organizations have made me a better writer and communicator while drawing out the real-world implications of my book. Most notably, I thank Reid Cramer and Justin King of New America, Maya Rockeymoore of the Center for Global Policy Solutions/Closing the Racial Wealth Gap Initiative, Anne Price of Insight CCED, Deborah Douglass and Michelle Weldon of the OpEd Project, Pamela Chan and Lillian Singh of Prosperity Now, Nikitria Bailey of the Center for Responsible Lending, and David Wessel of the Brookings Institute.

I'm deeply indebted to the large number of people who've taken time from their very busy lives to read or comment on parts or the entirety of the book: Eric Arnesen, Brian Balogh, Mehrsa Baradaran, Drucilla Barker, Taroue Brooks, Thomas Bynum, Rudolph Byrd, Sheryll Cashin, Sewell Chan, David Chappell, Marcia Chatelain, Julie

Chu, Simona Combi, Nathan Connolly, Reid Cramer, Joe Crespino, Sandy Darity, Rajeev Darolia, Rajeev Date, Michael Dreyer, William Elliott, Julia Elyachar, Mona Frederick, Norbert Frei, David Freund, Terri Friedline, Brett Gadsden, Margaret Garb, Vinay Gidwani, Andra Gillespie, Mary Graybeal, Walter Greason, David Greenberg, Darrick Hamilton, Claudrena Harold, Bob Herbert, Jesus Hernandez, Karen Ho, Andrew Kahrl, Michael Katz, Bob Korstad, Nelson Lichtenstein, Vincent Lloyd, William Roger Louis, Henry Knight Lozano, Geoff Mann, Waldo Martin, Timothy P. McCarthy, Deborah McDowell, Ajay Mehrotra, Zebulon Miletsky, Derek Musgrove, Jörg Nagler, Tamara Nopper, Rowena Olegario, Christian Ostermann, Mario Owens, Cassi Pittman, Paul Quigley, Carolina Reid, Caroline Rosenthal, Adam Rothman, Beryl Satter, Trina Shanks, Thomas Shapiro, Tracey Sharpley-Whiting, Brenda Stevenson, Joe Street, Pat Sullivan, Kathrine Sydor, Keeanga-Yamahtta Taylor, J. Phillip Thompson, Natasha Tretheway, Wallace Turbeville, Brian Ward, Adia Harvey Wingate, and Julian Zelizer. For research assistance, thank you to Krista Benson, Tim Boyd, Lathania Brown, Chayli Buenger, Tawanda Chabikwa, Natalie Dalea, Robert Donnelly, Rachel Fazzina, Michael Gawlick, Julia Istomina, Juwon Lee, Kimberly McKee, Haley Swenson, Lauren Todd, and Christy Wolf, and the University of North Carolina Center for Community Capital.

Thanks to Heather McGhee, Richard Benjamin, David Callahan, Tamara Draut, and Lew Daly for bringing me into the Demos family. During my tenure as a Demos fellow, I have had a perfect training ground to (re)learn the lesson that conveying complex ideas with clarity is what breathes meaning into scholarship in a liberal democracy. It has also given me the opportunity to meet and work with Robert Frank, Bob Herbert, and Wallace Turbeville, some of the most innovative minds in policy, finance, media, and journalism dedicated to the singular purpose of advocating for economic democracy.

The Rubicon Production team of Drew Perkins, Alex Jennings, Terence McArdle, and Marcus Smith gave me fresh insights into work, in the process helping me to reach an entirely new audience, by retelling it through the medium of film.

Of course, this book would have no foundation without the tireless work of countless archivists and librarians, including Kelly Barton

(Ronald Reagan Presidential Library and Center for Public Affairs); Brooke Clement, Tally Fugate, and Malisa Lewis (George W. Bush Library); Jason Kaplan (William J. Clinton Presidential Library and Museum); David Nickles (National Archives); Alex Rankin (Howard Gottlieb Library at Boston University); and Hillary Bussell (Ohio State University Library).

I've also been the beneficiary of supportive and caring colleagues. At Vanderbilt, Michael Bess, Richard Blackett, William Caferro, David Carlton, Kathrine Crawford, Dennis Dickerson, Marshall Eakin, James Epstein, Gerald Figal, Gary Gerstle, Joel Harrington, Yoshikuni Igarashi, Sarah Igo, Shafali Lal, Jane Landers, Liz Lunbeck, Moses Ochonu, Ruth Rogaski, Helmut Smith, Arleen Tuchman, and Eddie Wright-Rios were unflinching in their willingness to read some of the earliest drafts of my chapters and fellowships. Among other things, I'm grateful they selected Tom Schwartz as my mentor. A young scholar could have no better sounding board or ally. Similarly, at Hunter, Rick Belsky, Manu Bhagavan, Eduardo Contreras, Donna Haverty-Stacke, Daniel Hurewitz, and Jonathan Rosenberg helped me to think about the broader implications of my work while showing me and my family remarkable compassion during a challenging time. At Ohio State, my colleagues—Adeleke Adeeko, Leslie Alexander, Curtis Austin, Monika Brodnicka, Trevor Brown, Simone Drake, Kenneth Goings, Robert Greenbaum, Joshua Hawley, Dana Haynie, Katie Hogan, Judson Jeffries, Kwaku Korang, Valerie Lee, Stephanie Moulton, Lupenga Mphande, Linda Myers, Ike Okafor-Newsum, Jos C. N. Raadschelders, Molly Reinhoudt, Cheikh Thiam, Marquitta Tyler, and Katie Vinopal—helped me consider the impact of my research on America's most vulnerable populations. At Missouri, I've been welcomed into another wonderful community of scholars—Irma Arteaga, Christina Carney, A. Cooper Drury, Daive Dunkley, Keona Ervin, Tristan Ivory, Emily Johnson, Lael Keiser, Corey Koedel, April Langley, Victor McFarland, Ronald McGarvey, Jeffrey Pasley, Catherine Rymph, Jay Sexton, Stephanie Shonekan, Robert Smale, Jonathan Sperber, Mary Stegmaier, Barton Wechsler, and John Wigger—who've helped me bring the journey this book has taken me on to a successful end.

This book, too, is a testament to remarkable editorial, production, and marketing people working with Oxford University Press. My editor, David McBride, has been a master navigator—prodding, cajoling, and delegating with a discerning eye for detail, narrative, and the big picture. Erin Meehan, Damian Penfold, Claire Sibley, Reynesh Vittal, and Kathleen Weaver have brought both creative and commercial acuity throughout the editorial, production, and marketing phases of this book.

My family has been my chief source of comfort and counsel throughout the many twists and turns of this book. My six-year-old son, Devin Hiro ("Ziggy"), has brought a clarity of purpose to my life and urgency to my work. His curiosity is both boundless and endlessly reinvigorating. I come home each day to see the ways in which intergenerational mobility has (and has not) touched his life. And though he knows me only as his father, he has unquestionably made me a better person and scholar. If my writing comes with impatience, it is born out of knowing how the wrong choices made by my generation and previous ones have heightened barriers to mobility for him and his generation. In many ways, this book started with my brothers, Will and Troy, whose half century of knowledge about financial and regulatory culture helped in innumerable ways to explain the quotidian and systemic behavior of market actors and those the public has charged with overseeing them. On a more personal note, my family members—the Ferguses: Debbie, Sonia, Bella, Troy, Jr., and Tori; and the Itagakis and Louies: Dr. Brian and Mrs. Gale Itagaki, Lisa, Lori, Greyson, and Graden—have helped immensely by sharing their homes with me during conferences and research trips.

To my parents, Mr. Willie J. and the late Mrs. Jane Field Fergus, thank you for living lives well worth emulating and for teaching your children never to countenance or absolve injustice and inequality. Finally, to Lynn Itagaki, there's not enough space in this book to share the deep gratitude and love for what you mean to Ziggy and me. The only thing that I can think of that's better than the past we've shared is our future.

LAND OF THE FEE

Introduction

How you finance an asset can be as important as the asset.
                                                 —St. Louis Federal Reserve[1]

"WHAT BUGS AMERICA MOST?" Posed to the readers of *Consumer Reports* in the immediate aftermath of the Great Recession, this question had a simple answer: fees. Specifically, "unexpected" or "hidden" fees ranked as the American consumer's top complaint.[2]

While the Great Recession may have officially ended in 2009, fees continue to drain our bank accounts one drip at a time. Since the 1980s Americans have been increasingly subject to fees, often without knowing why they are being charged. We pay fees at home, at work, at school, and on our cars. Even retirement savings are not safe from the steady drain of fees. Fees are no longer merely an annoyance. The massive revenues collected from fees contribute to the "systematic transfer of wealth" from the pocketbooks of consumers to the coffers of wealthy corporations and individuals, according to the National Economic Council for an outgoing Obama White House.[3] This massive transfer may be even more so for fees and related expenses such as hidden rate or service charges and payments that are directly tied to consumer financial products or services that affect our everyday lives.

Subprime mortgages, payday lending, student loans, and urban auto insurance, for example, are now collectively costing working- and middle-class consumers in the United States more than roughly $1.46 trillion each year.[4] That eye-popping sum is greater than the revenue budgets of the United Kingdom and France, and nearly equal to that of Germany. It's also greater than the revenue budgets of Canada and Mexico combined. Reducing the cost of these financial products by just 1 percent would translate into roughly $14 billion each year in new spending power—additional monies families could use to reduce house-hold debt, increase their savings, or invest in retirement or income-generating assets.

Taking a more detailed look, a person making an inflation-adjusted national median salary of $30,240 in 2015 would have well over 50 percent of her yearly earnings *before* taxes eaten up by student loans ($4,212 per year), payday loans ($574 per year), auto insurance ($2,256 per year), and just the interest of a subprime mortgage payment ($7,313 per year).[5] She'd still need to pay roughly 27 percent of her earnings in income, sales, and real estate taxes. And while many might assume college graduates don't take out these short-term, high-cost loans, the college-educated are among those in the payday lenders' fastest-growing customer base, accounting for at least 20 percent of total industry revenue in 2016.[6] This example shows how the cascading effect of fees has lifetime and intergenerational consequences: a student loan makes it more likely one will be caught up in the progression of payday loan debt, and parents' subprime mortgage payments, auto insurance, and payday loans will force their child to take out a student loan, restarting the cycle of indebtedness. Reducing these fees can lessen the impact of these debts on future generations for the majority of Americans.

The growth of fees is due partly to the increasingly complex and underregulated financial marketplace that has developed. Fees for financial products frequently do not appear on an account statement.[7] In 1980, a typical contract for a consumer credit card was one typed page. By the early 2000s, it was more than thirty pages long.[8] These added pages, usually laden with seemingly endless fine print, are not necessarily included to protect companies from lawsuits. Companies have found other effective ways to protect themselves from litigation, according to Elizabeth Warren, the chief architect of the nation's first Consumer Financial Protection Bureau.[9] Instead, studies repeatedly show that, whether by aim or accident, longer contracts tend to trick or confuse consumers by obscuring the terms of a financial product. All too often the devil is in the details.[10]

As contracts grow ever more complicated, the time Americans have to make sense of them is ever more scarce. By 2008, Americans were spending more hours at the office or factory than at any point in the nation's recent history.[11] Those in a typical middle-income, two-earner household worked sixteen more weeks than in 1979, whether by putting in longer hours or taking second jobs.[12]

Along with working more, people are commuting longer hours than their parents did a generation ago. On average, the typical worker's commute is twenty-six hours longer each year than that of the same worker in 1980.[13] When not working and commuting, Americans are more involved in childrearing than ever before. Parents of Generation Z children—those born between 1995 and 2015—spend 2.5 times as many hours involved in their kids' lives, whether through soccer practice, language school, standardized test preparation, or some other activity, as their parents did in 1985.[14] As contracts become longer and more complicated and with Americans having less time to evaluate them than ever before, the broker state that protected financial consumers is being dismantled piece by piece.

Established largely during the New Deal era, from 1933 to 1938, the modern American broker state emerged as part of the federal government's evolving vision and role as mediator between the competing claims of consumers, workers, small farmers, and others, in ways that had once been available mainly to business interests.[15] Of course, stronger groups still often pressured and overwhelmed even an ostensibly more powerful federal government, as was the case during the New Deal when FDR's National Recovery Administration caved to big business on price stabilization.[16] While it may have been initially concerned with harmonizing industrial relations with corporate interests, the broker state may have gradually, if unintentionally, emboldened greater "counter-organization," in which weaker groups mobilized and challenged stronger ones.[17] For example, FDR's 1941 signing of executive order 8802, to stave off a march on Washington led by union and civil rights leader A. Philip Randolph, was a recognition of the limited but growing leverage that newly elevated and organized interests such as labor and civil rights possessed on the eve of war, particularly if it meant avoiding a face-saving international incident such as a protest rally. From 1942 to 1945, brokerism faded while America went to war, only to resurface with the 1946 Employment Act. The policies implemented under the act, like legislation before the war, generally looked to guarantee the rights of particular organized actors, oversee pluralistic competition in the national marketplace, and protect or advance the greater social good. Under Republicans and Democrats alike, the modern broker state continued and grew during the same post–World War II decades in which the middle class expanded and economic inequality remained largely stable or even decreased—a fact that is often unacknowledged.[18]

These decades were the days of regulated capital, strong unions, and economic growth. Conditions slowly changed in the 1970s, when a desire to open markets to previously excluded groups coincided with government efforts to reduce federal oversight, as competition and the market were increasingly touted as replacements for the regulatory state. The movement toward deregulation that followed—while perhaps having some salutary effects on economic growth and spurring new enterprise—brought with it a sharp increase in economic inequality.

During the mid-1970s, the federal government enacted a series of laws—the Equal Credit Opportunity Act of 1974, the Home Mortgage Disclosure Act of 1975, and the Community Reinvestment Act of 1977—designed to tackle "past practices of credit discrimination, service the contemporary credit needs of historically marginalized groups, and expand the pool of possible financial consumers for the financial services industry's [quest to annex] new markets and profits."[19] Yet almost simultaneously, the federal government was implementing a set of deregulatory policies that were quietly making credit, banking, mortgage, and insurance markets less accountable to governments and consumers. This deregulated space fostered the rise of a new fringe financial sector, one auguring a shift away from denying credit and services to extending them on high-cost terms.

This new fringe financial sector, draining the wealth from racial minorities and other historically marginalized communities since the 1970s, migrated to mainstream consumers beginning in the 1980s. In an era of declining wages, middle-class Americans increasingly relied on credit borrowing to simply make ends meet. In the process middle-class consumers became a highly profitable market for financial practices that had been primarily reserved for the nation's working poor and racial minorities. By the 2000s, the financial sector claimed as much as 40 percent of all profits for any kind of US business enterprise while producing just 5 percent of all jobs. In contrast, when it produced 40 percent of all profits in the 1970s and 1980s, the manufacturing industry supplied between 20 and 30 percent of jobs.[20] Not all workers were hurt by deregulation. Those in financial services often reaped the rewards of fellow workers in other industries toiling longer hours for relatively smaller paychecks. A financial service employee who earned roughly the same amount as a manufacturer or a blue-collar worker in 1980, for example, made 70 percent more than the same worker by 2006.[21]

As the subprime bubble grew ever bigger, more than half of prime-eligible borrowers with credit scores good enough to receive a cheaper conventional loan were nudged into an expensive subprime one.[22] By the mid-2000s, subprime was the norm. "We Are All Subprime Borrowers Now," proclaimed a 2007 headline in the *Wall Street Journal*.[23] The nation's foremost financial paper was exaggerating, of course, but not by much. Household credit spiked 106 percent, from 48 percent of gross domestic product (GDP) in 1980 to 99 percent in 2007.[24] Credit may have been easy, but it wasn't necessarily cheap, even when declining interest rates in the 1990s and 2000s made it seem to the average consumer that it was or should be.

Subprime was a significant factor in, though far from the sole contributor to, growing household debt. Fees up and down the financial food chain helped make subprime and other forms of household credit profitable. What made financial products lucrative were the fees hitched to them. For example, a $400 payday loan to buy school supplies for one's kid could end up costing a parent $120 each month in fees in addition to the loan principal, as preschool teacher and single mother Tracey Minda of Cincinnati learned before the school year started in 2006.[25] The expansion of household credit resulted in the ballooning of the financial sector—a sector funded in part by charging a variety of loan- or investment-related fees. These included fees tied to loan originations along with trading, management, brokerage, and/or withdrawal fees tethered to mutual funds, annuities, CDs and other fixed-income products, underwriting or administrative asset-backed securities, and derivatives.[26]

These fees, whether levied by the state or marketplace, have tradition-ally been applied as both a base and an add-on charge. In a mortgage, for instance, these direct costs might include a title search fee, appraisal fee, or loan origination fee rather than be applied to indirect costs like markups. Fees are often baked into the price of a good or service, mak-ing it nearly impossible for consumers to know its itemized cost. For example, auto insurers typically charge customers a hidden cost based on where they live but rarely disclose the premium differential. At other times fees may have been fully disclosed, but, like the list of ingredients on the side of a box of cake mix, they are impossible to sift out of the prepackaged product. And the transaction can't be completed unless these additional costs are paid. Such is the case with origination fees for student loans, title search fees for mortgages, percentage or flat-rate fees tacked onto the principal of a payday loan, "tuition and fees," and a host of other consumer financial costs. These hidden fees might seem small, five dollars here and there, or 1 percent of the loan, but when they are glued to the principal, the total amounts to billions of dollars in virtually undetectable fees—fees that are redirected from working- and middle-class households to the financial industry, the richest and still among the fastest-growing sectors of the global economy.[27]

For governments and corporations, fees were a backdoor way to gen-erate revenue while avoiding unpopular discussions over taxes or sticker price hikes. For the public sector, these fees have been a great revenue-generating source in recent decades when voters have resisted calls to raise taxes. Between 1970 and 2013, nontax revenue accounted for 92 percent of all revenue growth in the United States for the government (local,[28] state, and federal).[29] In the private sector, fees often cover wages, overhead, operational expenses, and other direct costs, as well as gen-erally increase corporate profits. As a case in point, from 1984 to 2009, overdraft bank fees grew exponentially, from $200 million to $38.5 bil-lion, and government fees mirrored this rise in the private sector.[30]

Of course, private-sector consumer fees are not a formal government levy that is paid to a municipal or state revenue collector or the Internal Revenue Service (IRS). Yet in many instances, these fees do the substan-tive work of a tax by underwriting a public good or service in which one group subsidizes another. In higher education, for instance, private lend-ers received a guaranteed minimum payment from the federal government on each student loan they made. These bank-issued educational loans had riders affixed to them called "origination fees." Banks made the loans, with this guaranteed payment to the lender, but the fees affixed to them were implemented to help balance the federal budget. In effect, the federal government subsidized the private sector while imposing fees on students to help balance the budget. Fee-generated profits are not merely about deregulation or innovative financial practices. Fees have climbed as cash-strapped borrowers, experiencing a decline in disposable income resulting mostly from stagnating wages, have had few alternative routes to access credit. Perhaps the most glaring example of these revenue-generating, no-option charges can be found in the world of higher education, where all institutions—public four-year universities and two-year community colleges, private four-year colleges and universities, for-profit technical schools and universities—encumber students with a bevy of fees. These include inescapable registration fees just to attend class or even higher discipline-related fees that dissuade students from pursuing lower-earning (humanities) majors and fields. In sum, fees boost school revenue without sparking the student or public backlash often engendered by unpopular tuition hikes or additional taxes earmarked for higher education. Similarly, agreeing to a student, mortgage, or payday loan often triggers a raft of extra charges like origination, transaction, or repayment fees that drain an individual's savings and, at the very least, have a cascading effect, making credit in the future more expensive. Student loans and fees end up putting the borrower in hock years beyond the stated loan repayment calendar schedule of ten years. Rather, a typical senior graduating from a four-year public university, who owes an average $35,000 (in May 2013)[31] in student loan debt and finds a job making $48,127 a year, should expect to be saddled with the loan(s) well into her forties—given that average BA degree holders take twenty-one years to pay off their debt.[32]

Consumer finance fees are nothing new, of course. They were a major part of consumer spending throughout the twentieth century. But what changed was the nature of these fees, as they rapidly evolved from being a primary means of offsetting administrative costs or risk to serving as a source of income themselves. Put bluntly, fees became a profit stream. Many date this turning point to the late 1970s and early 1980s.

The government has a checkered history of protecting consumers against this deluge of profits at their expense. Sometimes fees are a response to legislation, sometimes government fosters a fee-friendly environment, and sometimes the president and Congress step in to curb these abuses.

In the 1970s, banks turned to fees in response to the pro-consumer legislation known as the Truth in Lending Act (TILA). Passed in 1968, TILA required lenders to tell borrowers how much, as a percentage, a loan would cost them each year. In short, the legislation aimed to standardize the costs of loans through the use of annual percentage rates so potential borrowers might better shop and compare the length and amount of loans, interest rates, and other finance charges from lenders.[33] Concerned that TILA might cut into their profits, banks quietly countered by slowly increasing and expanding their use of fees, whose application under TILA was far more nebulous than that of a formal interest rate.[34] Consumers attempted to push back against these fees in the late 1970s.

At least one consumer fought the expansion of fees in the courts. Paul Perdue was a law student working part-time collecting income from rental units.[35] In 1978, he deposited these and other rental income funds into his local bank, Crocker National Bank of California, and wrote a check against these and other funds.[36] But one of Perdue's checks was returned for "non-sufficient funds" (NSF). While the bank charged Perdue a $6 NSF fee, the actual cost Crocker National incurred in processing the bounced check was only 30 cents, effectively netting the bank a 2,000 percent profit. Perdue's attorneys claimed the fee was therefore excessive and unconscionable, particularly since Perdue was blameless, as he, like the bank, assumed the check was in good faith.[37] California's law appeared crystal clear: it was illegal to punish customers with a charge such as this. "[A] fee or charge can only be an amount that compensates the financial institution for its costs" and should not punish customers. The California Bankers Association countered that it was good business to discourage customers from bouncing checks by levying prohibitive fines.[38]

In anticipation of the ruling in *Perdue v. Crocker National Bank*, which was ultimately settled out of court, the Office of the Comptroller of the Currency (OCC) issued an interpretive ruling in 1983 clarifying and establishing that service and other consumer user fees could legally be defined and treated as interest charges. Without warning and the customary period of public comment, the OCC reversed a century-old policy of letting states regulate bank fees and "prohibited states from curbing fees that banks could legally charge."[39] By the mid-1990s, these rules would be expanded. Around this time, additional deregulatory rulings and policies enabled banks to increase the products and services they offered customers, as well as the number and amount of fees they could charge.[40] In 1996, the Supreme Court settled the question of fees as interest in *Smiley v. Citibank.* A Citibank customer, Barbara Smiley, sued her bank for charging a $15 late fee, claiming the "fees charged by [banks] do not constitute 'interest' because they 'do not vary based on the payment owed or the time period of delay.'"[41] Late fees especially, Smiley insisted, should be regarded as a penalty, not interest.[42] The Court was unpersuaded and let stand the OCC's directive defining nearly all fees (e.g., NSF, membership, late payment) as interest.[43] *Smiley v. Citibank* authorized banks to disregard state usury laws and thus permitted the usage of fees across state lines.[44] While Smiley sued Citibank for its credit card practices, the ruling—like the OCC statute—offered an expanded definition of fees to include retail bank charges like membership, maintenance, and bounced-check fees.

Still, for consumers, bank fees did not rise dramatically until 2004. That January, the OCC "upset an unspoken delicate balance in the banking world" when it issued a new preemptive directive declaring that 2,200 national banks, controlling 56 percent of the nation's assets, were freed from complying with state consumer protection laws.[45] Seven of the ten largest banks in America were given the green light to charge limitless fees for limitless amounts without being in violation of state usury laws. The OCC was simply part of a larger laissez-faire trend that included lawmakers, state and federal judges, and other financial regulatory agencies that successfully pushed federal preemption in the 1980s and 1990s to restrain or roll back consumer protection policies at the state and, when necessary, national levels. Between 1984 and 2009, revenue from overdraft fees rose from $200 million to $38.5 billion—not to mention earnings generated from other fees like ATM withdrawals, minimum account charges, and checking balance maintenance. Even during the financial crisis, when pricing on most goods and products remained flat, the median overdraft fee charged by banks increased from $25 to $26, the first increase during a recession in forty years.[46]

Nonbank financial institutions such as check cashers, pawnshops, and some microloan organizations followed banking practices as they, too, used fees to circumvent regulations, especially on the state level. Although anti-usury state laws still provided borrowers a measure of consumer protection against high interest rates, many states had not defined fees as interest. By the 2000s, payday lenders were openly mentioning the term "fee," as its murky meaning conveniently fell in the liminal legal space beyond the purview of anti-usury laws. Whereas nonbanks charging interest remained subject to state and federal usury laws, borrowing fees were generally regarded as a non-usury charge and, according to many lenders, out of the reach of financial regulators. Consumer watchdogs countered that whether by design or default, the preferred use of the word "fee" over a term such as "interest" or "annual percentage rate" (APR) paradoxically added to the lack of transparency by obscuring the true costs of financial products. With all of these fees to sort through, many of which did not require any disclosure, the consumer's task of simple side-by-side, one-on-one rate comparisons became far more difficult and complex.

As consumers, we certainly bear some responsibility. Many of us fail to read contracts, and we've grown accustomed to mindlessly agreeing to terms with just a couple of clicks. For decades, regulatory, pro-consumer, and industry trade groups all have shown that consumers simply don't know what's in the papers they are signing. Poll after poll shows that consumers are unprepared, confused, or even indifferent to shopping around, preferring instead to ask a profit-driven credit card company, mortgage lender, or some other nonfiduciary institution about financial products such as checking accounts, student loans, and mortgages.[47] However, even when we take time for due diligence, contracts have grown thick with indecipherable legalese. And many industries, like auto insurance, protect their pricing systems as a trade secret. The confusion that results is not caused simply by a consumer's imprudence; it is also encouraged by the aggressive marketing of the financial services industry that lets it be known how quickly loans can be obtained. One example of aggressive marketing appeared during a Super Bowl commercial in 2016, when America's largest internet mortgage provider, Quicken Loans, vowed to make getting a mortgage as easy as going online to buy music or a pair of shoes. Today, a would-be homebuyer can complete a Quicken "rocket mortgage" application in eight minutes without ever talking to a live person or being told about the fees and payment terms that come with it. Ease costs. "You pay for the service," Erin Lantz of the housing website Zillow told *Consumer Reports*.[48]

Selecting financial products may have been a personal or family matter in a post–World War II industrial economy. But financial products and the sector as a whole have developed an outsized role in today's economy. Since 1980, financial services have accounted for more than a quarter of the growth of the service sector, nearly doubling their share of the overall GDP in the United States over this time. Fees have been crucial to this expansion.[49]

More than a petty, costly annoyance growing exponentially in recent decades, fees have impeded upward mobility. Rising consumer finance fees and related expenses have obstructed pathways long thought central to post-World War II upward mobility: housing, higher education, employment, and transportation. Policies triggering higher costs in these four spheres have not created equity stripping or economic inequality, but they have exacerbated them.

In housing, we get a clear picture of how financing an asset is as important as the actual asset itself.

Lifetime Drains on Wealth

Home

Homeownership is the main source of wealth accumulation in America. As a result of this asset concentration in housing, consumer financial practices that extract wealth, like subprime loans, have been particularly harmful to wealth accumulation, asset building, and social mobility. In basic terms, wealth is assets minus debts. Because of the high profits to be made in subprime, lenders shuttled would-be prime borrowers into these types of loans. As cofounder of a Dallas-based subprime mortgage company, Richard Bitner revealed in *Confessions of a Subprime*

Lender, "The only profit we made came from the fee[s] we charged the borrower."[50] Of the $2.5 trillion made from subprime loans between 2000 and 2005, more than 50 percent of these subprime loan recipients actually qualified for cheaper conventional loans.[51] By 2005, three years before the housing bubble burst, subprime borrowers had surrendered $9.1 billion annually in high interest rates, prepayment penalties, and other related fees. That's $9.1 billion each year in equity extracted from the most vulnerable borrowers in the housing market.

Given how important building wealth is to financial security and upward mobility, homeownership during the 1990s and 2000s may have unintentionally blocked entry into the middle class. In housing, wealth accumulation is compromised by a surfeit of fees and charges that strip equity from homes, which largely anchor the wealth of America's middle class. Though understandable, it is risky to conflate buying a home with building equity. Just because people own homes does not mean they are accumulating wealth. After all, at the same time homeownership rates soared to their highest levels, the net worth of the home was declining. By 2008, with homeownership rates still near record highs, the Federal Reserve noted that home equity fell below 50 percent for the first time on record since 1945.[52] This dip occurred despite the fact that home prices climbed steadily throughout the 2000s.[53] Lenders were approving mortgages. But the problem was the cost of the loans.

In California, where one-third of the nation's subprime mortgages were financed during the mid-2000s, a subprime borrower on average pays approximately $600 more each month than a prime borrower.[54] Over the fifteen- to thirty-year life of a loan, a subprime borrower in California can expect to pay anywhere from $108,000 to $216,000 more.[55] Put another way, on a typical loan of $166,000, a subprime borrower will pay $5,222 more in the first four years, or $109 more a month over the next forty-eight months, than if they had been offered a conventional loan. Amortized over thirty years, the gap between a subprime and conventional borrower is close to $36,000.[56]

Higher-cost mortgage products make it more difficult for borrowers to save, pay off mortgages, and cover household expenses.[57] Preventing access to the middle class, the rising costs of loans contribute to a growing number of homeowners who find themselves "underwater," or owing more on their home than it was worth.

The growth in subprime did not just affect first-time homebuyers. As Federal Reserve and HUD data reports from the mid-2000s show, the most stable middle- and lower-income populations who were long-time homeowners were often targeted for subprime loans because of the equity built up in their homes.[58] The more equity built up in the home, the greater the pool of cash available to the consumer and to the ambitious, enterprising lender.

Fees and related expenses tied to high-cost subprime loans were major drivers of default and foreclosure. By 2008, an individual with an adjustable-rate mortgage was 36 percent more likely to default, a borrower with a prepayment penalty was 52 percent more likely to default, and an individual with a balloon-payment mortgage was 72 percent more likely to default than someone with a conventional mortgage.[59] According to the Center for Responsible Lending, "Subprime mortgages originated from 1998 through the third quarter of 2006 wiped [out] $164 billion in homeownership wealth for 2.2 million American families," which equated to $74,545.45 per family.[60] For the average middle-class household, that drop in wealth might wipe out college savings, retirement, and more than a year's income.

Beyond the devastation to families caused by the loss of their homes, foreclosures had negative effects on entire neighborhoods, municipalities, and states. Not only did they erode the wealth of individual households, they set back entire neighborhoods of homeowners. In addition to the 2 million or so homes hit directly by foreclosure between 2007 and 2009, 69.5 million neighboring homes experienced devaluation because of their proximity to a foreclosed property.[61] Thanks in part to the foreclosure contagion depressing home values during the Great Recession, one in four of all residences had negative home equity value by as much as 8.7 percent.[62] The contagion radius extended as far as 0.6 miles from its epicenter and dragged down home prices for as long as two to six years after the initial foreclosure.[63] The Center for Responsible Lending (CRL) estimated a total decline of $501 billion in home values in 2009 alone, with a projected loss of $350 billion in state tax revenue by 2011.[64] With the typical local government drawing two-thirds of its revenue from property taxes, many communities were forced to cut police, road maintenance, and other civic services. Property values dropped on average some $7,200, according to a 2009 CRL study.[65]

While $7,200 may not sound like much to many in the Northeast and West, in poorer states where home values were already lower—especially throughout the South—and for those on fixed incomes, this relative loss was considerable.[66]

School

If homeownership is the largest financial investment an American household typically makes, a postsecondary education ranks second. Yet again, a once-reliable conveyance of upward mobility is increasingly fraught with unexpected fees and other hidden costs. A survey of consumer finances from 1983 to 2001 conducted by the Federal Reserve revealed that student loans more than doubled, from 28 to 58 percent, as a share of household debt.[67]

In 2015, a National Association of Realtors (NAR) survey found that "25 percent of first time [home] buyers said it was hard for them to save for a down payment, and within that group, 58 percent said student debt was impeding their savings, up from 54 percent the previous year."[68] The NAR poll is backed up by plummeting rates of thirtysomething homeowners. According to the US Census Bureau, homeownership rates for Americans under the age of thirty-five have shrunk since the mid-2000s, from 43.3 percent in 2005 to 34.6 percent in 2015.[69]

Nonborrowers have a "permanent advantage" in homeownership over student loan borrowers, according to Stephan Whitaker of the Cleveland Federal Reserve.[70] The latter have been less likely to purchase a home than nonborrowers, and of those who do, reports show that in 2009 student loan borrowers possessed 41 percent *less* equity than those with no debt.[71] The more students borrow, the less likely they are to own a home, concluded a 2016 Federal Reserve report on the impact of student loan debt on homeownership between 1997 and 2010. For every 10 percent more a student borrows, the likelihood of the student owning a home within five years of graduating from college drops by 1–2 percent.[72] In other words, if the average loan is $35,000, a student who borrows 10 percent more (i.e., $38,500) would be 1–2 percent less likely to purchase a home than someone who borrowed only $35,000. Whatever the amount of their loan, borrowing students lose home equity. For example, if they buy a home within five years, a higher debt-to-income ratio means that student borrowers increase their odds of facing add-on fee charges (e.g., private mortgage insurance), higher interest rates, and a larger down payment than nonborrowing students. If they wait patiently and pay off their student loan debts before buying a home, nonborrowing students will still have a decade's head start in building equity given that ten years is the standard repayment schedule for a student loan.

This cascading effect of student loans on homeownership and other wealth-building assets has a disparate gender impact on women, who comprise the majority of college students. "The average debt one year after graduation is higher for women than men." Student loan "debt takes up a higher proportion of women's [first-year] earnings than men's," according to an Institute for Women's Policy Research analysis of 2012 data from the US Department of Education. The gender debt-to-income gap applies to all racial and ethnic groups, with women having more of their first-year paychecks eaten up by college debt than men: Asian (women, 81 percent, vs. men, 65 percent), Black (111 percent vs. 89 percent), Hispanic (85 percent vs. 81 percent), or White (92 percent vs. 70 percent). One year after graduating with a bachelor's degree, for example, African American women still owe more (111 percent) than they actually earn.[73]

The Federal Reserve Board's 2010 Survey of Consumer Finances projects that "an average student debt burden for a dual-headed household with bachelors' degrees from four-year universities" ($53,000) leads to a lifetime wealth loss of nearly $208,000. Nearly two-thirds of this loss ($134,000) comes from the lower retirement savings of the indebted household, while more than one-third ($70,000) comes from lower home equity. This finding can be "generalize[d] . . . to predict that the $1 trillion in outstanding student loan debt will lead to [a] total lifetime wealth loss for indebted households of $4 trillion," or an amount roughly equal to the final White House budget proposed by President Obama for fiscal year 2017.[74] Median assets are 16 percent lower (or an average of $44,661) for graduates with student loans than for those without outstanding debt, according to a 2007–09 Federal Reserve Survey of Consumer Finance by the Center for Assets, Education, and Inclusion.[75] The hidden cost of student loan debt is too easily masked when mobility is examined with income benchmarks.

Conflating income with social mobility also masks the impact of student debt on career choices. Evidence from the National Bureau of Economic Research indicates that students burdened by higher debt costs were substantially more likely to choose higher-paying jobs over lower-paying public-interest jobs (e.g., in social work, healthcare, or early education) in the hope of paying off loans faster.[76] The impact of student debt transcends the individual, as it may well stifle innovation and entrepreneurialism. Joint research conducted by the Philadelphia Federal Reserve and Penn State University shows that between 2000 and 2010, relative student debt grew by about 2.7 percent in the same Pennsylvania counties experiencing a 17 percent decline in small-business growth.[77] Student loan debt may be dampening job growth within the small-business sector (i.e., companies with four or fewer employees), which accounts for nearly 60 percent of all new jobs and tends to be more reliant on personal credit to operate than larger companies, according to the Small Business Administration.[78]

Buried in student loan contracts are a trove of what I call "trick and trap" fees that too often go unexplained by financial aid officers and unnoticed by borrowers. These fees and related charges include add-on expenses like origination charges, deferment and extension costs, early repayment penalties, and default fines, in which lenders tack on collection costs as high as 20–30 percent of the balance before sending the delinquent loan off to collections, a process called "capitalization." Private student loans, which took off around 2001 and accounted for 14 percent of all student loans in 2008, often extracted even greater monies from borrowers. Some private loans went into default after just one missed payment. Ultimately, students often end up owing three to four times the original loan amount. And while the costs and terms may not have been hidden, the financial aid loan application forms and process were often so complicated (and some contend still are) that even education secretary nominee Arne Duncan admitted during his 2009 Senate confirmation hearing, "You basically have to have a Ph.D. to figure that thing out."[79]

"Fees" figure heavily in college attendance, justifying the spread and expense of student loans. To access almost any American college, a student must pay upfront the conjoined costs of "tuition and fees." Schools outside the United States simply call them "tuition fees." This more naked nomenclature directly links tuition and fees to the monetization of higher education. Similarly, the term "tuition fee loans" refers to fees attached to loans that are available to EU or UK students who wish to attend a British university or college and need money to cover their tuition fees.

Once trapped in debt, student borrowers are offered very little in terms of consumer protections to help them escape. Unlike other forms of consumer credit, key student loan–related statutes do not have private enforcement rights or attorney's fee provisions, so it is difficult and costly to challenge them in court. And compared with conventional debts, student loans may not be discharged by borrowers in bankruptcy court without clear proof of undue hardship. Along with add-on fees, which often hide in plain sight in student loan contracts, student loans in general could be regarded as an unexpected fee, since they were originally designed to play only a supporting role in financing students' education.[80]

Perhaps the most common and lingering perception about student loans is that those burdened with heavy student loan debt are much better off financially in the long run than are workers with just a high school diploma. As the US education secretary at the time, William Bennett, told an *NBC News* reporter in the early 1980s, "Having a $10,000 debt burden with the $600,000 advantage you get from going to college isn't bad. You need to put that in perspective."[81] Bennett's belief still holds sway. A three-part series published in 2015 by the New York Federal Reserve echoes Bennett's reasoning. The Fed concludes that college graduates earn 80 percent more than their high school classmates who didn't attend college.[82] While this comparison may be true, earnings are only one aspect of financial standing or wealth. Exclusive focus on a college graduate's earnings misses the cascading costs of a student's debt over the lifetime of the borrower. Because a person often takes out a student loan before assuming any other major financial burden—a mortgage, car note, or full-time self-employment, for example—its multiplier effect can be substantial. A student loan drags down one's credit score, resulting in higher interest rates on a car note, mortgage and equity loan, personal business loan, or credit card payment. These hidden, cumulative costs have lasting impacts on individuals and families far beyond the years of college enrollment or the twenty-year life of a typical college loan.

Monthly Drips of Wealth

While homeownership and higher education are likely to be episodic or once-in-a-lifetime financial expenditures, transportation and employment illustrate the cumulative effects and costs of more quotidian transactions, such as monthly or weekly auto insurance payments and the daily accrual of interest standard for a payday loan.

Work

Work has been another traditional pathway to the middle class. The Equality of Opportunity Project, for example, zeroes in on employment and income as vital measures of intergenerational mobility in America.[83] Yet disposable income is being lost to many consumer expenses. The rising cost of higher education has outpaced the average family income in recent decades.[84] The inability of incomes to keep up with expenses is symptomatic of a larger story: household debt has risen twice as fast as disposable income since 1981. By 2010, household debt had grown nine times worse over the last thirty-five years.[85] This income–expense gap exists despite the fact that Americans today are working longer and being more productive and efficient at their jobs than previous generations. By 2007, the typical American worker was 400 percent more productive than a worker in 1950, according to data from the Bureau of Labor Statistics.[86] Despite workers being more productive than ever, the median wage has actually fallen since 2000.[87]

Wage stagnation affects workers across the income/professional spectrum. In 1970, a nonsupervisory worker earned $18.08 an hour (adjusted for inflation), while that same worker in 2007 earned just $17.81 per hour.[88] In 1974, a male high school graduate in the twenty-five to thirty-four age group earned nearly $43,000 (in 2004 dollars). In 2004, a male high school graduate in that age group was earning just over $30,000 (in 2004 dollars). Similarly, adjusted for inflation, the income in 2004 of a male college graduate was less than it was in 1974, $50,700 (in 2004 dollars) and $51,223 (in 2004 dollars), respectively.[89] Given the higher output and better efficiency per employee hour, this increased productivity could have translated into working only about eleven hours per week for the same output for forty hours per week in 1974.[90] Instead, Americans work more today than at any other point in the twentieth century, and the United States is among the most over-worked developed nations in the world.[91]

Individuals and families have employed a variety of means to make up for the widening gap between incomes and expenses: working longer hours, establishing two-earner households as more women join the workforce, reducing spending, borrowing against credit cards, tapping home equity lines— and, perhaps most commonly, borrowing money from proliferating payday loan stores. By 2008, there were more payday loan stores than the combined number of the two modern-day monuments to consumption: Starbucks and McDonalds. These figures do not include the growing number of online payday stores that have popped up in recent years. A hidden shame of the middle class is that almost half of US households would have difficulty finding $400 to pay for an emergency, according to a 2013 survey conducted by the Federal Reserve.[92]

Payday lending emerged to fill the unmet demands of employed Americans, who watched their wages stagnate precisely as too-big-to-fail banks—which once offered retail services like low-interest, short-term loans—began chasing bigger institutional clients after the 1999 deregulatory law, the Gramm-Leach-Blilely Act, made doing so legal.[93] A 2012 Pew Center report on payday lending indicates that 85 percent of borrowers assume these loans to cover expenses that are either routine (utilities, gas, groceries, credit cards) or unexpected (car repair, emergency medical treatment)—the sorts of expenses traditionally covered by a worker's paycheck.[94]

As its name intimates, a payday loan requires all its customers to have a job—a unique condition of usage compared with almost every other form of short-term consumer credit. For example, unemployed children, life partners, and even pets have all been known to receive credit card applications. This is not the case with payday loans, for which a pay stub and bank account are standard requirements for obtaining a loan.[95] With the payday loan, there's no credit inquiry by Equifax, TransUnion, or Experian, nor is there a verification of a would-be borrower's assets or liabilities. In this sense, a payday loan is more closely correlated to employment and wages than other consumer financial products. Payday lenders recognize that wage stagnation is an industry boon. "There are multiple reasons fewer people are able to meet the[ir] expenses. First of all, overall wages have been stagnant for a long time," noted the Personal Money Store, a payday lender advocate and online marketer.[96]

Often overlooked is how recent free-marketers have responded to the crisis of middle- and working-class wage stagnation. This free-market cure for wage stagnation appears to have only caused more damage. "On average, a borrower takes out eight loans of $375 each per year and spends $520 on interest," according to Pew research on borrowers in 2010.[97] Mounting evidence suggests that payday lenders propel their users toward ever greater debt, making it difficult for them to build assets. What makes payday lending so profitable are the fees. For three out of every five payday loan borrowers, the total fees paid actually exceed the principal loan amount.[98] With borrowers charged fees the equivalent of triple-digit APRs, they end up in hock to their lender 212 days, or seven months, each year on average. According to 2016 Pew research on payday lending and the impact of the Consumer Financial Protection Bureau (CFPB), "The average payday loan requires a lump-sum repayment of $430 on the next payday, consuming 36 percent of an average borrower's gross paycheck. However, research shows that most borrowers can afford no more than 5 percent while still covering basic expenses."[99] Forced to pay more than seven times the percentage they can afford, borrowers must cover the additional 31 percent needed for basic expenses, likely taking funds from other crucial expenditures, possibly needing another payday loan, and potentially repeating this cycle of debt with each subsequent paycheck.[100]

Cumulatively, borrowers may have paid as much as $3.5 billion nationally each year in fees alone.[101] "The high cost of the loan . . . may itself contribute to the chronic difficulty such consumers face in retiring the debt," concluded the newly created CFPB.[102] Payday borrowers nearly doubled their chances of being behind in debt repayment and having to file for bankruptcy compared with similarly financially situated would-be borrowers denied a payday loan, according to a 2008 study by Vanderbilt University and University of Pennsylvania researchers.[103] The very product designed to help families avert or mitigate short-term financial disasters has, in the long run, eaten away at wealth accumulation and created yet another obstacle to upward mobility. As evidence shows, by making it far more difficult for consumers to pay their mortgages, rents, and other financial liabilities, access to payday loans creates barriers to rising to or staying in the middle class.[104] According to Pew, borrowers are more likely to be renters than are nonborrowers in the same or higher income brackets. For example, 8 percent of renters earning $40,000–$100,000 have used payday loans, compared with only 6 percent of homeowners earning $15,000–$40,000, according to Pew.[105] The high-cost transactions associated with a payday loan, relative to less expensive short-term credit options, may well strip wealth from future possible homeowners, creating another obstacle to increasing the personal savings that are necessary for such long-term wealth-building investments like the purchase of a house.

Transportation

Despite the higher profile of and greater media attention to mortgage lending, student aid, and even payday loans, nowhere is a de facto, hidden consumer tax more commonly assessed yet so little discussed than in the realm of auto insurance. For nearly 90 percent of American households, what links the three areas of consumer finance discussed so far—housing, education, and employment—is the automobile.[106] The car is the most commonly held nonfinancial asset in America and the second most commonly purchased durable good and necessity (after a home). By law in almost every state, one's car must be insured.[107] Relatively speaking, then, in the world of financial services, lenders are hardly the most advantaged class or the one most consistently promoted by policymakers. In fact, that privileged perch should instead be reserved for the auto insurance industry, which occupies a unique and protected status within the US economy: it offers a service that people are required by law to purchase, yet it is provided exclusively by the private sector on a for-profit basis. This public–private collusion resulted in skyrocketing premiums for insured motorists by the mid-1980s.[108]

The focus on auto insurance usefully reminds us that discussions of the wealth gap should include the "accumulated effects of repeating the same pattern," which tend to have a "dramatic [impact] on a consumer's overall financial picture."[109] Since "[p]eople drastically underestimate how much wealth they will amass" because of small (yet repeated) household decisions,[110] the impact of these small household decisions on the wealth gap frequently gets passed over in favor of attending to big-ticket, single expenditures such as home and college. Patterns exacerbating the wealth gap might be particularly instructive in the zero-sum world of auto insurance, where there is an active and ongoing transfer of wealth in the form of discounted insurance rates that funnels money from one pool of insured drivers to another.

Though often overlooked, transportation is a critical factor in upward mobility. Labor economists, sociologists, and urban policy historians have all documented the geography of opportunity related to reliable transportation.[111] Matching state data on auto insurance premiums to a microsample of car ownership and labor market outcomes, one study found that those with cars are 27 percent more likely to be employed, work on average eleven to sixteen hours more a week, and earn 40 percent more per hour than those without cars.[112] "Losing access to a car is equivalent to a reduction in income," the study's authors concluded.[113]

Within the realm of reliable transportation, auto insurance remains an inescapable financial expenditure. "Owning a car creates expenses far beyond the purchase price, including insurance, which is much more costly for city dwellers than it is for suburban motorists," sociologist William Julius Wilson writes.[114] A rate analysis of some 33,313 US zip codes (of the approximately 43,000 zip codes nationwide) from the six largest insurers reveals that the typical urban motorist pays $247 more each year in insurance premiums for mandatory liability than a suburban motorist with the same statistical profile (e.g., age, gender, make and model of car, annual miles driven) and driving record (e.g., no tickets, no accidents). Thus, simply moving from an urban area to a suburban one saves a driver, on average, $247 each year. While the financial costs of postal code profiling may not seem like much, the $247 is larger than the $227 the bottom 60 percent of taxpayers would have received under the proposed 2001 Bush tax cut[115]—a tax cut that was often justified publicly as a way to stimulate the US economy.[116] Extrapolated over the fifty years the average American drives, that $247 annual gap grows to $12,350. Worse, driving without insurance can result in imprisonment and fines and, in the event of an accident, astronomical reparations for loss of life and property. It's not that urban motorists are, in the abstract, unable to afford insurance; rather, it is that the zip code calculus used by insurers exacts a high-cost premium on them, often pricing these drivers out of the market altogether.[117]

The "transportation gap" that has grown over the past five decades is not only due to deindustrialization, which has led to the outmigration of manufacturing and industrial jobs from central cities to suburbs, the US South, and abroad. Changes in the structural economy have also been exacerbated by declining public support for mass transportation and the principle of integrated residential housing, evinced in numerous surveys and opinion polls since at least the 1960s.[118] As William Julius Wilson has written about the disappearance of upward mobility in the nation's inner cities, "Among two-car middle-class and affluent families, commuting is accepted as a fact of life. . . . In a multitiered job market that requires substantial resources for participation, most inner-city minorities must rely on public transportation systems that rarely provide easy and quick access to suburban locations."[119] The collapse of mass transit has been yet another factor contributing to the erosion of upward mobility.

In each of the domains outlined here, consumer financial products have served to extract wealth and even exacerbate inequalities. Whether a mundane product such as auto insurance or a payday loan, or episodic expenses such as a thirty-year mortgage or ten-year student loan, each is a vital area of analysis because these financial products and expenses are constitutive parts of domains or spheres—be they transportation, gainful employment, housing, or education—that have provided reliable routes to upward mobility in post–World War II America.

The American dream born in the land of the free has inspired generations of citizens and captivated immigrants and capital investments from around the world. But this dream has been eroded by a belief that the private sector could and would regulate itself rather than overstress financial markets. For many consumers, the erosion of this belief in a self-policing financial sector began at home.

I

House Money: The Story of Subprime in Three Acts

Prologue: The Conners and Goddards, Canaries in a Coal Mine—The Story of the Credit Crisis to Come

In June 1980, almost three decades before the global financial meltdown, Leland and Sherry Conner, a young couple from San Bernardino, California, bought their first home. With a joint income of $25,000, they found a place they wanted for $85,000. Through their real estate broker, the Conners put $5,000 down and financed the balance with a first mortgage of $45,000 at 8.75 percent interest, plus a one-year balloon loan of $35,000 at 11 percent. Their monthly mortgage payment was $750. The Conners' broker assured them that they could refinance the second loan (the balloon payment) with "only a small increase" in monthly payments. But when the balloon payment came due a little more than a year later, the couple's payments jumped to $1,200 per month. In an effort to meet their new monthly payment, they let all other bills go. The utilities were turned off. The $3,000 roof leak was left unrepaired. According to Sherry Conner, "There was nothing we could do to meet the payments." The Conners made three of the new, increased mortgage payments before finally giving up. They put the house on the market at $99,000 but had no takers. Bankruptcy was not an option. Leland, a bonded armored car company employee, would be fired if he filed for bankruptcy. By August 1982, the house had been foreclosed on. By October 1982, the Conners were living in rented quarters, some $15,000 poorer.

The story of Terry and Judy Goddard of Sierra Madre, California, also should have raised red flags about the pitfalls of exotic or nontraditional mortgage products and triggered stronger consumer protections against broker deceit, fraud, and intentional misrepresentation in home lending. Like the Conners, the Goddards faced a balloon arrangement that pushed their home into foreclosure. The broker bought the Goddards' foreclosed home for well below market value and sold it the next month, netting a $33,000 profit on top of the $5,600 original commission.[1]

Nor were the stories of others like the Conners and Goddards uncommon in California. Foreclosure sales there jumped 173 percent during the first six months of 1982 compared with the same period the year before.[2] The state's troubled economy exposed the potential shortcomings of creative financing in the mortgage industry, which exacerbated the foreclosure problem. With America's largest mortgage market operating in the state where the future is often said to arrive first, California should have set off alarms for Congress and the White House. But it did not. Instead, federal officials forged ahead, creating a "new world" financial order. They expanded the nation's first mortgage lending deregulation law, thus undoing consumer oversight lending protections—the first of which had been passed a mere two years earlier.

Through these changes and others, Republicans and Democrats set in motion the erosion of financial consumer protections. In particular, three congressional acts passed in the 1980s initiated a generation-long assault on financial regulations. This sequence of laws, passed with bipartisan blessings, gave rise to the modern subprime industry and the consumer abuses that followed. The first of these was the Depository Institutions Deregulation and Monetary Control Act of 1980 (DIDMCA), the awkwardly named gateway law to financial deregulation that was the genesis of the subprime market. Following in DIDMCA's footsteps, the Garn-St Germain Depository Institutions Act of 1982, described initially as an "aid bill" for the lending industry, introduced the new and incredibly lucrative loan instruments of variable interest rates, prepayment penalties, and balloon payments.[3] Finally, in the Tax Reform Act of 1986, Congress and the Reagan administration used fiscal engineering to legislate consumer behavior, carving loopholes and exceptions out of existing tax law that encouraged homeowners to borrow beyond their means in an era of stagnant wages. Significantly, these policies and the deregulation of the financial markets they engendered were part of a lobbyist-led, bipartisan agenda. Even entrenched foes of federal intervention and central planning such as President Reagan and many southern legislators—politicians whose rise to prominence came by way of running against a micromanaging Washington—became champions of preemptive action by the federal government. Those decisions that tended toward deregulation created space for the rise—and too often the exploitation, however unintended—of subprime markets. The statutory makings of today's subprime market, and the abuses that ultimately came to accompany it, started with a seemingly innocuous piece of revolutionary legislation passed toward the end of the Carter administration.

Act One: Depository Institutions Deregulation and Monetary Control Act of 1980 and the Making of a New World Financial Order

On March 31, 1980, President Jimmy Carter entered the East Room of the White House to sign the Depository Institutions Deregulation and Monetary Control Act (pronounced "DID-MAH") into law. At the signing ceremony, Carter remarked that the new law was the first "step in a long but extremely important move toward deregulation" of the financial services industry, liberating banks and savings institutions from "a wide range of outdated, unfair, and unworkable regulations." The end result, Carter predicted, would be a steadier flow of credit for housing, with finance costs held in check.[4] "Most significant of all," he added, "it can help improve our Nation's very low savings rate."[5]

Secretary William Miller, the only person ever to serve as both chair of the Federal Reserve and secretary of the treasury, spoke with even greater aplomb. DIDMCA augured a "new world," according to Miller. He believed that DIDMCA would not just change consumer lending as Americans had known it since the New Deal; the deregulation it initiated would also prepare the country for the decades and century that lay ahead. It was a way to "modernize . . . our economic system to deal with the issues of the '80s and '90s," Miller told the gaggle of reporters gathered that day.[6] In many ways, Miller was right. DIDMCA inaugurated a three-decade-long effort to undo the financial and banking regulatory policy that had developed out of the Great Depression and stood for half a century.[7]

Passed with bipartisan support—by a Democrat-controlled Congress and White House—DIDMCA effectively abolished state usury caps that limited the amount of interest banks could charge on primary mortgages. DIDMCA was among the first in a series of congressional acts, court cases, and White House decisions that helped lay the groundwork for a high-priced subprime market in housing, resulting in a market segment with a wider range of loan prices than found in the prime market.[8]

The initial intent of DIDMCA was to phase out the federal interest rate caps placed on deposit accounts and maintained by Regulation (Reg) Q. Having removed the rate cap, DIDMCA then mandated that federal laws could preempt state usury laws for banking and savings institutions. Federal preemption empowered banks and other lenders to bypass state laws to charge whatever interest rate they chose.

Next, the act loosened regulatory controls over financial institutions. This loosening was not an intellectual exercise to test free-market, laissez-faire capitalism. Rather, reduced oversight was meant to address a perceived social necessity: improved savings rates. According to President Carter, the savings rate was down to its lowest level in nearly thirty years. Carter and other DIDMCA backers contended that rolling back Reg Q would spur savings by individuals.

Finally, DIDMCA placed a greater burden on regulatory agencies to justify their existence. As Kansas senator and future Republican presidential nominee Bob Dole saw it, DIDMCA was intended to shift "the costs and burdens from the Nation's financial community" onto federal regulatory bodies, thus pressuring regulators to avoid conflicts and minimize compliance costs.[9] For regulators who ignored the new law's message and preferred to regulate as usual, pre-DIDMCA, with tight rate ceiling enforcement, their federal agency might well suffer budget cuts or Congress might simply legislate it into irrelevance.

Congress and the White House described DIDMCA as a win-win for both the financial industry and individual citizens. Financial institutions could now charge higher rates (about 11.3–12.9 percent by the fall of 1979) on mortgage loans.[10] Accountholders stood to gain as well. Ceiling-free federal rates on deposits would yield a higher rate of return on savings accounts, thereby making thrifts and other depository institutions more competitive with new financial products such as money market mutual funds. The resultant hiking of interest rates would help boost savings in the United States. This argument was so persuasive that groups like the Gray Panthers, a senior-citizen pressure group, for example, backed this original reasoning for ending Reg Q, claiming that the ceilings on interest rates for small savers had cost retired Americans an estimated $19 billion during the 1970s (and $42 billion for small savers overall).[11]

Savings and DIDMCA

The marked decline in savings in the United States began long before the 1980s. Several factors led to this decline, but the impact was widespread. One factor was growing income inequality. From 1947 to 1973, income equality was thought to have encouraged mass savings, but this outcome began to disappear in the 1970s as median incomes, adjusted for inflation, leveled out before flatlining in the 1980s. Adjusting for inflation, incomes stayed stagnant through the 1990s and 2000s.[12] The increasingly tenuous relationship between consumer spending and domestic production—as production moved overseas, it mattered less where goods were made—led to the creation of fewer and fewer American jobs. The rise of business and the growing consumer culture's emphasis on "indulging . . . desires and circulating money rapidly"[13] through the economy harmed savings as well. Reflecting the declining significance of savings culture in government and civil society, once-commonplace programs like school savings accounts were eliminated in the postwar decades. Similarly, the Tax Reform Act of 1986 also discouraged saving by using fiscal policy to incentivize debt. By the 1990s, both Democratic and Republican White Houses increasingly focused on the importance of consumption rather than on savings (as had often been the case in the earlier part of the century) as key to economic growth. Visiting Tokyo, President Clinton urged Japanese students to replace savings and exports with greater domestic consumption. His successor, George W. Bush, brought this story back home following 9/11. Bush II was the first president in modern history who did not propose higher taxes and greater savings to finance war. Moreover, when the House of Representatives authorized Patriot Bonds to help fund the War on Terror,[14] the Bush administration discouraged this form of revenue generation, contending it preferred Americans "spending money to buying . . . savings bonds."[15] As one car manufacturer advertising free credit in the weeks following September 11 urged consumers, "Don't let the terrorists get you down."[16] The globalization of finance also fed the decline in savings by US households. Since the 1990s, a global savings glut in China and elsewhere had resulted in vast foreign investments in the United States. This investment drove down American interest rates and spurred reckless institutional lending and consumer borrowing.[17]

While these other factors all had an impact, perhaps the single most important mechanism contributing to the decline in savings in the United States was the growth of credit in the housing and consumer markets. The salutary effects of extending credit as a means of promoting thrift were exaggerated. Buying one TV might allow consumers to reroute their entertainment dollars from games or movies, but multiple TVs? As buying more, and doing so on credit, became more commonplace, the purchases became more difficult to explain away financially. In comparison with Western Europe and Japan, "Americans became so accustomed to buying durables on credit that most forgot that consumption could be financed in other ways. Namely they might save first and buy later."[18] This shift in consumer behavior was inextricably linked to financial deregulation in the rise of the subprime mortgage industry, which would ultimately help to undermine thrift, exacerbate debt, and promote leveraged borrowing in high and low finance.

Although organized labor and consumer groups opposed phasing out Reg Q, fearing that ending interest rate ceilings would boost the mortgage rates of their members, DIDMCA had substantial support.[19] Even those most sympathetic to states' rights supported DIDMCA's federal preemption clause, which made the Federal Reserve the default setter of interest rates and then removed the Fed's power to set interest rate caps by phasing out Reg Q. However, most southern legislators and much of Congress welcomed the government intervention represented by DIDMCA, so long as it promised to override state regulatory laws and consumer protection by lifting usury caps. One of the few members of Congress to push for states' rights under these circumstances was Senate Democrat Robert Morgan of North Carolina. The usury laws of his state dated back to at least the Progressive fusion politics of the 1890s, when a coalition of Progressive North Carolina Whites and Blacks controlled the state legislature and defeated a cabal of corporate and industrial interests to pass consumer protection laws and usury caps. DIDMCA threatened to undo many of these protections. Chastising his colleagues, singling out in particular southern and western allies in the Senate, Morgan declaimed, "They want states' rights . . . and this goes to people of my home state, and then they want the federal government to move in and preempt State laws when it suits their convenience."[20] The bill nonetheless passed overwhelmingly.

Without even debating the phaseout of Reg Q, which had been in place since the 1933 Glass-Steagall Act, the House voted in favor of DIDMCA, 367 to 39.[21] It then sailed through the Senate, needing only a voice vote because of its near unanimous support. Most of the members of Congress reconciled themselves to the policy trade-off: exchanging state sovereignty for federal preemption if it meant greater freedom for financial markets. This bill represented the first step in what would be the slow, steady erosion of the Glass-Steagall Act, the most significant regulatory protection in American banking. Although disparities in the interest rates that financial institutions charged their customers did exist under the Glass-Steagall Act prior to DIDMCA, never had the disparity grown so great or so consistently as in the years after DIDMCA's passage. By effectively abolishing state usury laws, DIDMCA created a new market segment with a much wider range of loan pricing than had previously existed in the prime market.

Second mortgage lenders, which specialize in home equity or lines of credit lending and had been charging high-cost loans to consumers for years, noticed that DIDMCA appeared to allow them, too, to charge unlimited interest rates—provided that they took first lien (or refinanced the first mortgage) on the borrower's home. In other words, under DIDMCA, home equity lenders and even other consumer credit lenders could now charge unlimited interest if they persuaded borrowers to put up a house as collateral. That is precisely what happened to consumers taking out car loans in Pennsylvania.[22]

"We Don't Want the Car. We Want Your Aunt's House":
What DIDMCA Did

In 1986, Tito Manor went shopping for a car. At the lot, the car salesman informed Tito that he would need someone to co-sign, which
his aunt, Gloria Young, ultimately agreed to do. The car salesman,
who passed the completed loan application on to Fidelity Consumer
Discount Company, notified both Tito and his aunt that the loan had
been approved. Then the salesman instructed them to come to the deal-
ership and bring the aunt's house deed, just as verification that she was
indeed a homeowner. However, the dealer never informed Young that
the house was being used as security for her nephew's car loan. The
lender, Fidelity, took a first mortgage on Young's home at an interest
rate of 36.617 percent—far exceeding the Pennsylvania state usury cap
of 24 percent. Fidelity also added an origination fee of $544 on the car
loan of $3,613.86 (or an approximately 15 percent charge of the total
loan amount). Unable to keep up with the principal and interest on the
car note after several months, Tito tried to return the car to Fidelity, to
which the lender responded, according to uncontradicted deposition
testimony, "We don't want the car. We want your aunt's house."[23] Tito
Manor and Gloria Young would join other Fidelity customers in suing
the nondepository lender for violating Pennsylvania's state usury law.[24]
By enacting DIDMCA, Congress caused federal law to trump state
usury laws.

The changes DIDMCA brought paved the way for greater consumer abuse. Without DIDMCA, Fidelity would not have been able to
charge these incredible rates or to seize Young's home. The steep loan
terms made seizing the home not simply more likely, but also a more
profitable alternative than seeing the loan terms satisfied. Thanks to
DIDMCA, if a lender took out a first lien on a borrower's home and
that borrower defaulted on the car note, the borrower's home could
now be foreclosed rather than the car repossessed. Lenders preferred
the appreciative value of a home to the repossession of a depreciated
asset like a car. According to legal scholar Cathy Mansfield, "It didn't
take long after DIDMCA was adopted for some second mortgage lenders, and for other lenders who had been making high cost consumer
loans, to notice that DIDMCA appeared to allow them to charge an

unlimited amount of interest provided they took a first lien on the borrower's home. Thus a number of lenders, who would not have otherwise made first-lien home equity loans before DIDMCA, began to cast car loans, small consumer loans, and second mortgage loans as very expensive home equity first-lien loans."[25] High-cost lenders used loopholes in DIDMCA to bilk consumers out of their cars and homes. Such loan practices were possible, though, only because of federal preemption, which allowed lenders—those that wanted to charge borrowers large amounts—to bypass state usury laws.

Despite these sweeping changes to the mortgage industry, deregulation advocates argued that DIDMCA did not go far enough in creating a new world financial order. Both lawmakers and industry insiders continued to claim that bank regulations were strangling competition, putting banks and thrifts at a competitive disadvantage with money markets and other investment products targeting small investors. Two years later, in October 1982, they succeeded in passing the Garn-St Germain Act.

Act Two: The Garn-St Germain Act of 1982

On August 3, 1980, Ronald Reagan kicked off his postconvention presidential race by giving a speech just outside of Philadelphia, Mississippi. The site was hallowed ground for the civil rights movement: there, activists Chaney, Goodman, and Schwerner had been tortured and slain by the Ku Klux Klan in one of the most notorious murders of the era. Speaking specifically about economic policy that day, candidate Reagan vowed to redeem the value of limited federal government and home rule if elected. "I believe in states' rights," he told those in the Mississippi audience.[26] On Inauguration Day, January 20, 1981, delivering an address as the nation's fortieth president, Reagan reaffirmed the value of decentralization as a presidential first principle in perhaps the most frequently quoted line of his speech that day:

[Federal] government is not the solution to our problem; it is the problem. . . . It is my intention to curb the size and influence of the federal establishment and to demand recognition of the distinction between the powers granted to the federal government and those reserved to the states or to the people. All of us need to be reminded that the federal government did not create the states; the states created the federal government.

Most of the new administration's domestic policies—taxes, civil rights, judicial appointments, environmental protection, education, food stamps—sealed Reagan's reputation as arguably the staunchest White House advocate of states' rights in the twentieth century. Yet consumer lending proved a glaring exception to this record. In the landmark lending legislation of his presidency, Reagan urged Congress to pass the Garn-St Germain Act, a federal law designed to override state interests and insert central government further into the daily, personal financial affairs of the individual. Lauding federal encroachment and intervention as "historic reform," the Reagan White House actually championed expanding the influence of federal governance at the expense of oversight powers once thought to be reserved for the states and their people. In fact, because consumer protection advocates and attorneys considered the statute's preemption unequivocal in establishing federal supremacy over state law, this legislation was a thoroughly effective deterrent, and thus very few court challenges were ever mounted against it. Under Reagan, decentralization became a casualty of deregulation.

Passed in 1982, the Garn-St Germain Act expanded DIDMCA. Reagan described as a historic reform the law whose very success hinged on usurping states' rights. "I think we hit the jackpot," Reagan remarked at the signing ceremony.[27] The key clause in the bill was the Alternative Mortgage Transaction Parity Act, or AMTPA. AMTPA gave lenders across the nation access to a new range of exotic financial products: balloon payments, interest-only mortgages, prepayment penalties, late fees, and option alternative rate mortgages (ARMs). As these products were now clearly allowed by AMTPA, state laws prohibiting them were nullified. For both the primary market (e.g., lenders, brokers) and the so-called securities or secondary market—to which lenders sold these loans—the yields from this new creative financing proved extremely profitable, with a huge benefit for the capitalization of industry. Mortgage brokers, for example, who were typically involved in 60 percent of all mortgage loans, were paid on average 1.88 percent of the value of each subprime loan they secured. Those same brokers made only 1.48 percent on conventional mortgage loans. For a typical home loan—say, of $150,000—the broker could make an extra $600 by securing a subprime loan instead of a prime loan. Seeing the extra profits made on subprime loans, investors began snatching up these high-revenue-generating, mortgage-backed assets.[28] By 2005, at the height of the subprime mortgage boom, a majority (55 percent) of subprime loan recipients actually qualified for prime or conventional loans but were instead steered into the subprime lending market. The number of these very creditworthy borrowers continued to grow until the subprime collapse in 2007.[29]

These newfound financial instruments gave lenders flexibility and creative financing options during the high-interest-rate years of the early 1980s. These new instruments helped draw historically underserved communities into the primary and secondary mortgage loan markets. The problem lay in the law's opacity and lack of oversight and enforcement. AMTPA enabled lenders to make loans that often obscured the terms and total costs. For example, balloon payments offer borrowers low monthly payments initially but force them into larger payments later.[30] Problems of opaqueness were compounded by the lack of oversight, as lawmakers displayed little regulatory will to make sure these new practices did not turn out to be exploitative.[31] The combination of federal encroachment and lax federal enforcement helped foster a climate of borrower abuse.

These problems were most evident in Garn-St Germain's authorization of prepayment penalties and late fees, allowing state-chartered institutions to evade state laws. For instance, even when states passed aggressive laws to curb lending abuses, AMTPA empowered lenders to skirt state regulations under the guise of adhering to federal law. (Laws like these would, by the 1990s, have state regulators overmatched by the national and, indeed, global financial industries.[32]) Thus, brokers and lenders continued placing payment penalties on homes, even when state law clearly prohibited this practice, as long as these exotic packaged loans were covered by AMTPA (i.e., loans that had balloon payments or ARMs).[33] By 2001, according to Standard & Poor's, just 2 percent of prime loans contained a prepayment penalty—a fee assessed to mortgages if a loan is paid before a set time period to dissuade mortgagers from paying off loans early and guaranteeing lenders a minimum profit—as opposed to 80 percent of subprime loans, for which prepayment often incurred a penalty of 4–5 percent of the total loan.[34] This cryptic collection of charges and fees penalized borrowers who had worked to improve their credit scores and to refinance loans.

The abusive uses of AMTPA stemmed directly from its legislative origins. Because it was conceived and crafted primarily by industry lobbyists, American consumers were never the intended beneficiaries. Indeed, from the very start, Garn-St Germain was labeled an "aid" bill for the financial services industry—particularly the banks and savings and loan companies. The need for the legislation was real. More than 80 percent of the nation's 3,800 savings and loan institutions had suffered net losses by 1981. And the reason for the red ink appeared to be high interest rates.[35] These institutions lobbied hard for DIDMCA's expansion as they sought new streams of revenue to offset financial losses and to compete more aggressively with money markets.[36]

Lawmakers officially voted for the bill, but, in effect, the financial services industry had written it. As Fernand St Germain, chairman of the House Banking Committee, impressed upon the nation's top savings and loan regulator, Edwin J. Gray, "No legislation can pass the House without [industry] approval."[37] Lobbyists offered similar enticements to those running watchdog agencies at the National Credit Union Administration, Federal Reserve Board, and Federal Home Loan Bank Board. Reports surfaced later that the industry had also paid travel and entertainment expenses for Gray. Lobbyists defended these payments by calling them a common thrift industry practice.

House Money: The Rise of Fernand St Germain

There was no more illustrative example of the influence that the industry wielded than the political life of the bill's namesake, St Germain. His public service career as a Rhode Island representative and House Banking Committee chair made a millionaire out of this French Ukrainian son of a dye-factory foreman.[38] The foundation of the congressman's nouveau wealth was built on the cozy relations he sought or nurtured with bank tycoons, real estate developers, and financial service lobbyists. When questioned by a House Committee on Ethics panel years later in 1987, however, St Germain claimed not to recall who provided the original seed money used in his initial investments to amass his fortune.[39] These relations included taking monies and entering into business deals with companies that he was directly charged with legislating and regulating. After St Germain was elected to Congress in 1961, his public service became a series of quid pro quos with private investors who appeared to be in line to benefit directly from his official actions. Dating as far back as 1972–73, four Rhode Island lending institutions put up nearly 100 percent of the approximate $1.3 million purchase price for five IHOP restaurants that St Germain bought—which many wondered how he could afford on a congressional salary of $42,000.[40] Despite these questionable deals, St Germain spent the 1970s as a relatively obscure congressman, escaping the notice of moneyed interests as well as the scrutiny of a post-Watergate media. This would change by the early 1980s.

As St Germain's seniority increased, so did his financial fortunes. After St Germain's selection as chair of the House Banking Committee in 1981, the US League of Savings Institutions, the trade association for the savings and loan industry, lavished $2,000 on him each month to cover his entertainment expenses. Meanwhile, other financial lobbyists took care of the new chairman with corporate jet flights and corporate credit cards.[41] These close ties helped make St Germain one of the two largest recipients of campaign contributions from the three financial political action committees (PACs) lobbying for banking reform legislation at the time. According to a study conducted by the nonpartisan Public Citizen's Watch, in 1983 the average industry contribution per congressional representative was $2,438. (Each of the forty-one senators studied received $7,881 from the industry over a four-year span.) St Germain, however, received nearly nine times this amount in campaign contributions from the same PACs. By 1984, St Germain had amassed a net worth of between $2 million and $2.6 million (adjusted for inflation, that would be $4.6 million to $6 million in 2016).[42] Federal Election Committee filings captured how St Germain's coffers were filled after 1980, when he began chairing the House Banking Committee (figure 1.1).

Between AMTPA and the 1984 race, 81.3 percent of funding raised for St Germain came from industry (i.e., banking, thrift, securities, housing, and others), with 99.4 percent of St Germain's PAC funding coming from outside his home state.

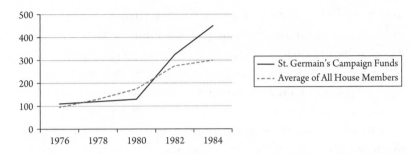

FIGURE 1.1 St Germain's campaign contributions increased exponentially after becoming House Banking, Finance and Urban Affairs Committee Chair in 1981

Source: Author's analysis of *Providence Journal-Bulletin*; Sunshine News Service based on Federal Election Commission reports (original in Gotlieb Archives, Boston University)

Funding St Germain's campaign in the early 1980s was akin to bankrolling a hidden retirement pension for him.[43] For any member of Congress assuming office before 1980, any unspent campaign dollars could go directly into their personal bank account once they left Congress.[44] No one expected the incumbent Banking Committee chair, who had breezed to victory in every election since 1976 by at least 61 percent of the popular vote, to face stiff competition for his seat. Rather, campaign dollars could be used to line the pockets of an incumbent congressman.[45]

In addition to amassing direct campaign contributions, St Germain used his perch as a lawmaker and regulator to enrich himself and others. According to the *Washington Post*, he received "lots of investment help from people and institutions."[46] The same individuals and lenders who helped make St Germain a millionaire stood to benefit financially from the legislation in front of him. Deeply interested in AMTPA and other legislation pending before the House Banking Committee, banker Raleigh Greene, Jr., founder and chairman of Florida Federal Savings and Loan, formed a business partnership in several real estate ventures with St Germain.[47] Greene and the heads of other savings and loans (S&Ls) stood to benefit from the October 1982 passage of AMTPA, which freed S&Ls to make riskier investments in commercial banking, real estate speculation, and the junk bond market, as well as to offer riskier mortgage loan products, like adjustable-rate mortgages, to potential homeowners.[48] In this and other deals, St Germain and Greene concealed their ownership from the public and the press by using anonymous trusts, thereby keeping both names off the deeds and mortgages.[49]

In defending his business partner, Greene may have only heightened suspicions. Describing three inside land deals he offered to St Germain but not to the public, Greene defended his business partner, saying, "It's like anything else. . . . You sit down with your buddies and say, 'Do you want in?' And you either say yea or nay."[50] The patience of constituents began to wear thin. Holly Rice of Newport, Rhode Island, wrote St Germain asking, "How can one accept over $100,000 from the banking bloc and not have that influence his actions as chairman of the House Banking Committee?"[51] (He left office with more than twice the amount Rice suspected.)

Pressured by the press and public that fall, members of the House Ethics Committee reluctantly launched an official inquiry of their colleague in February 1986.[52] The fourteen-month investigation led to a fifty-page report that noted the Banking Committee chair had accepted favors, including entertainment, meals, drinks, corporate jet flights, and corporate credit card use, from financial services industry lobbyists while championing a multibillion-dollar bailout of savings and loan banks.

But by then AMTPA was firmly ensconced.[53] Such revelations into how St Germain enriched himself as chair met with little opprobrium from the House Ethics Committee. Releasing its report in April 1987, the committee found he had violated six disclosure rules, including underreporting more than $1 million in assets (while claiming he had not gained financially), but it nonetheless recommended no punishment.[54] The committee's findings were met with deep skepticism if not outright incredulity. Conservative columnist Steve Chapman of the *Chicago Tribune* blamed the "self-contradictory" Ethics Committee for its "heroic lengths to spare" a colleague.[55] "Apparently the only thing worse than being suspected of corruption is being required to do something about it," Chapman wrote. Citing still unanswered questions about bribery, misconduct, and other allegations documented in the *Wall Street Journal*, House Republicans reacted by demanding a vote to reopen the investigation into whether St Germain grew rich by abusing his office.[56] An August vote was taken and rejected, 111 to 291, along party lines, with the exception of one Democrat voting for it.[57] Given that, at the time, only one member had been expelled from Congress since the Civil War, St Germain was likely never in any serious jeopardy of expulsion. Moreover, since 1922, Congress had censured only four of its members, and half of those were censured for sexual improprieties with House pages.[58] The House Ethics Committee rarely followed up on members after they left office.[59] Then-Georgia congressman and future Speaker of the House Newt Gingrich summed up the public message about the lax enforcement of rules in this way: "You now have a House where it is more dangerous to be aggressive about honesty than it is to be mildly corrupt . . . a situation [of Democratic leadership] where I think people feel almost invulnerable."[60] Despite the Republican Gingrich's indignation toward Democrats, lobbyist influence seemed less an individual party problem than a congressional one. By not checking the abuses of the Banking Committee chair, the Ethics Committee effectively took the issue out of the hands of the party in legislative power. The soft approach taken by the committee had a negative impact on all Democrats in the upcoming election, as it allowed the election to become a referendum on partywide corruption and a cover-up, rather than simply throwing a spotlight on a rogue congressman's putative abuses.

The concern swirling around St Germain morphed from an ethical issue into one surrounding his reelection. The minority party and many in the media suspected congressional Democrats of protecting their own, thus spurring the Reagan administration to intervene with a grand jury criminal probe. Having posed at a Rose Garden signing ceremony for the Garn-St Germain Act with the president just a few short years earlier, St Germain now found himself the target of that same president's Justice Department. The conclusions of the grand jury and the Justice Department proved severely damaging to the Rhode Island Democrat. The Justice Department released the jury's findings on October 31, 1988, just one week before the midterm election. The "October surprise" of Reagan's Justice Department claimed to have documented "substantial evidence of serious and sustained misconduct," including years of ongoing deals with bank industry lobbyists. Without pursuing a criminal prosecution, the Justice Department referred the matter to the House Ethics Committee for further inquiry. "This seems curious to me that it comes eight days before the election," was St Germain's reaction.[61]

A week later, Rhode Islanders voted the twelve-term congressman out of office. However, he escaped criminal charges and, thanks to the "hidden pension" loophole that transferred remaining campaign funds to his personal bank accounts, St Germain pocketed $248,000 in leftover campaign donations.[62] But his election loss and public disgrace did not bar St Germain from Washington; by the summer of 1989, he had returned to Capitol Hill as a savings and loan lobbyist.[63] Largely forgotten, however, is how St Germain, who was linked to the S&L crisis at the time, played a pivotal role as a legislative architect of subprime. Stated as generously as possible, the *Washington Post* described a myriad of allegations against those chiefly responsible for AMTPA's passage: "There is no indication that St Germain did legislative favors for Florida Federal individually, and no suggestion that he received preferential interest rates on his loans. But there is no doubt that all savings and loans—including Florida Federal—benefitted from legislation St Germain co-authored with Senator Jake Garn (R-Utah) in 1982 that restructured the industry."[64]

St Germain's fellow architect of AMTPA, Republican Utah senator Jake Garn, also reaped rewards from his close relationship with business. In 1987, the Garn Institute of Finance opened its doors at the University of Utah, thanks almost exclusively to $2.4 million in contributions made by industry executives at the US League of Savings Institutions—the financial services lobby—and three of the five largest savings and loans, as well as the nation's then-largest high-risk, high-yield securities company, Drexel Burnham Lambert, which financed Garn's pet project.[65] Funding tax-exempt foundations like the Garn Institute enabled the industry, in an effort to circumvent newly created campaign finance laws, to keep its access to legislators who were writing banking rules.[66]

When it came to banking deregulation, the line between ideology and influence blurred. Because AMTPA—the law that paved the way for the creative financing of the subprime market—originated from a policy process so awash in industry money, it is impossible to know where lawmakers' commitment to free-market principles ended and their loyalties to the interests of the financial services began. AMTPA may well have been a credible bill needed for legitimate reasons, designed by free-market principled policymakers. But given the strange (and regrettable) career of AMTPA and its impact on the US economy, it is difficult to sustain any serious defense of its deregulatory design and the financial fruits it bore. Doing so serves as little more than a ruse to disguise ulterior political and material motives. Summing up the shortcomings of Garn-St Germain, law professor Patricia McCoy stated that "there were no sub-regulations to make sure these new mortgages didn't turn out to be exploitative."[67] In effect, the average borrower was at the mercy of the financial industry, aided by Congress.

Act Three: The Tax Reform Act of 1986

These two laws—DIDMCA and Garn-St Germain—combined with a quiet revolution in fiscal engineering, the Tax Reform Act (TRA) of 1986. Before TRA 1986, consumers could take as a tax deduction the interest made from a range of installment purchases (e.g., credit card purchases, personal loans, and even home equity loans). After TRA 1986, only the interest of a home equity loan (aka second mortgage) was deductible, as lawmakers, hoping to steer borrowers away from credit cards, contended that homeowners were more responsible citizens than credit card borrowers. The act marked the first time since the Revenue Act of 1862 that the top rate of income tax was reduced while the bottom was increased. The long-term result of this last major simplification of the tax code was an increase in the after-tax return that benefited wealthy households more than wealth-poor households. As Kirk White of the US Census Bureau wrote in 2004, "I find that the tax reform can account for nearly all of the increase in wealth inequality observed in the data" since 1986.[68]

Overlooked, however, is the extent to which the law attempted to legislate and alter consumer behavior. Nowhere is this more evident than in the Home Mortgage Interest Deduction, which legislators intended to encourage taxpayers to purchase homes and increase home equity spending by phasing out incentives for rental housing and eliminating deductions for interest on small-scale consumer loans like credit card debt. Under TRA, 10 percent of the interest of conventional loans was tax deductible by 1990. However, a homeowner could take out a home equity loan to buy a car and have the interest deducted in full. The message that *Black Enterprise*, a magazine marketed to African American businesses and professionals, took from the new tax system and passed on to its upwardly mobile and financially savvy readers was that Uncle Sam played favorites (figure 1.2). TRA sheltered citizen mortgage holders from a host of expenses, including those associated with buying multiple homes, while leaving renters to fend for themselves in weathering a storm of taxes.[69] Furthermore, thanks to the act's elimination of investment incentives for rental properties, the number of rental housing units decreased by some 50 percent over the next fifteen years after the 1986 law's passage. A tightened supply resulted in increased expenses faced by tenants.[70]

By 1988, the TRA had "cleared the way for increasing securitization of real estate," thereby increasing the incentive to take out primary residence mortgage loans over consumer loans.[71] What followed next was a rapid rise in subprime mortgage lending.[72] Securitization enabled mortgage and equity lenders to pool, repackage, and sell the loans they made to investors. With the lenders' accounting ledgers no longer holding these loan debts on their books, they had additional capital to loan. And so the securitization finance process increased cash flow exponentially

FIGURE 1.2 The 1986 Tax Reform Act incentivized and protected homeowners over renters
Source: Black Enterprise, 1989

for lenders. This process started slowly. The first substantial (private-sector) securitization of low- and moderate-income loans began in 1997 when Bear Stearns bought Community Reinvestment Act (CRA) loans.

The Tax Reform Act of 1986 eviscerated the postwar tax advantages of consumer credit. The new law, according to savings and consumer historian Sheldon Garon, "elevated the home equity loan—a minor phenomenon before the mid-1980s—to the American homeowner's favorite form of consumer credit."[73] In order to secure the big tax break, consumers increasingly used their homes as their primary source of investment and savings.[74] Banks quickly swooped in and began encouraging customers to tap into their home equity to pay for a vacation, car, or wedding. Touting the tax benefits of using home equity, Chemical Bank advised its customers, "If you're looking for your cheapest source of money, check your home."[75]

Home equity proved more tempting to homeowners than credit cards did. Secured by property, the interest rate for a home equity loan was half that of a credit card. With housing prices rising, homeowners had more equity to take out of their homes. By 2004, one in four homeowners had assumed a home equity loan. Little of this money went toward increasing the value of one's home. Instead, only one-third of the proceeds of home equity loans financed home improvements, while one-quarter went to school debt, medical bills, weddings, cars, and vacations, and approximately one-third was used to pay off credit card debt. Comprising between 67 and 70 percent of home value in the late 1980s, home equity (as a share of home value) continued declining through the Great Recession because of these loans—even as housing prices climbed. From 1989 to 2007, "debt as a share of household disposable income rose from 86 percent to 141 percent." Soaring debt was largely attributable to the near doubling of household debt to 103 percent.[76]

Of course, the question naturally arises: If DIDMCA, Garn-St Germain, and the Tax Reform Act were products of the 1980s, why did the subprime mortgage markets (and predatory abuses) surface more than a decade later?

The Market and Subprime

Despite the lowering of regulatory barriers and the erosion of consumer protections in the 1970s and 1980s, the private sector essentially avoided subprime markets until the 1990s. The 1990s ushered in changes in both the American housing market and international economies that allowed subprime lending to take off by the decade's end, making securitization a phenomenon despite the fact that it had been an option since the 1980s.

Rising interest rates, combined with the collapse of international and national real estate, helped to dry up investment dollars in the prime mortgage market. These factors caused the sales volume of residential and commercial properties to drop precipitously. This bubble-to-bust cycle (along with leftover investment capital from the bursting of the dot-com bubble in the late 1990s) also caused mortgage brokers and companies to rely more heavily on subprime mortgage markets in order to maintain volume. From 1995 to 2003, subprime loan securitization rates nearly doubled, from 30 percent to 58 percent of all securitized mortgage (e.g., conventional, jumbo) loans. Over this same period, prime securitization also grew, though at a lesser rate, from 50 percent to 75 percent.[77]

At this time, international investment in the United States grew, particularly capital investment from commodity-producing and manufacturing countries in Asia, the Middle East, and Eastern Europe that were eager to park their cash in the world's safest, largest economy. Initially, overseas investors bought US Treasury Bonds, because they produced a low but safe return. But the desire for greater returns increasingly turned these global investors to more high-risk, high-reward financial instruments, such as subprime mortgage–backed bonds and securities.[78]

These factors alone would not have produced the subprime boom without the near-perfect storm for lenders: skyrocketing home values, plummeting interest rates, and stagnating wages. While home values continued to climb, interest rates steadily dropped, so that by 2000, the rates were at an almost forty-year low. This combined with a factor all too often overlooked by policymakers and the media: the stagnant wages of workers and the concomitant escalating cost of living, most evident in climbing healthcare expenses. With house values higher than ever and the average homeowner's paychecks worth less than at any point since the end of the nineteenth century, the home operated effectively as a piggy bank. Working homeowners used equity not for investment purposes like home improvement, but, increasingly, to make up for declining real wages or to pay bills. The deflationary drag—often attributed to the massive influx of low-cost Chinese goods into US markets that caused prices to fall almost everywhere else—was of little consequence to this long-term trend, given that the surge in Chinese exports was a relatively recent occurrence by the end of the twentieth century. At most, China was a late contributor to the suppression of American workers' wages. As economist Mark Zandi has written, China's arrival in the global market, which triggered a "lowering of trade barriers and accelerated a massive shift of global manufacturing to the formerly closed communist mainland," was a consequence of China's joining the World Trade Organization in November 2001.[79] Wages for US workers had already been stagnant for the previous three decades. In other words, Chinese-manufactured low-cost goods may have made the crumbling cost of living standards in America more difficult to shore up, but they did not create the problem. Rather, the gap that grew between the rich and the rest was largely a domestic problem of America's own doing, one that had been decades in the making. Each of these was a salient factor in the explosive growth of the subprime market. Yet subprime also depended on the deregulated space cleared by the three laws, DIDMCA, AMTPA, and TRA, that opened the door for the subprime market.[80]

The conditions also allowed investors and borrowers to believe the system would increase their wealth, as home prices kept rising. But rather than narrowing the wealth gap, this new world financial order, marked by the rise of subprime lending, facilitated the transfer of wealth to the rich from the rest. The mortgage meltdown only intensified this transfer. As Robert Shiller, a leading economist on subprime mortgages, pointed out in November 2008, "Many Americans thought that they would rise in the economic hierarchy from one or another of these investments, and their disappointment is profound. . . . As dreams have been lost, the gap between the wealthiest and those struggling to provide basic items for their families will become more evident and more painful."[81] Nor was the fallout quarantined to defaulting homeowners. Instead, the foreclosure and boarding up of homes harmed property values for entire neighborhoods. As a result, municipalities saw their revenues vanish at the same time that the costs of local public services skyrocketed and state and federal funding dried up.

Much has been written about what this new world financial order has meant in the fifteen- to thirty-year mortgage market arena. This focus is understandable given that homeownership is traditionally an individual's single largest investment. Yet, if owning a home is the largest investment an American consumer makes, paying for a college education is second. And in the borrowing cycle of a consumer, a student loan typically comes first. Years before consumers assume a mortgage, they will take out an education loan if they are like a majority entering college today—with the class of 2015 the most indebted in US history. Nor does the student loan debt simply come first; in addition, it actually *increases* future costs for a mortgage loan. How financing a college degree today has helped mortgage the American future, then, is the subject we turn to next.

2

Tax Eaters: The Origins of the Student Debt Bubble

AMERICAN HIGHER EDUCATION IS not usually considered a mechanism driving wealth disparity. Indeed, particularly since World War II, a college degree in the United States has been regarded as a social leveler. However, this belief has slowly been changing in recent years as the growing costs associated with a degree have increasingly turned college campuses into sites of indebtedness rather than upward mobility. Two out of three college students graduate with student loan debt.[1] Data from the 2010 Federal Reserve's Triennial Survey of Consumer Finances show that in 45 percent of US households one or more people have student loans.[2] Student loan debt is the only form of non-mortgage household debt that has continued to grow since the Great Recession began in December 2007, according to the New York Federal Reserve.[3] With consumer spending responsible for up to 70 percent of America's economic growth, the consequences of this heavy concentration of debt have rippled through the US economy.[4] And as we've seen in the introduction, student loan debt has had a cascading effect: an increase in a borrower's debt-to-income ratio results in the borrower's delaying the purchase of a home or car, or paying more in interest rates for a credit card, home, or car.

Student loan debt erodes savings needed for homeownership, which is widely regarded to be the most reliable driver of wealth in a free-market economy built on notions of private property.[5] First-time homebuyers, who rely on savings for down payments, traditionally represent 40 percent of the home-buying market; with increased and more widespread student loan debt, their numbers have consistently dropped to around 30 percent of the market in the years following the Great Recession.[6] People are delaying taking on new financial obligations like buying a home or car, the Consumer Financial Protection Bureau reported in May 2013. Recent college graduates also struggle to qualify for mortgage loans because their student debt skews their debt-to-income ratio, according to the National Association of Home Builders. In addition to housing, high-debt burdens appear to affect other major financial necessities, including retirement security, healthcare,[7] and entrepreneurial formations—the last two of which are primary forces of US employment.[8]

Despite these drawbacks, the share of students assuming a student loan has climbed markedly since the 1970s. In 1976–77, one in three graduates were borrowing for college. [9] Through the 1980s and 1990s, the number of graduating seniors who borrowed grew steadily from 43 percent in 1983–84 to 52 percent in 1995–96.[10] By 2001, fully 64 percent of students were taking on loans, reversing the percentage twenty-five years earlier.[11] Guaranteed loans had existed since 1965 to encourage an unenthusiastic private lending market to lend widely to students. Leery, private lenders at the time thought it too risky to make unsecured loans to a college student with no expectation of repayment for at least four to five years, as opposed to the customary thirty, sixty, or ninety days of a standard personal loan. Such a speculative bet on a teenager required handsome compensation from the government. Hoping to help the private sector warm to the idea of the college student loan, the federal government offered private lenders two incentives: subsidies and a federal guarantee.[12] Under guaranteed student loans, government subsidies paid lenders upfront to cover fees associated with loans and compensated them for any costs of collection and default while (ostensibly) keeping interest rates low. Subsidies paid all interest costs on the loan while the student was in school, in the loan grace period, or in deferment. (With an unsubsidized loan, borrowers may defer paying interest, but it still accrues, and the borrower is responsible for paying all interest costs on the loan while in school, the grace period, or deferment.)

In addition to offering this subsidy to private lenders, the federal government guaranteed the loan against default. If a borrower defaulted, the federal government guaranteed the bank a minimum return on investment, as much as 80 percent. If the borrower paid in full, a lender recouped the loan principal plus any additional profit in interest, fees, and charges. Not only did a federally guaranteed loan promise lenders a minimum return, it also allowed them and processing agencies—called state guarantee agencies—to add on expenses for originating, administering, managing, and collecting these loans.

The current student aid crisis has its roots in the 1980s, when the Reagan administration, with help from a coalition of congressional Republicans and conservative Democrats, pushed through Congress a combination of tax- and budget-cutting measures. In part, these measures reduced the federal government's financial commitment to the student financial aid system by shifting many of the costs of college away from American taxpayers and on to student loan borrowers. In the early 1980s, the costs of student loans might have been spread over 100 million or so taxpayers (currently there are 139.5 million taxpayers); subsequently, these costs were passed on to about a third of that number (currently there are 44.2 million student loan borrowers), student borrowers from primarily working- and lower-middle-class backgrounds.[13] While subsequent federal and state choices continued or accelerated matters, these tax cuts and budgetary reductions in the early 1980s marked the starting point of the transformation of the student financial aid system: cutting grants and elevating and expanding loan programs as the primary means to offset rising college costs. These fiscal policies represented a fundamental shift in the public discourse about student borrowers and the cultural and economic role of higher education, a shift that politicians from both parties reinforced. Prior to the 1980s, students needing government assistance were once thought of and described as America's deserving future tax contributors—fulfilling a compelling public interest to advance the nation's macroeconomic and security agenda, national and state governments should and did underwrite these promising individuals. This image would slowly be undone in the 1980s, with students no longer cast as future tax contributors but as so-called "tax eaters" who, like other undeserving Americans, were leeches on the backs of the American taxpayer. It was the fiscal decision-making that laid the groundwork for the presentation of students as parasites rather than the next generation of taxable-income earners.

Reagan Shrugged: Debt and Taxes

In 1981, President Reagan, newly elected, pushed through Congress a $38 billion budget reduction bill and a three-year 25 percent reduction in both individual and corporate tax rates. The tax and spending cuts passed thanks to a disciplined Republican majority in the Senate and a Democratic majority in the House that was, to quote one historian, "riddled with defectors" such as the so-called boll weevil Democrats—a caucus of conservative southerners led by Texans Charles Stenholm and Phil Gramm, Trent Lott of Mississippi, and Larry McDonald of Georgia.[14] In addition to supporting tax cuts, the twenty-nine boll wee-vils embraced military spending and deregulation. Having recently survived an assassination attempt, and as the first president since JFK to face such a serious threat to his life, Reagan may have also benefited from a groundswell of public sympathy, and the goodwill toward him flowed to his policies.

Perhaps equally significant was Reagan's promise not to campaign in the upcoming midterm elections against any Democrat who voted for both tax and budget cuts.[15] Having lost thirty-four House seats to Republicans in the preceding election, even Democrats who may have been predisposed to vote against the largest cuts to public spending in US history appeared a bit more willing to accommodate the new administration. Such genuflection to the Reagan White House was part of a larger trend of congressional acquiescence. In areas that included the confirmation of court nominations, this Congress was the most submissive the nation would see for the next thirty years.[16]

This dutiful Congress passed two laws—the Gramm-Latta budget and the Kemp-Roth tax cut—that combined to give the Office of Management and Budget (OMB) and its director, David Stockman, license to reduce the federal role in education and slash federal financial assistance. Gramm-Latta required major spending increases in military aid and mandated the Kemp-Roth tax cut while simultaneously forcing major cuts in discretionary spending, including Pell Grants, and entitlements, such as guaranteed student loans. The US Department of Agriculture famously attempted to meet the spending cuts imposed under Gramm-Latta by telling parents and their children that pickle relish was a vegetable so that it would survive the skimpier budget while meeting federal nutritional guidelines. However, the student aid program—along with employment, training, and social services programs—was marked for the deepest cuts.[17] These fiscal measures, signed into law in August 1981, targeted grants and student loan programs. Spending on higher education and federal student aid was slashed by some 25 percent between 1980 and 1985. In raw dollar figures, the Gramm-Latta budget was responsible for cutting $594 million in student assistance and $338 million in Pell Grants.[18]

At least initially, starving these government programs did not automatically create an enlarged role for the private sector. In contrast to bankers' avid support for housing deregulation, they lobbied infrequently for student loans until the 1990s. Loan officers were skittish about lending to students who possessed shaky credit profiles. These students were, after all, most often teenagers with virtually no employment or credit history, no collateral, and no spouse and kids depending on them to behave responsibly by repaying the loan. Unlike the subprime mortgage industry, student aid was not designed primarily by the private financial sector. Instead, the architects of the Reagan-era rise of the student loan were fiscal engineers and cultural warriors in Washington.

The command center for the fiscal assault on student financial aid was the Office of Management and Budget. Supply-siders at Reagan's OMB had regularly contended that tax cuts would generate sufficient revenue to balance the budget. OMB director Stockman, however, was skeptical that tax cuts alone could eliminate the deficit; he knew spending cuts would be required to accompany the new fiscal policy. Student aid "isn't a proper obligation of the taxpayer," Stockman explained to the congressional subcommittee on postsecondary education. "It seems to me that if people wanted to go to college bad enough, then there is an opportunity and responsibility on their part to finance their way through the best way they can."[19]

As the last cabinet member invited to join the Reagan administration, Education Secretary Terrel H. Bell had no illusions about the priority the president placed on education. Having served under the previous two Republican presidents, Bell was certainly attuned to the ways of Washington. Nonetheless, he was stunned by the budgetary choices emanating from OMB and its director. "I could not fathom . . . [the] rationale for the budgetary choice of cutting student aid and retaining such other less worthy expenditures as subsidies for growing cancer-causing tobacco."[20] Bell's career in the Reagan administration would come to symbolize the serious shift in policy and rhetoric on education and the ascendancy of New Right politics that was nearly unthinkable to lifelong Republicans like Bell. He found a sympathetic ear in Defense Secretary Caspar Weinberger. Weinberger understood the connection between education and the administration's budgetary commitment to military spending, and he lobbied the president and OMB privately not to slash higher-education expenditures. But no other major cabinet member thought it important, and Weinberger's attempts to sway either Stockman or Reagan were unsuccessful.

In addition to cutting the funds available through federal grants, the Kemp-Roth tax cut led to the very first set of consumer fees on student loans, so-called origination fees. An origination fee was a 5 percent activation charge added to set up a guaranteed student loan, but this was not to offset or cover the administrative costs of the loan. Rather, the origination fee for student loans was created to help pay for tax cuts and to help lower government debt.[21] Origination fees were actually higher than 5 percent, as they became part of the loan to be repaid with interest. Though originally introduced as a temporary measure, origination fees would become a permanent fixture of all student loans. (Before his tenure ended, Reagan looked to double these fees but was rebuffed by a Congress with more resolve than the one he had faced in his first term.) Origination fees bore no direct benefit for the borrower. As one onlooker bristled at the time, these dollars would never be "seen or available for expenses yet students had to repay [them] with interest."[22] At the same time, a new means test for families earning more than $30,000 was instituted. In the brief time between the law's passage and the implementation of these new fees and means testing, students rushed to get loans, making more than $2 billion in new requests.[23]

Beyond the Beltway, financial aid workers at the local, state, and regional levels felt targeted by the Reagan administration. They saw

Gramm-Latta and Kemp-Roth as cudgels not simply for attacking spending, but also for turning public opinion against the very idea of government student aid. "It appears that the Administration is conducting a campaign to discredit student aid and its administration in the public and legislative arenas in order to support budget cuts," said Mary Haldane, the head of the Midwest Association of Student Financial Aid Administrators (MASFAA), the leading trade association for the region's public and private higher-education aid officers.[24] The OMB, in particular, put pressure on financial aid officers to make sacrifices so that the administration could ratchet up military spending. Rather than costs being cut, Haldane noted at the time, "budget expenses will be at an all-time high this year primarily because of defense spending."[25]

Cuts in education in the 1980s also came via regulatory rollbacks, attrition, and layoffs. In addition, government reduced spending in the enforcement budgets overseeing higher education and financial aid in particular, as OMB posited that less funding would translate into less federal intrusion.[26] An exception to the administration's drastic cuts was the Education Department's Office of the Inspector General (IG), which saw its enforcement budget expand under Reagan. The IG's office added new personnel, augmented its authority, and increased its operational budget so that it might crack down on fraud and abuse in the submission, evaluation, and disbursement of student financial aid. The administration also expanded the office by empowering it to go beyond complaint collection, its only authorization, in order to initiate investigations. It added at least 130 audits while making ten more investigations into criminal activity.[27] In contrast, enforcement was relaxed wherever the administration's commitment was less than zealous, as was the case with the Education Department's Office of Civil Rights, where compliance review claims were summarily dismissed or limited.[28] The Education Department's staff was reduced overall by 1,600, which included 74 staff layoffs (or roughly 6 percent of the 1,046 total) in the Office of Civil Rights. Overall, from 1981 to 1983, budgetary cuts caused discretionary appropriations to fall by 6 percent. By contrast, between 1975 and 1982, discretionary appropriations increased 20 percent.[29] However, the Reagan administration's student aid policies not only marked changing fiscal priorities but also altered access to higher education for some of the newest and most vulnerable groups of future borrowers.

The Early Reagan Years: Gender and Class in the Hidden Benefits of Loans

These policy changes deeply affected the gender, racial, and class character of higher education. During the first months of the new administration, cultural conservatives recognized that there could be parallel, stealth benefits to winding down federal grant programs. Put simply, some conservatives recognized that the shift to student loans might weaken the enforcement mechanisms and regulatory triggers of Title IX.[30] Passed in 1972, Title IX guaranteed that no person shall, on the basis of sex, "be excluded from participation in, be denied the benefits of, or be subjected to discrimination under any education program or activity receiving Federal financial assistance."[31] The story of Grove City College bears this out, showing how cultural conservatives sought to roll back the federal grant program as a way to sidestep Title IX. In the early 1980s, allies of Grove City College, a Christian college in Pennsylvania with long-standing institutional ties to various right-leaning think tanks in the United States and abroad, balked at complying with Title IX regulations. Faced with these regulations they regarded as burdensome, Grove City officials turned to the Reagan White House for help.

Colleges and universities were required to comply with Title IX if they accepted grants from the federal government, but it was less clear whether that was the case with indirect (or even direct) loans. The Reagan Justice Department contended that, unlike Pell Grants, guaranteed student loans "do not constitute 'federal financial assistance' and thus do not trigger the regulatory scrutiny of Title IX."[32] The administration's logic was simple: shifting to student loans from grants would help greatly reduce, if not eliminate altogether, the need to comply with Title IX. Thus, leading Reagan administration officials, including future Supreme Court justices John Roberts in the Justice Department and Clarence Thomas in the Education Department, strategized a more narrowly drawn student aid program—one that would effectively help Grove City and other conservative outfits skirt compliance with Title IX.[33]

Of course, not everyone in the administration viewed lowering the compliance bar on antidiscriminatory policies like Title IX as a positive outcome. White House special assistant Elizabeth Dole opposed it. As chair of a presidential task force on equal rights for women, Dole raised concerns that this shift away from Pell Grants would have detrimental effects on women and African Americans, pointing out that the federal Pell Grant was "one of [African Americans'] primary vehicles for upward mobility."[34] Dole's admonition was largely ignored.

By 1986, federal student aid had declined by 10 percent in the five years since Reagan had taken office.[35] This decline was not only a result of the administration's deep cuts to funding. The federal government also tightened grant guidelines that made fewer people eligible following the passage of Gramm-Latta. Stricter guidelines had the net effect of redirecting student aid recipients from the grant program to student loans. These students tended to be from lower-middle- and working-class families that earned too much to be considered below the poverty line but earned too little to be able to pay for their daughter's or son's education.

So began the slow rollback of federal financial student aid. The decision to rewrite aid eligibility guidelines had dramatic consequences. From 1980 to 1985, the years immediately following the guideline changes, freshman participation in the Pell Grant program declined by nearly 50 percent, but freshman participation in the guaranteed student loan program increased by almost 25 percent. Changing eligibility rules disqualified 267,000 freshmen from receiving Pell Grants between 1980 and 1986.[36] Families and students who were eligible for grant assistance in the year before were now told that they had to take out student loans to cover the remaining years of their education. Other grant programs were targeted as well, notably Social Security educational grants and GI Bill educational grants for student veterans. At the request of the Reagan administration, federal funding for these two programs was dropped to almost zero.[37]

But these cuts tell only part of the student financial aid story in the early 1980s. While the Reagan administration froze grant funding for the nonprofit higher-education sector, it poured money into the federal student loan program. For example, during the Carter administration, consumer price index–adjusted figures show that Pell Grant amounts spent by the federal government jumped from $910 million in 1976 to $2.36 billion in 1980. From 1980 to 1984, Reagan's first term, the federal needle on Pell Grant spending barely moved compared to previous administrations, going from $2.36 billion to $2.80 billion. The flatline for Pell Grants during the first Reagan administration stood in stark contrast to the rising trajectory of guaranteed student loans, which almost quadrupled from $2.9 billion in 1980 to $7.93 billion in 1984. Comparatively speaking, the Carter administration spent approximately 2.5 times more on student loans in 1980 ($2.9 billion) than it did in 1976 ($1.3 billion).[38] In an internal memo, the chair of the House Committee on Education and Labor captured the effect Reagan's policies had on students: "After 1981 students turned to the [guaranteed student loan] program to help replace the other lost sources of income to meet the rising costs of higher education."[39]

The eligibility criteria of guaranteed student loans were changed as well, having a small but growing impact on the middle class. At the beginning of academic year 1980–81, for middle-class households, low-cost, low-interest, subsidized federal loans were open to all students regardless of income or family size. By academic year 1982–83, these same loans were now limited to families with incomes of less than $30,000—regardless of family size.[40] To make up for the sudden, substantial decline in federal support for students, schools began using their own institutional funding. The proportion of first-year students receiving campus grants and scholarships from 1980 to 1986 rose at both public universities (64 percent) and public colleges (69 percent). School funds once set aside by colleges for salaries, program enhancement, and facility repairs and improvements were now being reallocated—along with tuition and fee hikes—to close the federal gap in financial aid to students.[41] So students, even those whose families were not in need of aid, often bore the brunt of rising costs as colleges offloaded additional deficits onto them by ratcheting up tuition and fees. Changing federal aid polices forced families to pick up the expenses of what colleges did not or could not cover, according to the American Council on Education in its 1986 study of 372 American colleges and universities.[42]

Wesleyan University was one of the first major universities to change its aid policy because of the Reagan cuts. Trustees at the private liberal arts college in Connecticut adopted a policy that allowed the school to reject applicants not because they did not qualify, but because they were unable to pay full tuition.[43] One month later, Dartmouth College adopted a similar policy. Some schools, such as the University of Pennsylvania and Harvard, dipped into their own endowments to preserve aid-blind admissions policies. More typically, private universities passed on the newfound expense of the 1982 budget to students. The decline in federal financial aid "put real pressure on the middle class," said the dean of undergraduate admissions at Georgetown, Charles Deacon, whose university made students pay more by affixing a special top-up fee to regular tuition, specifically to offset the loss of federal dollars for financial aid. "You saw a shrinking percentage of middle-class students at these top universities," Deacon added.[44]

Even universities assumed to be insulated from such fiscal vicissitudes were affected. Harvard's first-year classes had steadily become more racially and economically diverse after 1968, the year of the assassination of Martin Luther King, Jr. This trend abruptly stopped in the early 1980s. Though the aid Harvard offered to students was unaffected by the Reagan cuts, the percentage of both racial minorities and first-generation college students enrolling at the university dropped between 1981 and 1982. The decline in aid discouraged working- and some middle-class families, leaving them with the clear impression that there would be no way they could afford private colleges and universities such as Harvard. "We all assumed that the graphs would continue to go in that upward direction, but we got blindsided by the federal government making these announcements that hit news wires across the country," Seamus P. Malin, acting director of financial aid in 1982, told the *Harvard Crimson* some years later.[45]

The Case for Transforming Student Financial Aid

The OMB and Reagan White House had several rationales for slashing aid to college students. Some argued that it would reduce the deficit, and others averred that less money meant less federal intrusion.[46] Still others insisted that government's active financial support of students upset the natural order of the nuclear family, supplanting parents and their primary obligation to provide for their children. Thus, the argument went, by limiting aid, the government would be restoring traditional family values. Collectively, these various perspectives coalesced around a shared view: students were "tax eaters" who were "a drain and drag on the American economy."[47]

From the perspective of Reagan's White House, students attending college on aid were feeding on the American body politic. Secretary of Education Terrel Bell's 1988 book, *The Thirteenth Man: A Reagan Cabinet Memoir*, sheds light on exactly how the administration was able to displace decades-old views of higher education. Bell disagreed with the president and many of the president's leading advisors on the policies and the ways they were enforced. To the Reagan administration, Bell wrote, students needing financial assistance were part of the problem, not very different from other "undeserving" Americans. Stockman and others saw no difference between these students and "welfare queens," out-of-work fathers drawing unemployment insurance, poor families on Medicaid, the elderly in need of Medicare, or even farmers relying on subsidies. They were all tax eaters and a drain on the economy, and the Reagan administration was "going to pull those leeches off the backs of decent, hardworking people," Bell wrote.[48] With this ultimate goal, Stockman "ripped into [my] departmental appropriations with fanatical intensity . . . slashing [our budget] like a wild dog."[49] Reagan officials did not deny that education was an important investment, but it was deemed a personal or private—not societal—responsibility. Not surprisingly, in testimony to Congress, Reagan officials often held up the food stamp program as the analogue of student financial aid, claiming that the same restrictions, rules, and regulatory coverage (or lack thereof) placed on grocery stores participating in the program should be applied to universities receiving federal student aid.[50] But financial aid administrators noted that unlike food stamp recipients, student loan applicants were charged a fee for accepting assistance.[51]

This view of students as tax eaters marked a significant departure from the way the federal government previously saw students. For three decades, national lawmakers had regarded students primarily as future tax contributors, in whom the federal government should invest. This bipartisan belief had held sway since the Eisenhower administration and the early days of the Cold War.[52] Eisenhower's backing of federal aid in education, evinced by his support and signing of the National Defense Education Act (NDEA) in the summer of 1958, stemmed from his belief that investing in students was a matter of national security.[53] (Eisenhower did not support federal grants for nonveteran student education, but his support for federal aid for college education created the basis and foundations for a program where none had existed previously.[54]) The National Defense Student Loan Program (authorized under NDEA) charged 3–5 percent interest rates (to be repaid in ten years) on loans ranging between $1,000 and $5,000 for college students wanting to teach sciences or foreign languages.[55] (The latter amount, adjusted for inflation, would be approximately $8,060; in 1958, undergraduate tuition at an Ivy League institution such as the University of Pennsylvania was $1,050.[56]) By contrast, Reagan implicitly claimed that educational aid not only was inconsequential to the nation's defense interests, but competed with or even weakened them.

Meanwhile, despite his public support for Reagan's policies, Bell was becoming persona non grata for not being a team player. Administration insiders complained bitterly that Bell too frequently contradicted the Reagan education proposals at congressional hearings, was too conciliatory in his relations with Congress and special interests, and was perhaps even bent on "sabotaging" Reagan's program of budget and student aid cuts, vouchers, school prayer, and tuition tax credits.[57] He was never trusted by the more conservative members of the administration because of his suspected "left-leaning tendencies." Edwin Meese, director of the Reagan transition team, and Stockman, both of whom were counselors to the president, were especially suspicious of him.[58] Unlike his last stint in DC with the more moderate Ford regime, Bell had his testimony regularly vetted by those he dubbed the "zealots at OMB"—his apparent reference to Stockman—to ensure he challenged the need for student aid and legislation for disabled students.[59] "Confidential memos" from Bell's office were widely circulated and then leaked to reporters at conservative newspapers. As Stockman recalled, "We shackled Ted Bell with a sweeping retrenchment at the Education Department."[60] While administration insiders viewed the secretary skeptically, Bell's colleagues in higher education remained deeply disappointed in him for the loyalty he demonstrated to his boss. They did not believe the secretary fully endorsed Reagan's budget cuts, yet Bell nonetheless defended White House higher-education cuts in appropriations hearings time after time.

The end of Bell's tenure actually started with what most regard as his signature achievement as secretary. *A Nation at Risk* was a report on the state of education produced in 1983 by an eighteen-member commission led by Bell.[61] The report highlighted the deficiencies in US public schools, concluding that primary and secondary public education systems were failing to prepare America's workforce.[62] Although President Reagan had originally refused Bell's request to appoint a presidential commission, this did not stop the White House from taking credit following the glowing reception the press gave Bell's *A Nation at Risk*. The positive press offered the White House a perfect opportunity to continue its cuts: now the administration cast its reworking of education as a way to improve it while simultaneously underfunding it.[63] Published a year before the election, Bell's report was touted by Reagan, who quoted it on the campaign stump to show that his administration was serious about fixing failing schools. Reagan's surrogates boasted that while liberals such as Democratic presidential nominee Walter Mondale talked a good game about improving education, promising to throw money at the problem, the Reagan administration had been quietly immersing itself in a serious study of the crisis engulfing American education. To Bell, the campaign's use of *A Nation at Risk* in the run up to Reagan's landslide victory over Mondale was naked political exploitation with him as a political pawn.[64]

Bell's resignation was as ignominious as his tenure. Putting a kinder, gentler face on education served no useful purpose once Reagan won reelection. Thus, Bell's efforts to restore education funding to its earlier levels went nowhere. In fact, compared with other departments, Education was singled out for additional cuts after the November 1984 election. Even the secretary's "efforts to rearrange dollar allocations while keeping in budget [were] rebuffed."[65] For Reagan and his fellow conservatives, who regularly called for the Department of Education to be abolished, even a deep cut in the educational budget was regarded as a compromise.

Two days after Reagan's reelection, Jim Baker, the president's chief of staff, met with Bell to set the tone for the next four years. Baker told Bell he expected more "deep budget" cuts and conveyed a renewed desire by the president to abolish the department.[66] Through Baker, the president also made it clear that Bell's pet passion, the *A Nation at Risk* project, would not be a high priority now that a second term was secured. Bell, who went into the meeting with Baker hoping to stay at least two more years, instead submitted his resignation to the president by special courier early the next morning. "I never heard a word. No one telephoned. Three days later the president announced to the press that I had resigned for personal reasons."[67]

Bell was replaced by William Bennett, a self-described "recovering Democrat." Unlike his predecessor, Bennett had come to the GOP not by dint of birth, but by conversion. The forty-two-year-old political philosopher displayed the fervor of a new convert, possessing a missionary zeal and unflinchingly pressing the education policies of the White House. Bennett, who had previously overseen the National Endowment for the Humanities, was hired, as he explained during his first press conference, because of his affinity for the administration's vision of students on federal financial aid as the educational equivalents of welfare cheats. The problem was not simply that students were draining the tax system, according to Bennett. They were defrauding and abusing it.

Student aid abuse was an endemic rather than isolated problem for Bennett. He believed that for most, financial aid cuts would "require for some students divestiture of certain sorts—stereo divestiture, automobile divestiture, three weeks at the beach divestiture."[68] Bennett was careful not to be accused of demonizing too indiscriminately: "I do not mean to suggest that this be the case in *all* circumstances."[69] Nonetheless, the message delivered by Bennett was plain, according to *New York Times* education reporter Edward Fiske: there were a great many students who neither needed nor deserved a loan or grant and were bilking taxpayers for four years (or more) of state-supported luxury.

The president liked what he heard from his new secretary. "I've been following those press reports of your interviews," Reagan joked with Bennett at a public appearance shortly after the new secretary's first press conference. "I just wish you'd stop mincing your words."[70] If Reagan appeared to cotton to the new secretary's attacks, it may have been because Bennett's words were seemingly lifted directly from the president's own policy playbook and apocryphal yarn about the Cadillac-driving welfare queen. In Reagan's telling, the woman was a welfare cheat who possessed eighty names, thirty addresses, and twelve Social Security cards and collected veteran's benefits on four nonexisting deceased husbands—while receiving Social Security checks, Medicaid, and food stamps, plus collecting welfare under each of her assumed names. "Her tax-free cash income is over $150,000," Reagan often added for good measure.[71] In Bennett's updating of Reagan's yarn, the welfare queen had decided to get a degree or at least enroll in college to get more free money—a Pell Grant and student loan this time —and again all on the taxpayer's dime.

Politicizing Education: The Results of Reagan's First Term

The installation of Bennett reflected how deeply politicized the Education Department was by the mid-1980s. According to Congress's nonpartisan General Accounting Office (now called the Government Accountability Office), Education had "the greatest percentage of political appointees among its high officials of any cabinet, 45 percent." As the department became more ideological, its overall staff shrank by almost 38 percent by 1986.[72]

The 1986 budget cuts in student aid reflected the values of the new cabinet secretary. With Bennett's support, the administration looked to push between 500,000 and 2 million students off the federally subsidized loan rolls. They tried to revise the budget calculus so no households with incomes above $32,500 would receive federally supported loans and the total amount of loan, grant, and work-study funding would not exceed $4,000.[73] Even though Congress modified the budget somewhat and raised the income cap, it failed to take on the fundamental shortcomings of the Reagan aid cuts: underfunding student aid and shifting the expense to the states.[74] Although other cabinet members typically fought initial budget cuts in internal negotiations or, in the case of Defense Secretary Weinberger, begrudgingly accepted a modest increase, the new education secretary willingly accepted his department's cuts without any negotiations.[75]

Bennett and other critics of financial aid programs consistently argued that more aid simply gave universities the incentive to inflate tuition. Thus, the logic went, toeing the line in aid would slow or stop tuition increases. The rising cost of education in the 1980s (and subsequent decades) belied such reasoning, however. With few exceptions, reducing federal aid compelled colleges and universities across the country to raise tuition. "The growth curve in federal student aid leveled off sharply in the first half of the 1980s," but tuition continued to climb, wrote Lawrence Gladieux in a Department of Education report.[76] Tuition hikes had two measurable effects on student enrollment. First, they priced students out of the private college market, resulting in a shift in enrollment to lower-cost public universities, where expenditures and resources were already stretched thin.[77] Second, with less aid available but more tuition to pay, minority and low-income students were less likely to enroll. Not surprisingly, minority enrollment declined at state and private schools throughout the 1980s.[78] This was important, because there was lingering national concern about minority enrollment as an indicator of equal access to education and of economic progress.

The costs of higher education continued climbing for the next generation—despite the fact that government spending, adjusted for inflation, declined. Between 1982 and 2006, tuition and housing costs grew at three times (439 percent) the rate of median family income (147 percent).[79] Rising tuition also created an impediment for students in the lowest income quintile, who were graduating at the lowest rates in thirty years.[80] Reducing government aid failed to stem the inflationary costs of college, as had been predicted by OMB and others, and it began the slow and steady decline of the purchasing power of the Pell Grant, the nation's main source of government funding for working-class students.

Reagan's Second Term: Cuts Continued

Reagan introduced more budgetary cuts to higher education in his second term via the 1985 Gramm-Rudman-Hollings Act, the Tax Reform Act of 1986, and the White House 1987 fiscal year budget, indicating that the administration was not yet satisfied with the effects its first-term policies were already having. Passed at the beginning of Reagan's second term, the Gramm-Rudman-Hollings Act introduced an across-the-board cut of 4.3 percent to a wide swath of nondefense federal programs. Bryant College president William T. O'Hara lobbied the administration to exempt financial aid from cuts emanating from the act—given that previous Reagan fiscal decisions had resulted in a

12–15 percent loss in real dollars and a $500,000 reduction in Pell Grant awards for the tiny Rhode Island college. To make up for this Pell short-fall, Bryant substantially increased institutional need-based grants. If faced with further reductions from Gramm-Rudman-Hollings, which the college estimated would result in a $1.5 million shortfall for its students the next academic year (1987), O'Hara feared the college could not absorb the loss.[81] At Williams College in Massachusetts, a number of economic analyses indicated that policy changes regarding tax deductions would result in a decrease by at least 30 percent of gift income from private sources to postsecondary institutions. "My fundamental concern with the proposal for reducing and revising the Federal student aid programs is the strategic purpose that underlies the proposed change: the attempt to shift to the states those higher education costs now borne by the Federal government," wrote Williams president John W. Chandler.[82] With students no longer receiving the same or greater aid to attend private institutions, their alternatives would be to enroll in public universities, which would place heavier demands on campus facilities, staff, administrators, and faculty while only further stretching the already more limited college budgets.

Even Reagan's unalloyed allies in higher education thought deeper aid cuts were a bad idea. Nichols College president Lowell C. Smith enthusiastically endorsed drastic cuts in or eliminating federal dollars for higher education altogether, recommending twelve areas of college funding where the administration might introduce cuts, including the National Education Association and the National Endowment for the Humanities, which he thought had become "more political than cultural." Yet he carved out financial aid as an exception. Smith wrote, "This is the only title in . . . law that deserves significant support. The whole question of student access to higher education is at risk here and without significant federal aid there is a genuine risk that thousands and thousands of students will be deprived of the opportunity to pursue college level work. . . . The increases in these amounts are quite reasonable compared with the percentage for most of the other titles."[83] Similarly, Kenneth LaValle, who worked for Reagan's election and reelection and was chair of the higher-education committee for the New York Senate, criticized reductions in the guaranteed student loan program, by which New York would lose as much as one-third of the loans awarded in 1985. "Further reductions in aid," LaValle told the White House, "generated greater tax burdens upon individuals and businesses as the states attempt to maintain collegiate access levels."[84] While ruled unconstitutional a year later, Gramm-Rudman-Hollings would be built upon by subsequent legislation like the Tax Reform Act of 1986 that carried it out.

The following year, the Tax Reform Act of 1986 had the practical effect of converting any student on aid into a student taxpayer. It did so by taxing fellowships, scholarships, tuition remission, and other nonloan financial assistance. The act recast scholarships, grants, fellowships, stipends, internships, and prizes as taxable income and placed the onus on students to declare the gross income portions of all this funding. Only expenses exclusively related to school, such as tuition, fees, and books, could be legally exempt. Still, the student taxpayer had to document these school-related expenses for at least three years. After 1986, for example, Lisa Jones, a college student receiving $10,000 in scholarships and grants who spent $8,000 for tuition and another $800 for books and supplies, now had to report $1,200 to the IRS as taxable income.[85] This new tax hit professional and graduate students, many of whom were married and had children, particularly hard, although the graduate student population did narrowly escape the doubling of origination fees on loans.

By December 1986, the first wave of reports of a student debt crisis came in. A congressional report entitled *Student Loans: Are They Overburdening a Generation?* expressed the concern that too many students were assuming too much debt before taking jobs. Students borrowed more at that point than ever, with nearly 50 percent of all students leaving college in debt. In 1975–76, loans constituted one-fifth of student aid; by 1986, they totaled almost 50 percent.[86] Student indebtedness had implications well beyond individuals' financial well-being, affecting the future health of the overall national economy, according to the report. Secretary Bennett dismissed Congress's report as exaggerated, countering with his frequent retort about the earning power of those with college degrees compared with those holding only a high school diploma: "Having a $10,000 debt burden with the $600,000 advantage you get from going to college isn't bad. You need to put that in perspective," he said in an exchange with *NBC News* reporter Irving R. Levine.[87] The next year, 1987, the administration pressed to further reduce the number of aid recipients, placing more downward pressure on the Pell Grant program—even after studies showed that a declining number of freshmen had enrolled in college. It pressed for the continuation of a stronger emphasis on student loans than on grants. The Pell Grant program funded one of every four college students. The administration proposed to reduce the number to one in six.[88]

Historic levels of personal debt led to unprecedented defaults. Guaranteed student loan net default rates had steadily declined since 1978 but started to move up again in 1985 (from 8.4 percent in fiscal year 1984 to 8.9 percent), the first year that student borrowers under Reagan's new financial aid policies were asked to begin repaying their loans.[89] By September 1987, the Education Department projected the guaranteed student loans default cost for fiscal year 1988 to be $1.6 billion, up from $2.4 million in 1980.[90] Defaults in Parent Loan for Undergraduate Students (PLUS) and other supplemental loan programs, often with higher loan limits or repayments that began just sixty days after disbursement, would cost the government an additional $32 million.[91] Bennett and others stamped loan defaulters as undeserving "deadbeats" who were all too happy to stiff taxpayers.[92] "A deadbeat is as a deadbeat does," Bennett replied when asked by a reporter to characterize the student in default, defined by the Education Department as a borrower who was supposed to pay in fiscal year 1985 but had not done so by September 1986.[93] The department was zealous about collection on its loans and proved the most successful by far of any federal department in collecting outstanding debts. As an OMB official put it, "If you owe a debt to the taxpayer of America, you can run but you can't hide." OMB coordinated with the IRS and Department of Education to confiscate more than $116 million in only six months from 217,000 former college students.[94]

Bennett's profile of the student loan defaulter was at best inaccurate and incomplete, according to the department's own Office of the Inspector General. Rather than fleecing the financial aid system, the typical defaulter was more likely to be a struggling, minimally employed or unemployed twentysomething from a working-poor family, according to Dallas Martin, president of the National Association of Student Financial Aid Administrators (NASFAA), the largest trade group with a primary focus on postsecondary community and student aid legislation.[95] The troubled borrower was also far more likely to have dropped out of a vocational or technical school than a four-year university.[96] More important, the administration neglected to recognize its role, if unintended, in fomenting the crisis, Martin lamented in his testimony before a Senate subcommittee in December 1987. Students were not intended to depend "entirely on loans or accumulate large amounts of debt," Martin said. But he added, "Overall reductions in federal student aid since 1980 have reduced the percentage of grant and work-study dollars available," compelling students from working-class and increasingly middle-class families to rely on college loans.[97] The Department of Education showed far more institutional will in going after struggling former students defaulting on their loans than it did in pursuing the major institutional culprits: fly-by-night and other for-profit schools that took grant and loan funds despite having low graduation rates, low placement rates, and more than 20 percent of students in default.[98] Federal marshals entered homes of defaulted students in order to drag them to court, but these schools got off with warning letters.[99]

The savings to taxpayers—the rationale for making the cuts—were often dubious. For example, one putative cost-cutting administration measure was the outsourcing of student loan debt collection. But as OMB's own records indicate, this failed to produce any net savings or reduce federal activity.[100] What it did lead to was the greatest debacle in the history of student financial aid, when United Education and Software, a company responsible for tracking and collecting the debts of nearly five hundred thousand students, lost track of hundreds of thousands of student loan files, sent threatening letters to student borrowers in good standing, and ignored actual delinquent borrowers. This mess would take years to clear up, with the total losses estimated to be approximately $650 million.[101]

By the mid-1980s, the purchasing power of the Pell Grant had declined by 50 percent.[102] For nearly nine years in the 1980s this trend continued, as college costs grew and outpaced inflation.[103] As the purchasing power of the Pell Grant declined, what it covered shrank as well. In 1980, a Pell Grant covered 56 percent of tuition costs, but by 1988, it was only 47 percent.[104] At the dawn of the decade, when President Carter submitted his budget for fiscal year 1980, a maximum Pell Grant promised to cover 50 percent of the price of attending a four-year public institution: tuition and fees payable to the institution, books and supplies, room and board, and transportation to and from the school. By decade's end, when President Reagan proposed his 1989 budget, the share had dwindled to 35 percent.[105] With for-profit colleges taken out of the equation, Pell outlays to traditional two- and four-year colleges and universities were even paltrier. Students were not simply more reliant on loans; thanks to Reagan policies that introduced origination fees, these loans now cost student borrowers more for years, if not decades.

Summing Up the Reagan Legacy on Education: "Mixed Picture"?

In Reagan's final State of the Union address in 1988, he struck a familiar educational theme: spend less, but expect more.[106] Reagan's outgoing fiscal budget provided much more for education than had previous budgets, but as Wisconsin Democratic congressman David Obey reminded Secretary Bennett, "Kids go to school every year, not just in election years."[107] The House Education Committee chairman, Augustus Hawkins, also a Democrat, shared Obey's assessment, reminding the press, "The last time Reagan proposed to spend more on education than Congress appropriated was during his own reelection campaign in 1984."[108] The nonpartisan College Board, best known for administering the SAT and other standardized examinations, was also cynical, dismissing the budget as typical "election year program increases."[109] The College Board was kinder when handing out its report card on the Reagan years, describing the period from 1980 to 1988 as a "mixed picture." The bad news was that federal student aid in inflation-adjusted dollars had declined 17 percent from 1980 to 1988. At roughly the same time, the percentage of Pell Grant dollars for students at for-profit colleges more than doubled between academic year 1980–81 and academic year 1986–87.[110] The post-Reagan 1990s would further cement this new normal, as loan policies and state funding in the next decade shifted costs even more firmly to students.

Trickle-Down Taxes: The States

The shift to family and student accountability trickled down to the states as well. Starting in the 1990s, state support for higher education represented a declining share of *all* state budget expenditures.[111] Faced with tight budgets during the recessionary years of the early 1990s, states shifted spending away from discretionary expenditures (e.g., higher education) to government-mandated or entitlement programs like public assistance caseloads, Medicaid costs, federally mandated healthcare, and increases in K–12 public schools and corrections budgets.[112] Consequently, in 1990–91, state general fund expenditures allocated 33.7 percent for primary and secondary education, 10.5 percent for Medicaid, and 14.1 percent for higher education (figure 2.1).[113] By 2010–11, general fund expenditures had been redistributed away from discretionary expenses to mandatory state outlays, with larger shares reallocated, often for very understandable and good reasons, to primary and secondary education (35 percent) and Medicaid (17.4 percent), while, at the same time, support declined proportionally for higher education (from 14.1 percent to 11.5 percent).[114]

The result for college tuition was predictable: raising prices when students and families could least afford it. During this time, the proportion of revenues public colleges and universities received from state appropriations would steadily decline as well, from 38.3 percent in

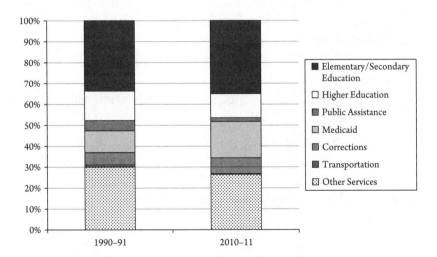

FIGURE 2.1 State general fund expenditures, by category, 1990–91 and 2010–11

Source: National Association of State Budget Officers, State Expenditure Report, various years

fiscal year 1990–91 to 24.4 percent by 2010–11. (And while both the early 1990s and 2010–11 were recessionary times, cutbacks signaled a larger trend.) After controlling for inflation, states collectively invested $8.75 per $1,000 in 1990–91, compared with only $6.12 per $1,000 in 2009–10. And no state invested more than it had twenty years before (table 2.1).[115] This drop, again, signaled the public's declining interest in investing in higher education.

By 2010, states devoted less wealth to higher education than they did in the early 1990s. The figures are starker when population growth is factored in. A cursory look at aggregate state support for higher education suggests it increased 0.8 percent per year from 1990 onward. But, in fact, state support failed to keep pace with the growing young adult population, which grew at a much faster annual rate (1.2 percent) than state support (0.8 percent).[116] Funding for public full-time-equivalent (FTE) students kept with these downward trends. From 1990–91 to 2009–10, real funding (exclusive of the 2009 American Recovery and Reinvestment Act [ARRA]) per public FTE student dropped by 26.1 percent, falling to $6,360 from $8,608 (table 2.1). Moreover, real per capita funding for higher education dropped from $261 to $244, or 2.3 percent, and public FTE enrollment figures increased at more than double (1.8 percent) the annual rate of state investment (again, 0.8 percent). Had state-level funding kept pace with enrollment since 1990–91, total appropriations in 2009–10 would have been approximately $102 billion, or 35 percent greater than the actual amount.[117]

As funding at the federal and state levels covered less and less of a student's higher-education expenditures, student financial aid failed

TABLE 2.1 Average Support for Higher Education by States in the United States

	1990–91	2010–11
Funding per Full-Time-Equivalent Student	$8,608	$6,360
Funding per $1,000	$8.75	$6.12
Funding per Capita	$261	$244

Sources: Edward R. Hines, Appropriations: State Tax Funds for Operating Expenses of Higher Education, 1990–1991; for 2010-11 figures, see John Quinterno, "The Great Cost Shift: How Higher Education Cuts Undermine the Middle Class" (March 2012), at http://www.demos.org/sites/default/files/publications/thegreatcostshift_0.pdf

to keep up with college costs during the 1990s, according to a 2002 study on the affordability of higher education.[118] With governments doing less, students' share of the cost of education spiked. Students and universities had to pick up the tab in the form of ever-higher tuition fee costs. The question is not whether states allocated relatively less for higher education in the 1990s, but why. The reasons for this did not originate in state legislatures alone.

Beyond the States: Why the Federal Matters

At first glance, the great cost shift for a college education appears to be a problem hatched as much in statehouses and governors' mansions as at Pennsylvania Avenue. After all, from the 1970s to 2013, the costs of college paid by states dropped from 65 percent to a mere 30 percent.[119] At the same time, the federal government actually appeared to increase its commitment, from 10 percent in the 1970s to 16 percent by circa 2013.[120] But such statistics, without their larger political economic context, may conceal more than they illuminate. Specifically, unmooring federal figures from the context that anchors them obscures how important these subterranean forces, just beneath the surface of the trending statistics, were for the seismic shifts in state outlays toward higher education. They are also essential in ultimately explaining why states allocated less. Take, for example, the issue of government deficits. While the federal government was free to run deficits to pay its expenses, every state, with the sole exception of Vermont, possessed a statutory or constitutional requirement to balance its budget.[121] This fiscal reality meant that states lacked the flexibility in spending that the federal government had. Despite this flexibility, the federal government impressed on state and local municipalities that the nation was entering an age of "recognized limits," in terms of both foreign interventions and domestic spending, which would necessitate belt-tightening.[122] By the early 1980s, this age-of-limits thinking would apply primarily to domestic social policy, as the Reagan White House ratcheted up defense spending. By the 1990s, states were faced with paying for a growing number of costs once covered at the federal level.

Given their limited options vis-à-vis Washington, state elected officials made the political calculation that it was safer to rob Peter to pay

Paul—that is, to divert existing funds from discretionary costs to non-discretionary costs—than to raise Peter's or Paul's taxes. Elected officials along the electoral food chain noticed that Reagan had paid no electoral price for cutting higher-education spending, evinced by Reagan's landslide reelection in 1984. And although George H. W. Bush's successful 1988 election campaign was boosted by his pledge "Read my lips: no new taxes," his "broken promise" was later used as political fodder by both Republican primary challenger Patrick Buchanan and Democratic presidential nominee Bill Clinton to hamper his 1992 reelection campaign. These same voters were far more likely to punish lawmakers for raising taxes than for cutting them. What ensued was a race to the budgetary bottom, with cities and states often outdoing one another to see who could cut corporate and personal income taxes more.

In this way, Reagan's tax policies had a cascading effect on state budgets. Most states followed Reagan's tax template of the 1980s. According to economist Ronald Ehrenberg, these tax cuts resulted in budget shortfalls in many states: "There simply have not been sufficient revenues available to fund public higher education generously, and dramatic reductions in the share of state budgets devoted to higher education have taken place."[123] These state deficits were particularly palpable with respect to the most rapidly growing public cost: healthcare.

The expansion of Medicaid eligibility, which effectively shifted costs away from the federal to state government, also drained funds available for higher education.[124] The shift was especially severe in the early 1980s.[125] Since the 1960s, Reagan had held a long-running ambivalence toward Medicaid recipients, whom he reportedly described around the law's passage in 1965 as "a faceless mass, waiting for handouts."[126] Now, as president, Reagan seized the chance to push many of the 22 million Medicaid beneficiaries off the federal rolls by making major cuts or at least requiring that the states pay much more to keep them there.[127] Under Reagan, federal expenditures were cut by $4 billion between 1981 and 1984. These cuts placed downward pressure on states to cut or cover these healthcare expenses.[128] While some states responded by making Medicaid cuts of their own, others sought to close the gap by "making up the difference using other state revenues."[129] Moreover, even when states did attempt to impose cost containment controls (e.g., limits on hospital stays or physician visits), these measures did little to reduce utilization and spending. Despite cutbacks and cost controls, states maintained basic services, however. As a result, they still were required to make up the cost somewhere.[130] Increasingly, these costs were made up through discretionary spending transfers from higher education to Medicaid funding.

A series of economic shocks was another subterranean factor in states' decreased support for higher education. Three economic recessions over the span of a decade (January 1980, July 1981, March 1990) further dried up states' revenues while simultaneously sparking increased competition for ever-shrinking dollars among rival state agencies responsible for funding Medicare, corrections, and education, among other programs. As a last resort, then, states turned to students. By the mid-2000s, "every public official [knew] that colleges and universities [could] raise tuition to compensate for state cutbacks," concluded JBL Associates, a leading team of postsecondary policy experts.[131] As a consequence, higher education took the "worst beating of any major spending category" at the state level.[132] Hiking tuition and fees at moments of fiscal crisis and apparent federal indifference, cash-strapped state governments looked on college students as the equivalent of well-heeled relatives with seemingly bottomless pockets who could always be relied upon to help make budgetary ends meet during tough times.

The New Consensus: A Bipartisan Cost Shift Through the 1990s

In 1995, Benjamin Weisman saw unprecedented government cuts in higher education as an opportunity to bring free-market practices to his resistant colleagues and administrators at Mercy College, a private liberal arts college in Dobbs Ferry, New York, where Weisman chaired the economics and business department. Faced with deep cuts of 25 percent to all campus programs and losing $2.2 million of federal and state support,[133] yet fearful that offsetting these losses with additional tuition and fee hikes would depress student enrollment, Weisman proposed that professors' salaries be pegged to student enrollment (rather than teacher instruction and class performance).[134] The plan was simple: faculty members would receive a 7 percent pay raise if student enrollment rose by four hundred or more or take a 7 percent cut if the quota was not reached. It was an incentive structure modeled largely on Weisman's experiences as a Wall Street consultant. By a 4-to-1 vote, the Mercy faculty adopted the Weisman plan. "It was presented to us by the Administration" as a "no-choice option," said the American Association of University Professors chapter president Marvin Karp.[135] Pink slips were the only alternative. "We made the trade off of gambling . . . on student enrollment rather than see significant numbers of our colleagues decimated [by layoffs]," Karp added.[136]

The incentive was widely credited with increasing enrollment 20 percent by the next year.[137] Mercy president Jay Sexter seized on this engineered collapse of higher education to impose a new and permanent economic paradigm on campus employees.[138] Sexter and Weisman also hoped this new approach would give the college a distinct competitive advantage over other schools. What began as an emergency, stopgap measure to avoid large-scale and massive layoffs increasingly looked to become a university fixture. Within three years, the bonus system at Mercy appeared firmly entrenched, even turning a tidy profit for the university by 1998.[139]

Whether the Weisman plan ultimately worked is debatable. What is clear is that, after more than a decade of severe government cuts and threats, higher education was forced to make certain compromises, making schools fundamentally change the structures under which higher education had functioned for centuries. As the Mercy case illustrates, college administrators and many faculty members were not opposed to the laissez-faire capitalist approaches to problem solving that had gained such adulation in the Reagan era. Such a system of commodifying and monetizing public services reimagined taxpayers as shareholders more interested in quarterly returns than in making multigenerational societal investments. Indeed, similar stories cropped up on other campuses. "We are struggling with good faith efforts to restructure, and they aren't satisfied," said Russell Adams, chairman of the Afro American Studies Department at Howard University in Washington, DC; his institution faced a total of nearly $200 million in federal cuts. "We still have massive defense budgets with no real enemy, and they are saying we can't afford a Howard."[140] Public colleges and universities were even more vulnerable than private ones such as Mercy and Howard. At public colleges, cutbacks resulted in larger classes, heavier teaching loads, fewer student services, and poorer maintenance. The loss of state support for higher education was an even bigger blow to previous funding models.[141] With an emaciated government student aid system, the choice was no longer between grants and loans, but rather what would be the preferred loan product the government would offer the student-consumer. Although a surfeit of loan options was available to students by the early 1990s, two vied for dominance of the market: direct loans and guaranteed student loans.

The Early Clinton Years: The Origins of Direct Lending

As President Clinton closed out his first one hundred days in the White House in 1993, a *Money* magazine headline predicted, "Count on Big College Aid Changes under Bill Clinton."[142] However, most of the items on Clinton's agenda—loan forgiveness in exchange for community service, loan repayments tied to income, and penalty-free individual retirement accounts (IRAs) to pay for college—either failed to pass Congress or were ultimately thought too incremental and modest to matter much.[143] His most ambitious early effort to tackle runaway private and public debt was establishing a direct lending program. Direct lending would also fail, although it suffered quite a different fate than his other efforts.

Direct lending was not a new idea. It was originally raised in the late 1950s by Chicago economist Milton Friedman and others as part of the National Defense Education Act. Friedman's plan was to minimize bureaucracy by directly using US Treasury funds to help the non-rich pay for college, instead of having the federal government subsidize private lenders to provide loans to, or collect them from, needy students. By eliminating the middlemen or bankers, the government would reduce the service costs of loan delivery and repayment and thereby pass those savings on to student borrowers (and ultimately taxpayers) in the form of cheaper loans. Direct lending would get tabled in the 1960s for a more expansive guaranteed student loan program. But eager to balance the budget, the Clinton White House resurrected it, seeing direct lending as an important component of the administration's overall deficit reduction plan.[144] Direct lending, the administration argued, was simpler, faster, and cheaper—saving about $1.9 billion, or $190 per student, starting in 1996.[145] The plan was to expand direct lending from 4 percent of new student loans in 1994–95 to 100 percent by 1997–98.[146] A direct loan was simpler, faster, and cheaper because it did not require the kinds of subsidies and guarantees that the federal guaranteed loan system did.[147] The loan would be issued by the US Department of Education (with money from the Treasury) and not a private lender. Whether from an interest payment or origination fee, the money made from a direct loan would go to the government and not a private lender.[148] Multiple cost-benefit analyses of direct lending concluded that it was a more efficient and cheaper alternative than the incentive-laden deals of guaranteed loans.

The banking industry, not surprisingly, contended that direct lending had major flaws.[149] Direct loans would deprive students and parents of private lenders' financial expertise. Higher education, or more specifically college financial aid offices, would be ill prepared to handle the rush of additional expenditures (personnel, equipment, etc.), and direct lending would be less efficient and lead to more government waste and potential abuse. Lenders also hinted that they had a higher mission. "Guaranteed student lending is a marginally profitable business," said Phillip Hamm of Meridian Bank, adding that Meridian and other lenders were lending not for profit but "for students."[150] Finally and perhaps most significantly, lenders argued that direct lending would be costly to taxpayers. Bankers claimed that once start-up and administrative costs were factored in, direct lending would add between $75 billion and $100 billion to the federal debt (then estimated at $4 trillion).[151]

Some outside of the banking industry also criticized the shift to direct lending. Many opposed it on inflationary grounds or as another example of expanding government. Others argued that the "easy money" of state and federal grants was a perverse incentive that would lead to higher costs for families. As John Hood of the libertarian-minded John Locke Foundation put it, "Why should anyone be surprised at the huge increases in college costs and government spending on higher education" when loans gave students and, by extension, schools access to such easy money? Continuing to underwrite higher education with government money would only encourage universities to charge students more, he added. "By taking private risk out of the system," Hood argued, "the government has only transferred that risk to taxpayers." For Hood and others opposed to direct lending, too much public support, not too little, was the central problem plaguing higher education. They believed government aid, as opposed to market priorities, was the reason why the number of new faculty members (often in unnecessary academic programs, Hood and others claimed) had risen faster (76 percent) than student enrollment (59 percent) from 1970 to 1990.[152]

Direct Lending: "The Best Thing since Microwave Brownies"

Despite concerns, direct lending ultimately proved a more efficient and cheaper system. The first wave of media reports on the direct lending pilot program was quite positive. Funds were disbursed to students in weeks rather than months. In the first week of the 1994–95 school year, for example, $13 million was disbursed to students, compared with only $3 million the year before, when schools used the guaranteed student loan.[153] "It's the best thing since microwave brownies," proclaimed Anthony Gallegos, a twenty-two-year-old journalism major at Colorado State University, one of 104 colleges and universities using direct lending during the program's inaugural year.[154] Colorado State University financial aid director Kay Jacks shared the student's enthusiasm for the pilot project, praising direct lending as a "spiritual experience" compared with the guaranteed loan program. "It helps us provide students with a better service, period," Jacks added.[155] In addition to students receiving aid in a fraction of the time, the paperwork proved simpler and easier to navigate.

The direct program also appeared to work well for universities. Rather than deal with the seven hundred or so different lenders and the forty state guarantee agencies used to administer and collect guaranteed student loans, college financial aid departments dealt with only one federal office. "We would characterize our first year in the [direct lending] program as being very close to an unqualified success," the director of financial aid at the University of Washington told the *New York Times*.[156] This was the general sentiment among financial aid administrators nationally. Although noting that the choice should ultimately be left to schools, the president of NASFAA, Dallas Martin, acknowledged that the program's first year was "successful" and had "received high marks" from fellow financial aid practitioners.[157] At the University of Florida, direct lending was thought to be so far superior that the entire financial aid office threatened to quit if the university returned to the guaranteed loan system.[158] Ninety percent of universities polled rated the new direct lending system "excellent," according to one survey regularly touted by Education Secretary Richard Riley.[159]

Approximately 2,300 schools applied for the direct loan program by the start of the next school year. But because lending capacity had a cap at 40 percent of the total federal student loan volume, the Department of Education accepted only 1,500 schools. The remaining 800 schools were waitlisted for the next round, beginning in July 1996.[160] By 1996, direct lending had captured about one-third of the student loan market share, cutting a sizable chunk from banks and guaranty agencies.[161] (Guaranty agencies, among other things, loaned money supplied by banks at higher rates but on easier terms.[162]) Buoyed by this early success, the Clinton administration made plans to expand the program to include 1,641 colleges and universities by the 1996–97 school year.

However, the GOP-controlled House disputed the White House's positive assessment of direct lending and its cost-saving advantages for students and taxpayers. House Budget Committee chairman John Kasich argued that direct lending did not offer lower interest rates than guaranteed student loans. Citing a Congressional Budget Office (CBO) report that appeared to lend credence to his position, Kasich claimed the guaranteed loan program would save taxpayers $1.5 billion more than the direct program over a seven-year period.[163] Alice Rivlin, director of the Office of Management and Budget, pointed out, however, that at least two-thirds (or $1 billion) of the GOP's cost-cutting plan would come from removing federal oversight of the loan program—a deregulatory move that put students and ultimately taxpayers at considerable risk.[164] The higher cost Kasich attributed to direct lending was also the result of GOP congressional changes to federal accounting rules. Under these new rules, the CBO was required to count the administrative costs of direct loans in its overall project budget, but not the full government costs to administer the guaranteed loan program.[165] Later calculations would show that, when adjusted to incorporate administrative costs associated with these two loans, direct lending actually saved taxpayers more, not less, than guaranteed student loans.

For example, guaranteed student loans cost taxpayers $8.91 per loan, whereas direct lending yielded $2.06 in *revenue* for taxpayers.[166]

Concerned that the guaranteed student loan system fleeced taxpayers, not all fiscally conservative Republicans sided with the GOP House majority. "Making the change the industry proposes without looking at other changes which might be necessary is problematic," Lawrence Lindsey, a Republican economist serving a term as the Federal Reserve governor of consumer finance, informed one Republican senator in a letter. Lindsey added, "As long as it is necessary to provide a profit to induce lenders to guarantee student loans, direct lending will be cheaper."[167] Administration officials and financial aid officers also claimed that competition from direct lending spurred the industry to offer better terms, and indeed, at a minimum, competition from direct lending appeared to push banks to offer more attractive terms to student borrowers. While pronouncing the group's neutrality, NASFAA president Dallas Martin acknowledged to fellow panelists on a federal advisory panel that guaranteed student loans "is a better program" because of direct lending.[168]

Direct borrowers also maintained lower default rates (7.9 percent) than guaranteed student loan borrowers (8.8 percent), according to a 1999 report.[169] Under federal direct loans, the government could more easily garnish a borrower's paychecks, and direct loans also featured income-contingent repayments, which pegged student loan repayments to one's monthly earnings rather than a simple flat monthly rate, thus reducing the number of defaults.[170] Lower rates of default benefited taxpayers, too, as there were fewer losses to be covered or written off. Ultimately, direct loans may have lessened the debt burden for guaranteed student loan borrowers. The lower costs meant that subsidized private lenders needed to offer better rates, origination fees, rebates, and repayments—which often lowered the overall cost of a student loan—if banks wished to stay competitive.[171]

Perhaps most important, direct lending remained a better deal for taxpayers. Even if direct lending could not offer lower interest rates, as Kasich claimed, it nonetheless remained cheaper for borrowers and ultimately taxpayers. That was, in large part, because there were fewer fees and administrative costs than were typically charged or tacked on by the host of private lenders—the so-called private middlemen—that the federal government relied on to fund guaranteed student loans. "Estimates from all of the government's budgeting and auditing agencies showed that direct lending would deliver the same loans to students at significantly lower costs to taxpayers."[172] A guaranteed student loan cost the government $12.80 for every $100 borrowed. By comparison, direct loans brought in 22 cents for every $100 borrowed, even after administrative costs were deducted, according to one study.[173] Direct lending saved $1.9 billion, or $190 per student, more than a guaranteed student loan. After the program was established and the government was no longer covering its start-up cost, the gap between the programs was expected to widen. Banking on this, the Clinton White House envisaged direct lending as contributing to its goal of balancing the budget, expecting direct lending to save taxpayers $4.3 billion once the program was up and running.[174] Even the 2006 Bush White House educational budget showed that a guaranteed student loan cost $11 more per $100 loan than did a direct loan.[175]

Evidence also indicated that direct lending could potentially create a long-term stimulus to the overall financial economy. Certainly, investors believed an expanded direct lending program would undercut the stock values of Sallie Mae and many publicly traded student lenders and the securities market they often served. That said, other large-scale institutional investors, particularly those in equity markets, endorsed low-cost direct loans as a way to lower the deficit and thus reduce interest rates, spurring domestic growth. Morgan Stanley bullishly touted direct lending in its newsletter as a "budgetary winner" that "will lower government spending and reduce the deficit."[176]

Post–Republican Revolution: The Defeat of Direct Lending

Direct lending could never gain a permanent foothold, however. Despite the advantages of direct lending and the Clinton vision of having direct loans be the only option by 2000, these loans never topped more than one-third of all undergraduate loan allocations during the Clinton and Bush years (figure 2.2). In fact, after 1996, the proportion of direct loan allocations declined each year until 2007. It wouldn't be until the 2010–11 fiscal year that direct lending would again gain political favor.

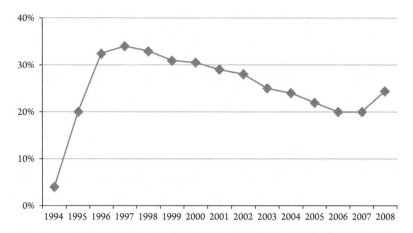

FIGURE 2.2 Direct loan share of annual new federal loan volume, 1994–2008

Sources: US Department of Education; New America Foundation

After the initial flush of interest, guaranteed student loans quickly regained dominance. Three major factors contributed to their resurgence and the generation-long undoing of direct lending: the Republican revolution of 1994, lender lobbying, and the thaw in Clinton's relations with the GOP, which was reflected in his embrace of tax credits.

The 1994 Republican victory ushered in congressional leadership whose main education proposals centered on shifting a larger share of education costs to student borrowers while expanding the market's role in student lending. At the same time, an otherwise cost-conscious Congress passed a series of measures that embraced the guaranteed student loan program, including loosening rules on banks, expanding a costlier and less efficient version of the program, and lowering Department of Education oversight of student lenders.

In Congress, the mood harkened back to the Reagan administration. As Congressmen William Goodling (R-PA) and Howard "Buck" McKeon (R-CA) wrote in a 1995 *Washington Post* op-ed, entitled student borrowers still insisted the government give them "something for nothing."[177] For Goodling, McKeon, and other congressional conservatives, the only thing worse than the existing system was one that would expand government's role while crowding out the private sector.[178] The broader aim was to apply the revenue generated from increased borrowing costs (e.g., charging student borrowers interest on their loans while in school) to help balance the federal budget by 2002.[179] In theory, the House Republican position appeared quite logical. Those directly benefiting should pay more; moreover, the private sector was assumed to be more efficient in handling and dispensing financial services.

By 1995, proponents of the guaranteed student loan program had pushed ahead legislation in the 104th Congress, promptly enacting a de facto muzzle law on supporters of direct lending. The law prohibited the Department of Education from requiring or even encouraging colleges to switch to the direct loan program, effectively stopping the program in its tracks.[180] While the Department of Education was blocked from marketing what many considered a cheaper, more streamlined direct loan alternative, private student lenders were free to lure universities to stay in the guaranteed loan system by almost any means they deemed fit.[181]

Once Republicans in Congress marginalized or silenced the competition, private lenders launched a charm offensive for the guaranteed student loan program, aggressively lobbying members of Congress and wooing financial aid officers. Between 1997 and 2003, Sallie Mae lobbying expenditures were the third highest of any company in the credit industry.[182] In 1995, the new Republican majority passed legislation that capped the proportion of direct loans to no more than 40 percent of all student loans.[183] Such lobbying efforts also may have helped the industry win other legislative battles at the time; lobbyists persuaded Congress to create a new interest rate formula and to table planned interest rate deductions, as well as keep the muzzle on direct lending.[184]

The muzzle law, coupled with state and federal cutbacks that made new, large-scale government subsidies unlikely, fostered an environment of codependency between increasingly solicitous aid administrators and their corporate suitors. Once reluctant financial aid administrators reconciled themselves to the fact that their new reality was predicated on a "pay-to-play" relationship with banks and other lenders, they began courting the guaranteed lending industry. "Send a note of thanks to our sponsors," the chair of the corporate committee at MASFAA prodded fellow executive council members. "They enjoy and appreciate hearing from us."[185] In fact, in the aftermath of the 1995

muzzle law, the bulk of MASFAA correspondence was often dedicated to "thanking" PNC, Bank One, Chemical, Household Bank,
Quodata, Fifth Third Bank, Educaid, US Bancorp, and other student
lenders for sponsoring various workshops, institutes, and other func-
tions for the trade group.[186]

Major lenders also appointed university officials to ad hoc advisory
boards, flying them first class to retreats at swanky hotels or villas. Ellen
Frishberg, financial aid director at Johns Hopkins University, described
getting "an endless stream of invitations," recalling that earlier in the
month she had declined concert tickets from Sallie Mae to see the pop
rock band Huey Lewis and the News. "It's quite comical at times,"
Frishberg added.[187] In addition to junkets, lenders enticed resource-
poor colleges with goods and services that many institutions otherwise
could not afford. One lender, for example, promised to provide the
financial aid office at Tuskegee University free loan counseling, com-
puter software, and temporary employees to help reduce the workload
of overworked financial aid employees.[188] Sallie Mae tried to lure even
more schools with so-called opportunity loans, available only to schools
that promised to abandon the direct loan program and work exclusively
with the mega-lender, even though this appeared to violate a federal
law prohibiting lenders from offering direct or indirect inducements.
Another inducement used at the time was the "school as lender," in
which lenders extended a line of credit to cash-strapped universities.
Schools used the equity line to make loans to graduate and professional
students, then sold the loan debt back to partner banks, typically charging them a premium between 2 and 6 percent of the total loan portfolio.[189] The more students borrowed, the more income was generated for
the institution—in terms of both the originating loan interest and fees,
often as much as $1 million, that private lenders awarded to schools for
bringing in loan business. "We figure it'll bring in about $1.3 million a
year," the financial aid director at Wayne State University, Bryan Terry,
told a reporter for US News & World Report. "We make more money
by making more loans," said Karen Fooks, financial aid director at the
University of Florida. "The linkage is so obvious it ruins our credibility," Fooks added.[190] In exchange, lenders expected an exclusive relationship with the school, not the government's direct loan program,
when it came to making undergraduate loans. Within the decade, US

News & World Report would be comparing Sallie Mae and other private student lenders to "old time political ward bosses, [who] used money and favors, along with their friends in Congress and the Department of Education, to get what they wanted."[191]

By 1998, hoping to seal direct lending's fate, Congress had passed legislation allowing students to pay lower interest rates on guaranteed student loans than private lenders would receive, with the federal government picking up the difference, at a cost to the federal government of $1.5 million to $3 billion over five years.[192] The Clinton White House opposed the move in an effort to protect the direct lending program, according to Goodling. The Clinton administration eventually backed down when the legislation was passed as a temporary measure and was included as part of a transportation bill.[193] This was the final blow to direct lending.

Those in the private lending market felt vindicated in their belief that the guaranteed loan was the preferred option. According to them, discounts on origination fees and interest rates, among other things, proved their worth. By 1999, "the direct lending market [was] struggling to hold on to a one-third market share of student loans," according to the Consumer Bankers Association (CBA).[194] However, the CBA's selective reading failed to acknowledge how various pay-to-play schemes tilted the financial aid playing field in the private lenders' favor and how an otherwise cost-conscious Congress had passed a series of measures that embraced the more costly guaranteed student loan.[195]

The biggest loss for taxpayers occurred in the spring of 2003 when the second-largest participant in the direct loan program, Michigan State University, with $183 million in loans each year, was lured away by private lenders promising to deliver the school a profit of at least $2 million when it purchased the notes from the school. The Michigan State deal was projected to cost federal taxpayers $23.5 million annually in subsidies and federal guarantees to the bank, according to a study done by *US News & World Report*.[196] What made this exchange arguably the most bitter pill to swallow for direct lending supporters was that the $2 million incentive that direct loan competitors promised to give Michigan State came directly from a special federal subsidy guarantee the federal government gave to lenders. "It's a windfall that has no benefit to taxpayers or students," said Thomas Wolanin of the Institute for Higher Education Policy.[197] The guaranteed student loan industry had successfully stemmed the once-rising tide of direct lending and had begun to reclaim its share of the college loan market, consigning students to more expensive financial products and costing taxpayers more money.

The other signature student aid initiative at the time was tax credits, which, like the direct lending program, was consistent with what Clinton labeled his New Covenant agenda of balancing the budget while also reducing costs for taxpayers.[198] Sufficiently chastened by the first Republican Congress since 1952, Clinton engaged Republicans on their own terms, countering a Republican tax cut bill with a triangulated tax revenue reduction proposal of his own: the 1997 Taxpayer Relief Act. Clinton was famous for triangulation—adopting a popular conservative Republican idea and reappropriating and rebranding it as his own to claim he embraced an ostensible nonideological third way. Among other things, the Clinton tax plan (or TRA 97) offered tuition-paying households tax credits and deductions. The most heralded of these tax tuition breaks was the Helping Outstanding Pupils Educationally (HOPE) Scholarship Credit, which allowed families who earned less than $75,000 (or individuals who earned less than $55,000) to deduct up to $10,000 in tuition from their taxable income or receive a tax credit of $1,500 for the first two years of undergraduate education for members of their household. The problem with the HOPE credit, however, was that it required families to pay their children's tuition upfront, something few working-class families could do. "There's no way that I could have come up with $1,500 to begin with, and most people without money aren't going to understand what a tax credit will do for them," said Audrey Dismuke, a Georgia HOPE Scholarship recipient and mother of three enrolled at Albany Technical Institute to become an X-ray technician.[199] Unlike the Georgia model program, which covered tuition and $100 for books upfront, the Clinton plan would come on the back end, in the form of an after-payment tax credit.[200]

Tax credits were bad economics, but good politics.[201] Pell Grants and other direct expenditures, according to many economists, were far more effective in closing the opportunity gap, something Dismuke knew instinctively and experientially.[202] Economists in particular were skeptical that tax credits would help keep college costs down because of the subsidy fear factor. Economic reasoning suggests that subsidies typically lead to higher prices. This subsidy, the tax credit, essentially gave families of college-bound students more income, and universities could simply raise tuition knowing they would not lose buyers because these students and their families would have more money to spend. The administration countered subsidy fears by applying the tax credit for only the first two years. If schools raised tuition, students would be left with steeper costs for their last two years of college without the benefit of the tax subsidy. "Economy theory would not suggest that that would be a prudent policy for the college," Clinton's education secretary, David Longanecker, reasoned.[203]

Despite these reservations, tuition tax credits were popular. They polled well with voters and enjoyed consistently wide support throughout the 1990s, particularly with the all-important, deficit-minded suburban voters and the growing number of middle-class voters who were increasingly imagining themselves as members of the investor class.[204] Therefore, despite skepticism among experts, politicians voted overwhelmingly for tuition tax credits, and President Clinton signed the bill into law in August 1997.[205] Tuition tax credits also exemplified the success of Clinton's favored strategy of triangulation. Through triangulation, the president was able to insulate himself from criticism by the oppositional party while simultaneously appearing unbeholden to special interests of his own political party—a perception that had dogged Democratic leadership since at least the 1970s. The triangulation strategy and the tax credit approach cemented as bipartisan common sense the logic that had seemed so radical only a decade before when introduced by Reagan: the primary role of the government in higher education was not to fund students or fund universities, but to step back and intervene as little as possible in families' efforts to pay for schooling.[206]

Student Loan Making in the New Millennium

The George W. Bush administration would continue to favor guaranteed loans and lenders while further politicizing the Department of Education. Rather than appoint members of the department to oversee federal direct loans who believed in the program and wanted it to succeed, the Bush administration appointed four longtime opponents of direct lending. These appointees were either student loan executives or private loan lobbyists whose careers were built, in large part, on their opposition to the very programs they were now being asked to run. For example, the second-highest-ranking official at the Department of Education, Deputy Secretary William Hansen, was a former CEO of the Education Financial Council, a student loan trade group. Hansen testified on the Hill and elsewhere against direct lending, in addition to leading a political action committee whose purpose was to defeat pro–direct lending candidates. The administration even attempted to sell off the government's direct loan portfolio to a private investor, a move that would have eviscerated the program.[207] When selling off these loans fell through, the Bush administration's Education Department gutted the direct lending program, with nearly 100 percent of all new loan volume coming from guaranteed student loans between 2005 and 2007—only the drying up of private-sector credit and lending beginning in August 2007, a spate of private student loan scandals that same year, and 2008 election year pandering would slow the guaranteed student loan trend in 2008.[208] With direct lending no longer crowding out private capital amid a general climate of hyper-deregulation, corporate influence over financial aid grew into one of the largest pay-to-play schemes in US history.

When students and their parents stepped onto a college campus, they frequently did so with the expectation that the school's financial aid officer had reviewed lenders in a competitive process and was committed to helping advise the family of the best possible bargain for the student.[209] These expectations were betrayed in the predatory lending landscape of financial aid, full of kickbacks and other inducements, that would come to define the 2000s, when students and their parents became mere marks to be exploited for personal benefit and corporate gain.

With direct lending marginalized, lenders now jockeyed for position among each other to be placed, or moved up, on the so-called college-approved preferred lender list, where some nine out of ten student borrowers went to select their lender.[210] To make the list was an achievement; the higher up on the list a company was, the more likely students would perceive it as favored by a school. In exchange for being added to or moved up the preferred lender list, lenders granted financial aid administrators nearly every quid pro quo imaginable. For example, in 2002, the lender Student Loan Xpress controlled 5.15 percent of the loan volume at Columbia University. That figure more than doubled to 12.17 percent, however, after financial aid officers at Columbia received SLX shares from company president Fabrizio Balestri.[211]

In addition to stock options, lenders rewarded financial aid officers with various inducements, including consulting and "speaking" fee payments; in-kind compensation such as cupcakes, spa treatments, and Yankees and Phillies baseball tickets; all-expense-paid golfing trips and stays at the Four Seasons and other five-star hotels; and even personal tuition and fee remissions. If a financial aid administrator did pit lender against lender, it was often not so that the companies would compete to offer the best possible rate or terms for students; it was, as one financial aid officer boasted, to see which lender would give him the best NBA playoff seats.[212] Lenders launched a "rewards program" for increasing student loan volume. "Congratulations," a representative from Student Loan Xpress greeted one financial aid officer in an email, letting him know that he'd won an online shopping spree.[213] Citizens Bank induced one financial aid official at Rutgers University with the "carrot" of a lucrative advisory board appointment to encourage him to increase Citizens' market share among Rutgers' student borrowers.[214] Other times, the "stick" was the motivator of choice, especially over concerns of sagging loan revenues. For example, when a financial aid officer at Puget Sound University inquired if NorthStar Education Finance could donate basic office supplies for an upcoming conference, the sales representative admonished the administrator to get loan sales up the next year.[215]

Inducements were the rule more than the exception. As many as nine out of ten students relied on the preferred lists when choosing a lender. At least twelve lenders, including the eight largest in the country, engaged in various quid pro quos on hundreds, if not thousands, of campuses, from Chaminade University in Hawaii to the University of Southern Maine, from community colleges to most Ivies. The Illinois state attorney general alone counted 270 colleges participating in rigging the loan process via preferred lending lists and other dubious practices.[216]

"Cobranding" was another common inducement practice employed by lenders. Lenders paid or promised to share loan-generated revenue with universities, school athletic departments, and alumni associations in exchange for the use of the school's name, insignias, mascots, logos, and other university-affiliated paraphernalia. The use of the school's image was intended to deceive students and their parents into thinking the company was the official lender of the school or actually a part of the school.[217] Other lenders gave $50 cash incentives to students for referring their classmates.[218] What all these inducements had in common was that no one at these schools—from students and their parents to university administrators, financial aid officers, athletic directors, or members of the alumni association—evaluated the quality of the student loan marketed and sold by lenders. Instead, for steering them to new student borrowers, lenders cut schools, athletic departments, and alumni associations in on the profits.[219]

While federal anti-inducement laws on student loans had been on the books since at least the late 1980s, they were meaningless without the authority or will to police rogue lenders and financial aid officers. By the late 2000s, Congress possessed the will but had only the authority to tighten regulation and investigate allegations of lender abuse, which the Senate Education Committee, chaired by Senator Edward M. Kennedy, did in 2007. The power to enforce anti-inducement abuses rested primarily with the executive branch, which demonstrated little will or desire to go after student loan company executives, some of whom were former co-workers of officials in the Education Department.

The Department of Education in the 2000s went beyond the omission of oversight. Department officials worked for or actively profited from student loan companies they were responsible for regulating. The story of former Sallie Mae employee Matteo Fontana reflects the permissive regulatory culture that seems to have been de rigueur at the Department of Education.[220] In 2002, forty-year-old Fontana joined the Education Department and later would come to oversee private lenders in the Federal Family Loan Program.[221] As the federal official primarily responsible for overseeing inducements and related abuses in student lending, Fontana overturned a lower department official's decision to reject the expansion of the student lending operations of a company in which Fontana owned 4,500 shares of stock. More troubling, fellow officials appeared to be aware of their colleague's stock ownership yet did not report it—despite at least three egregious instances of conflicts of interest, each of which violated federal ethics law.[222] Rather, the deceit and cover-up came to light only after a state attorney general, New York's Andrew Cuomo, investigated inducements of student loans in 2007 and uncovered the criminal deeds of Fontana, who pleaded guilty to making false statements in 2009 and was ordered to pay a maximum fine of $115,000, or an amount totaling less than half of the payout price when he cashed in his stock while a federal official.[223] "The fact that this financial conflict of interest was apparent on the face of Fontana's disclosure forms but was not addressed by the Department raises grave concerns about the effectiveness and impartiality of the ethics process at the Department," Massachusetts Democratic senator Ted Kennedy wrote in a letter to Education Secretary Margaret Spellings.[224] "These facts demand hard scrutiny of the Department's ability to police itself," added Kennedy, who then chaired the Senate Education Committee.[225] As Andrew Cuomo stated in another lender abuse case, which was settled for $15 million around this time, "Choosing the wrong loan can lead to devastating consequences" that affect millions of people.[226] What these pay-to-play schemes cost students and their parents in higher interest rates and fees is unknown and may never be known. What is clear, however, is that higher-cost loans ultimately increased the chances of default, loss of federal revenue, and a cascading set of wealth-building delays for student borrowers and their families. Financial analysts sensed the potential of the student loan industry to threaten the national economy yet again.

In 2011, as the global economy was still struggling to recover from the Great Recession and the housing crisis, Moody's was already bracing its investors for the next bubble: student loans. Despite a new federal law making direct loans to students the sole government-backed lending program a year earlier, the "long-run outlook for student lending and borrowers remains worrisome," *Moody's Analytics Report* informed its readers. The report added that "the boom in student lending," coupled with delinquency and loss rates on outstanding balances, posed even worse implications for the larger economy: dragging down consumption while simultaneously making America less educated, less productive, and less competitive in the global marketplace.[227] If student loans are the next debt bubble, its origins are not ratings agencies, financial risk assessment firms, or secondary capital markets. Instead, that bubble began in Washington, born at least as much out of the 1980s political culture as today's financial economy.

Though the Reagan administration's motive for cutting student aid was largely fiscal, the shift to loans was never truly a matter of number crunching. Rather, it was embedded in the cultural and political conversations of the day, the repercussions of which we still face today. The tax-eater mindset toward students would translate into a set of fiscal and education policies designed ostensibly to close the debt gap while restoring traditional family values at home. As Reagan's czar in the Education Department, Secretary Bennett, liked to remind fellow conservatives, the intent was to roll back the aid program not simply to control spending, but "to restore the traditional role of parents and students in financing college costs."[228] These policies were an attempt to make parents and their children financially accountable for their college education and less reliant on government assistance to defray tuition costs. Yet by constructing a system so heavily dependent on high-cost, subsidized loans in an era of wage stagnation for American families, the architects of modern student financial aid helped to all but close off one of the nation's most reliable postwar routes to upward mobility: affordable higher education. And although more students today are pursuing a postsecondary education, they are also more burdened by its costs for much, much longer.

Over the past three decades, high-cost, private, and subsidized guaranteed student loans have increasingly come to fill the void left by hemorrhaging federal and state grant programs. In the 1970s, grants covered 70 percent of college costs. By 2008, they covered just one-third. As wages stagnated, household debts rose, government aid evaporated, and family savings dried up, more students borrowed. In 2007, two out of three students borrowed through loans, up from just over one in two (52 percent) in 1995. More students were also paying more for what they borrowed as the economic downturn and credit crunch put an end to low-interest loans. By 2007, rates on student loans were often more than twice as high as they had been a decade prior, increasing from 8 to 18 percent.[229]

In recent years, the surging student loan crisis has forced lawmakers to ameliorate the worst excesses of the financial aid system. In 2007, Congress, which was under both House and Senate Democratic control for the first time since the Republican revolution in 1995, created the Public Service Loan Forgiveness Program, which offered loan amnesty to borrowers who worked full-time for ten years in qualified public-sector jobs and made 120 on-time monthly payments under a qualifying repayment plan.[230]

The Obama White House would tackle runaway student debt by going back to the future. Most notably, with the help of Congress, the first Obama administration put an end to the nearly twenty-year practice instituted by Congress in the 1990s of making private banks the primary lenders for federally insured student loans, and resuscitated the direct loan program. Nonetheless, for those saddled with debt, a generation of damage to credit scores and wealth-building aspirations has already been done. An estimated three thousand student borrowers default each day, according to Rohit Chopra, the former student loan ombudsman at the Consumer Financial Protection Bureau.[231] This figure, though, is almost certain to climb and bury even more students deeper in debt if Trump's first budget plan—which includes cutting education spending, eliminating the subsidized loan program, cutting in half work-study support, hiking monthly repayment and debt collection fees, and rolling back the student loan forgiveness program by narrowing the definition of "public service" (or the repayment equivalent of calling relish a vegetable)—is any sign of things to come. Finally, while missing from this budget proposal, the return of private banks as the issuers of federally backed student loans remains a perpetual concern—particularly given the influence of the lending industry on the Hill.

Few efforts by any recent Congress or administration to rein in student loan debt have mentioned let alone actively addressed the root of the problem: the public's disinvestment in higher education. That disinvestment has resulted in the shifting of the costs of access to higher education to the next generation and increasingly America's middle class in the form of higher tuition and fees.

Student loans and thirty-year mortgage loans are episodic events, ones that a borrower may take on only once or perhaps twice in a lifetime. These episodic events often overshadow more quotidian, high-cost consumer transactions that are hidden or appear unremarkable yet, nonetheless, contribute to circumscribing wealth building and upward mobility. Comparatively little is known about this slow financial extraction and the ways it has reallocated wealth since the 1970s. The ostensibly mundane world of everyday high-cost, low-finance auto insurance is the slow, steady drip that precipitated the deluge that I will turn to next.

3

Driving While Broke: How Auto Insurance Drives the Wealth Gap

ZIP-code profiling in insurance has been one of the most tenacious forms of discrimination. For decades good drivers in Black residential neighborhoods have been charged more. Basic economic fairness should mean that my driving record, not my ZIP code, would shape [my] premium. This history of economic discrimination must end, and the new regulation [Proposition 103] is a long-overdue step in that direction.

—James Lawson, Southern Christian Leadership
Conference of Greater Los Angeles[1]

WHILE SUBPRIME MORTGAGES AND student loans have headlined the front pages and homepages of major news outlets, nowhere is there a de facto, hidden consumer financial fee that is more commonly charged but so little discussed than auto insurance. There was a time, not very long ago, when the "auto insurance wars" did dominate news. On the eve of the post–Cold War era in 1988, America found itself embroiled in a crisis of national identity later known as the culture wars. That year Colorado, Arizona, and Florida placed immigration and English-only initiatives on their ballots. In Michigan and Arkansas, abortion dominated election conversations. For Maryland, the issue was gun control, the National Rifle Association, and a ban on cheap handguns; in South Dakota, voters debated whether to accept gambling. Yet of all the hot-button social issues that have dominated domestic discourse since the late 1980s, none was more costly and hotly contested in 1988, according to the national television news networks, than the so-called insurance wars.[2] With drivers required by law to purchase auto insurance, in almost no other realm did government touch so many pocketbooks.[3]

With the world's eighth-largest economy and a population 50 percent greater than that of any other state, California was where the future happened first. That was certainly the case with Proposition 103, a package of auto insurance reform initiatives passed in 1988 intended to tie pricing to a driver's record while disentangling pricing from factors unrelated to driving, such as zip code and marital status.[4] Civil rights and consumer groups, national media, and policymakers anticipated that Proposition 103 would provide a model for the nation. Believing that as California went so would the nation go, more money poured into the state to defeat Proposition 103 than either of the presidential candidates, Michael Dukakis or George H. W. Bush, spent on their campaigns that year. Despite the massive influx of opposition money, the ballot measure passed. Proposition 103, which the *Wall Street Journal* once anticipated would be "the next populist revolt," did not produce the results expected, however.[5] For a generation, none of the major reforms were implemented.

Since 1986, California motorists had watched their insurance rates go up 58 percent, giving them the third-highest rates in the country by 1988. In an effort to stave off escalating insurance costs, consumer activists launched Proposition 103.[6] While there were several initiatives on the ballot that year, all geared toward fixing auto insurance rates, none of them garnered the ire of insurers or the imagination of the electorate as much as Proposition 103. The proposition's main provisions stipulated, among other things, a rate cut for policyholders, an independent regulatory agency to oversee the industry, and an elected insurance commissioner. But no feature of Proposition 103 proved more popular among consumers or more troubling to insurers than its stipulation that insurance be based primarily on one's driving record, not geographical factors.

Insurers contended that Proposition 103 was seeking to remove the free market from pricing. As insurers' logic went, the ballot's stated initiative—"to encourage competition in the insurance marketplace"— was based on the false premise that high rates were the consequences of an insurance monopoly that ignored related costs like hospital expenses, auto repairs, and litigation. More generally, insurers argued that they were a private business, which needed to safeguard industrial trade secrets like how rates were calculated. An insurance industry spokesperson charged that by overturning the use of zip codes as a primary factor in determining rates, supporters of Prop 103 were bent on *"seeking to redistribute wealth"* in California and, potentially, throughout the nation.[7] For insurers, Proposition 103 was yet another example of creeping socialism and further government encroachment on the sanctity of the free-enterprise system, empowering the state to set their rates, not just review them.[8] "What [Prop 103 proponents] actually want is a state takeover of the insurance business."[9]

While Proposition 103 would not have abolished territorial rating, requiring only that insurers put greater weight on merit-based driving, insurers stringently opposed any concession to diminishing the role of postal codes in formulating rates.[10] On the particularly controversial issue of postal code profiling, the insurance industry argued that it had the objectivity of science on its side. It pointed to the "wide agreement among actuaries that territory should have a greater weight than is allowed by Proposition 103."[11] The industry contended that its statistics-driven analysis stood in stark contrast to the rights-based appeals of 103's civil rights and consumer advocates, for whom emotions ostensibly outweighed evidence. Backers of 103 believed, as the industry advisor and Berkeley law professor Stephen Sugarman explained with apparent sarcasm, "It simply isn't right for individual motorists to be ruled by the impersonal tyranny of actuarial science."[12]

In the campaign's final stretch, insurance companies waged a fierce financial battle. Envisioning California as the firewall state in which to stop any potential national consumer backlash, insurers outspent 103 proponents $65 million to $2.3 million.[13] Up to 70 percent of the insurance industry's October campaign budget went to negative advertising. These ads targeted Proposition 103, claiming its passage would lead to wealth redistribution among Los Angeles–area drivers by unhinging auto insurance from postal codes. Insurers put much of their money behind a series of television spots that attacked 103 with the tag line "Why should we pay more so Los Angeles can pay less?"[14] The ad contended that a rate hike for a majority of California's drivers would result if Proposition 103 succeeded in "eliminating rate-setting based on claims within ZIP codes." These and similar television attack ads ran statewide except in the heavily minority media markets of San Diego and Los Angeles.[15]

What made the 1988 insurance wars the most contested issue in California and the costliest nonpresidential campaign in US history was not merely the fear of uncoupling postal codes from rate pricing; it was also the fear of the ripple effect should the proposition pass. Californians had watched their rates jump in the 1980s, as had residents of other states, making the rate increases a national issue. In more than a dozen states at the time, either ballot initiatives or legislative reform were proposed.

As its influence spread, the most popular provision of 103 among consumers across the country was reform of postal code profiling. After California's election, territorial rating as a political issue took hold in Ohio, Florida, Maryland, and Pennsylvania, as drivers in Cleveland, Miami, Baltimore, and Philadelphia realized they paid more than their statewide averages.[16] New York was also fairly typical. There, 79 percent of drivers living in the Bronx's urban core were assigned to the high-cost risk pool versus 41 percent of the rest of Bronx motorists and 16 percent of drivers in the rest of the state.[17]

It was anticipated that if the reform measure passed in California, similar if not more aggressive rate-cut initiatives might sweep through other states. Fearing a national ripple effect and the subsequent loss of billions of dollars, the $60 million or so that insurers spent fighting the California campaign was considered a smart, preemptive investment. Given the national implications, nearly three times as much was spent on trying to defeat 103 than on any single political campaign in California history; the biggest financier came from outside the state, from Illinois-based State Farm, which gave $3.6 million.[18] Despite unprecedented contributions (in both financial and in-kind spending, as insurance workers allocated more than $2 million in man-hours) and eroding popular support for Prop 103, insurers remained behind in three major statewide polls.

On November 8, voters narrowly approved Proposition 103 by 51.1 to 48.9 percent.[19] Despite the razor-thin margin, the election was not as close as the final numbers might suggest. The electorate clearly favored 103 above the other insurance options on the ballot that year. No other initiative received more than 42 percent of the yes vote. For example, the insurer-backed no-fault initiative, Proposition 104—requiring motorists to collect from their own insurance companies, regardless of who caused an accident, limiting contingency fees for plaintiffs' attorneys, and preventing more stringent state regulation of the insurance industry—was rejected 3 to 1 by voters.[20] In this way, Proposition 103's victory signaled perhaps an unparalleled moment in modern proposition movements: a progressive proposition cause that was backed by civil rights, consumer, and immigrant groups and was met with democratic approval.

As expected, urban and inner-city motorists in Los Angeles, San Diego, and San Francisco intensely supported Proposition 103. Los Angeles County voters pushed it to victory, providing a six hundred thousand vote margin. The proposition fared worse outside the Bay Area in northern California.[21] But the crucial swing vote tended to be cast by a suburban couple, often married, parents of children, and White. They backed the measure, believing that doing so would result in their own insurance rates being cut. The promise of Proposition 103 stemmed from its unifying consumer appeal. The proposition galvanized the average California consumer against moneyed interests in ways that previous initiatives, which often pitted Whites and suburbia against racial minorities and the inner city, had failed to do. Nor did those arrayed against it fit neatly into preconceived patterns. For example, Democratic senator Dianne Feinstein, the former mayor of arguably America's most liberal city, San Francisco, didn't just back Proposition 104; she co-wrote it. Generally regarded as more anti-consumer than most ballot choices, Proposition 104 capped nonfinancial damages and restricted future regulations on the industry.[22]

Nationally, the reactions of Wall Street and Main Street to Prop 103's passage captured the clash of interests distinguishing finance capitalists from consumers. On Wall Street, the market reacted with a stock sell-off of publicly traded auto insurance companies, as insurers saw their prices drop. Meanwhile, in the afterglow of the 103 victory, consumer groups from thirty states contacted Proposition 103 architect Harvey Rosenfield's office to inquire how to launch a voter revolt of their own.[23] As the *Wall Street Journal* editors braced its readers, Proposition 103 augured America's next great populist revolt on the coattails of auto insurance.[24] But insurers had more fight left than either the *Wall Street Journal* or many Proposition 103 supporters anticipated.

Within twenty-four hours, the auto insurance industry struck back. The day after the election, Wednesday, November 9, the nation's sixth- and ninth-largest insurers, Travelers and the Fireman Fund, announced they would stop underwriting insurance in California and pull out of the state altogether.[25] Meanwhile others, including Safeco, Geico, and the marker leader, State Farm, stopped writing good-driver policies for new customers; instead, regardless of record, they shunted them off to higher-cost subsidiary insurers, where new policyholders were charged as much as 60 percent more than premiums paid by existing holders.[26] By November 15, eighteen of the fifty-seven largest insurers had rejected all new applications or stopped accepting auto insurance at all.[27]

The insurance industry's response contributed to rising apathy and disaffection, especially among voters of color. According to one study of the next major election season after 103's passage, the June 1990 primaries, three out of four eligible adults did not vote. Usually reliable older voters signaled the loss of confidence.[28] "I just got fed up," said one retired man, sixty-eight, from San Pablo. "We passed Proposition 103, and then they're fooling around with it."[29] Given that seniors, the most reliable voting segment, increasingly found themselves politically disaffected, it was unsurprising perhaps that the stalled implementation of 103 only further depressed turnout among African Americans, Asians, and Latinxs, who represented 30 percent of the state's adult population but, on average, only 15 percent of voters. Conversely, White voters over the age of sixty typically made up 30 percent of actual voters while representing only 21 percent of voting-age Californians.[30] If noncompliance characterized the insurers' response to Proposition 103 before 1995, the industry was only emboldened by the upset election victory and tenure of the new state commissioner of insurance, Charles Quackenbush, a Silicon Valley Republican assemblyman.

The Stickiness of Race: Proposition 187, Insurers, and Postal Code Profiling

Insurers consistently claimed that their policies were color-blind, but the stickiness of race remained an inescapable if submerged theme.

Language, culture, and citizenship, as well as conceptions of the unde-served, often function as discrete categories of discrimination in their own right and may also serve as proxies for race.[31] The intertwining of race with these proxies was pivotal in 1994, when insurers seized the political-cultural moment to help elect Charles Quackenbush as the state's first elected insurance commissioner. It was a stunning victory over the once heavily favored Latinx candidate, East Los Angeles Democratic state senator Art Torres. In return, Quackenbush would ultimately be captured by the very business he was charged with regulating.

How much Torres's late-campaign collapse was tied to that year's highly controversial ballot battle over Proposition 187 may never be fully known. Still, it would be naïve not to take Prop 187 into consider-ation. Southern California Republican assemblyman Daniel Mountjoy introduced the bill to the state legislature in 1994 calling it the "Save Our State" (SOS) initiative. Prop 187 made it illegal to, among other things, offer undocumented immigrants public services such as education and nonemergency medical care. Whether it was intended or not, many read a racialized subtext encoded in this proposition. Critics of SOS perceived that the initiative was meant to rescue White Californians not so much from undocumented immigrants, which this proposition officially targeted, as from the sense of siege many Whites felt amid a rising presence of immigrants of color, especially Latinx, be they legal or not. That the highest-profile Latinx running for office in 1994, a time of heightened racial tension between Whites and racial minorities in California, was bidding to become the state's next insurance regulator did not help Torres's bid for the post of commissioner. Equally impor-tant was an October infusion of insurer financing, totaling nearly 75 percent of all money spent. Insurance dollars underwrote a series of anti-Torres television ads, which branded him as being too sympathetic to criminals and as the "king of special interests."[32] Such attack ads paid huge dividends, according to Field Poll reports. Before the ads, Torres had maintained a double-digit advantage since the primaries; after they aired, he fell behind Quackenbush and never recovered.[33]

Nationally, Torres was swept up in the onrushing Republican elec-toral tide, which in 1994 lifted the GOP to newfound control at the federal and state levels. In Congress, Republicans took over for the first time since 1952. In the states, they possessed a majority of governorships for the first time in three decades, while taking control of a majority of state legislatures for the first time in fifty years. The national Republican surge helped to end California Democrats' twenty-five-year majority rule in the State Assembly. Business-friendly GOP candidates running for statewide office rode this electoral tidal wave as well—despite the fact that registered Democrats outnumbered Republicans 2 to 1 in California.[34] All this boded well for the insurance companies.[35] Not surprisingly, the industry exhibited even further reluctance to abolish postal code profiling under Chuck Quackenbush, whose victory was, in the editorializing words of the *Sacramento Bee*, "bankrolled" by insurers.[36]

Quackenbush took office in January 1995, and his first thirty days confirmed civil rights and consumer advocates' worst fears. He enacted a series of new emergency regulatory measures that gave insurance companies even greater authority to base rates on criteria primarily unrelated to driving safety records, rolled back consumer-friendly settlement arrangements, and called for further hearings on auto insurance rather than implementing recommendations in the exhaustive report of his predecessor, John Garamendi, whose study of 10 million policyholders was generally regarded as the most thorough of its kind in California's history.[37] The new regulatory commissioner spent much of his remaining tenure shifting premium burdens and costs away from corporations and onto consumers. While the growth of insurance rates, adjusted for inflation, had slowed down from 1994 to 1996, rates increased twice in three years during Quackenbush's time in office. But no policy remained more guarded than zip code–based profiling. Effectively disregarding Prop 103, California's new insurance head tightened the tethering of rates to where one lived rather than how one drove. He did so by allowing factors related to geography, such as an area's average wage and income level, as well as zip code, to be used in computing rates.

In response, three of California's largest cities, representing more than 8 million Californians, successfully filed suit against redlining policies by the insurance industry in March 1998. Los Angeles, Oakland, and San Francisco sought "to force Quackenbush to put an end to that subterfuge," which, in the litigants' words, freed insurers to deepen their "Jim Crow regulations." City attorneys were joined by several civil organizations, including consumer groups, the civil rights–based Southern Christian Leadership Conference, and the Spanish Speaking

Citizens Foundation.[38] Latinx and Black civil rights organizations saw zip code redlining in the historic vein of centuries-long discriminatory practices and charged Quackenbush with colluding with insurers in perpetuating economic hardships and the disenfranchisement of minorities. "California needs leadership from the insurance commissioner in ending unfair zip code rating," proclaimed Genethia Hayes, the executive director of the Southern Christian Leadership Conference of Los Angeles.[39] "This history of economic discrimination must end," added veteran civil rights activist James Lawson some years later, when the case was still tied up in courts because of insurance interposition.[40]

At the hearing of the lawsuit against Quackenbush, it was charged that the commissioner continued the discriminatory practice of redlining by allowing insurers to give too much weight to zip codes. The law required that rates be based primarily on three mandatory factors within a motorist's control, in decreasing order of importance: driving safety record, annual mileage driven, and years of driving experience. Insurers were then permitted to use up to sixteen optional factors if they "had a substantial relationship to risk of loss," which could not have a greater impact on rates than the mandatory factors approved by the electorate.[41]

Quackenbush, however, introduced regulations that allowed insurers to take an average of all optional factors rather than award individual numerical weights for each optional factor. In this way, public and consumer advocacy groups could not determine how much weight was given to neighborhood factors. By using this averaging method, which plaintiffs dismissed as "voodoo mathematics," insurers were able to give greater weight to non-driving-related factors such as zip code, gender, marital status, and school grades and to mask the actual value at which these specific factors were assessed. Exactly how much numerical weight was given to zip code was unknown because, along with gender, it was combined with other optional factors. Thus, when averaged, the mean weight for all optional factors could be less than any of the three mandatory factors of driving record, miles driven, and experience—allowing zip codes to still have an inordinate impact. Such statistical sleight of hand by the industry under Quackenbush kept the public in the dark, as consumers never quite knew how much postal codes factored into a company's decision.

It was estimated that Quackenbush's zip code–rate calculus exacted a financial cost well into the millions on urban and working-class motorists—a segment of Californians assumed to be least likely to possess either savings or investments. For example, a twenty-two-year-old male driver in South Los Angeles paid quadruple ($7,844) what a similar (twenty-two-year-old, male) San Luis Obispo citizen did ($1,706) over his lifetime, despite their identical driving profiles. Oakland experienced a similar disparity between upscale Montclair ($3,398) and Fruitvale ($4,417). As James Hahn, Los Angeles's city attorney, said, "What Quackenbush has done is undermine the will of the people, who overwhelmingly voted to enact Proposition 103, by letting insurance companies hide the ball on redlining practices."[42]

Beyond using complicated math, Quackenbush significantly protected auto insurance redlining by allowing the industry's silence on "trade secrets." At issue were voter will and the public's right to know versus the corporate right to privacy. These matters had a direct bearing on postal code profiling. Data were considered essential to track the practice; otherwise, it was unclear how much race, gender, and geography inequitably affected rates. One intent of Proposition 103 was to require fuller disclosure from insurers: it mandated that insurance commissioners collect pricing and other underwriting information and then make it available to the public, thereby bringing greater transparency to rate-setting practices. But Quackenbush's failure to enforce the full-disclosure provision allowed insurers to continue postal code profiling.[43] Put simply, postal code profiling remained "politically correct." Over the past three generations, governments, the private sector, and civil society have taken public stances on rooting out gender, racial, ethnic, sexual orientation, age, and religious discrimination and their vestiges from contemporary life. Postal code profiling and zip code discrimination, however, remain both persistent and illustrative of a last refuge of acceptable prejudice in multicultural, free-market liberal democracies such as the United States. In America, one's zip code is routinely used by local governments to apportion tax dollars, for example, and despite the outlawing of gender and racial discrimination, banks and other members of the financial services industry still deny or charge extra for loans, credit, and insurance premiums to households in low-income or working-class neighborhoods as delineated by their zip codes.

Campaign Finance Reform, 1998–2000

Postal code profiling was inseparable from campaign finance. With Quackenbush up for reelection in 1998, insurance dollars drowned out his opponent with a flood of television and radio campaign ads. At least a dozen insurance companies with direct interest in his office's decisions donated to Quackenbush's coffers. Outspent by approximately 4 to 1 and down by double digits, Diane Martinez, a three-term Democratic assemblywoman, did not have the insurance industry financing to run television ads to catch her opponent in the final days, as Quackenbush had done to beat Torres four years earlier.[44] Heavily indebted to insurers, Quackenbush began his second term by making it easier for them to drop drivers for minor violations. In a state where insurance was mandated by law, this new "driver cancellation" policy had the net effect of rerouting hundreds of thousands of motorists into the highly lucrative subprime (predatory or high-risk) auto insurance market.

Quackenbush's policies were not merely a fortuitous alignment of political philosophy and industry interests. By 2000, Quackenbush had resigned from office to avoid impeachment, as he faced a surfeit of scandals. He was charged with waiving up to $3 billion in industry fines in exchange for campaign contributions.[45] Even the insurance industry had accused him of extortion. Industry executives recounted how his lieutenant, William Palmer, had attempted a massive shakedown following the 1994 Northridge earthquake. One insurance official recalled that Palmer told his company "to put up the money [in Quackenbush's foundations] or face much bigger fines and attendant bad publicity for [its] alleged lack of fair treatment of quake damage claimants."[46] "He's the most egregious example we have currently with respect to elected officials raising campaign contributions from those they regulate or have an impact on with respect to legislation," Tony Miller, California's former secretary of state turned campaign reform advocate, told reporters.[47]

The problems transcended Quackenbush. They were systemic. Quackenbush, a Notre Dame graduate, US Air Force veteran, and Silicon Valley entrepreneur, became a corporate vassal whom campaign finance reformers named Exhibit A. His detractors claimed that Quackenbush provided the best public case of money's ability to influence policies and taint politicians. Yet before taking office as commissioner, Quackenbush spent a decade as a state elected official without a hint of financial scandal. As a primary candidate, Quackenbush was one of the few Republicans running on a platform of rejecting industry money, telling the *San Diego Union Tribune* during his 1994 primary race that taking company money is "like handing a loaded gun to the Democratic strategists. . . . They'll just accuse you of being bought and paid for by the industry."[48] That Quackenbush—a likable moderate Republican regulator once thought to have a bright political future—morphed into California's "most egregious example" of an ethically challenged elected official illustrates how special interest money in the political system distorts social policy and democratic will. Even the free-market-friendly *Economist* summed up the relationship as too corrupted by conflicts of interest: "Surely it is a little absurd to allow insurance commissioners to raise money from" those they regulate.[49]

A state audit in the fall of 2000 corroborated this view. The fifty-seven-page report found that Quackenbush's lax enforcement was the result not of independent policy considerations but of political and personal financial payoffs. Under Quackenbush, obfuscation replaced transparency—preventing "policyholders and consumers from obtaining critical information about the business practices of insurers," concluded the auditors.[50] By refusing to enforce full disclosure, Quackenbush enabled insurers to continue profiling motorists based on zip code. Despite an eighteen-month investigation and a guilty plea from his deputy commissioner, federal, state, and county prosecutors believed they lacked sufficient evidence to indict Quackenbush.[51] Voters themselves shouldered some of the blame. Preoccupied with more hot-button social issues like immigration, affirmative action, abortion, and flag burning, voters paid little attention to the erosion of oversight, though the insurance issue directly affected more than 20 million Californians—a far greater number than immigrants, African Americans, pregnant women, or flag burners.

Redistribution and Risky Business

Throughout the 1990s, the insurance industry resisted the implementation of Proposition 103. Insurers frequently claimed that attempts to end postal code profiling were little more than a socially engineered effort to redistribute wealth to the least deserving drivers. By claiming that the majority would subsidize the minority of bad and uninsured drivers, the state's leading insurance lobby wing allowed it to seize rhetorically on contemporary cultural critiques about rewarding society's undeserved.

From the view of the state's leading insurance trade groups, rescinding the territorial rating system was tantamount to wealth redistribution. "Examples abound as to what happens when government arbitrarily tries to control the price of products and services," said Jim Snyder, president of the Personal Insurance Federation of California, a trade association whose members included California's largest insurers. Three of the nation's largest insurance trade associations proclaimed that government intervention would result in a "mass subsidization" program. Insurance consortiums like the Personal Insurance Federation, the Association of California Insurance Companies, and the National Association of Independent Insurers warned that merit-based initiatives like Proposition 103 "would result in discriminatory pricing by, in effect, forcing subsidies for high-risk drivers at the expense of others."[52] Insurers then turned their focus to the supposed recipients of the subsidy. High-risk drivers, they contended, were the least deserving. Defenders of the current system argued that under any alteration of the territorial rating system, the drivers ostensibly behaving badly—including those without insurance, with a higher incidence of traffic accidents and citations, and sometimes with poor credit or with a personal history of bad life choices that resulted in their living in a poor neighborhood—stood to be the primary beneficiaries of any insurance reform.

But insurers were concerned with more than redistributing wealth and rewarding risky behavior. As they saw it, good drivers stood to be victimized by such social engineering. Adhering to Proposition 103 would result in "a giant subsidy program that would force good drivers . . . to pay more for their auto insurance so bad drivers could pay less," wrote Barry Carmody, president of the Association of California Insurance Companies, in a 1995 op-ed column.[53] Appropriating the contemporary language of victimization, Carmody expanded his analysis in a second op-ed one month later, saying that Prop 103 punished merit to reward the unworthy. Citing a study of one of California's largest insurers, Carmody claimed that insurers stonewalled the proposition not to protect their profit margin but to protect deserving drivers: "66 percent of California's bad drivers would get rate decreases while 53 percent of the good drivers would see their premiums increase."[54] If rates were too high, Carmody concluded, it was because so many Californians—14 percent by some estimates—remained uninsured. "The uninsured motorists problem in the state . . . penalizes people who buy insurance with an additional financial burden." For Carmody, "It all boils down to fairness . . . pure and simple."[55]

Proposition 103, according to industry insiders, sacrificed fairness at the liberal altar of equality. Insurers impressed on suburban and exurban motorists that they were the victims of a liberal regulatory elite that rewarded the bad behavior of mostly urban drivers. Proposition 103, then, was part of a larger pattern in which the worthy majority of society ended up paying the social costs of the personal failures of society's most undeserving—in this case, uninsured as well as insured motorists who were either unable or unwilling to move out of their impoverished neighborhoods. The fact remained, however, that insurers' bottom line hinged on defending values that conservatives, moderates, and a growing number of liberals at the time found most objectionable: namely, the privileging of social and physical environmental factors and identity politics over individual merit.

Individual Merit versus Identity Politics

In fact, throughout the history of postal code profiling, auto insurers highlighted the importance of social and physical environmental factors over individual motorists' merit. This was the case in 1962, when George Joseph, the founder of Mercury General Corporation, helped pioneer the use of neighborhoods and zip codes in calculating rates. By the 1970s, privileging social forces had become a state and national mainstay in auto insurance pricing.[56] Environmental factors outside an individual driver's control—traffic congestion, local litigation rates, auto thefts, accidents, higher medical and car repair costs, and the like—explained rate differentials among neighborhoods. But for the insured with clean driving records, such as Brendan Mulholland, a forty-year-old Oakland geologist debating whether to move two blocks away, where his new zip code would save him 20 percent every year on his auto insurance, the issue was how territorial rating resulted in the unintended consequence of undermining the ethos of individual merit. To Mulholland, "The whole premise of basing auto insurance premiums on locality as opposed to individuality is wrong."[57] For insurers, however, arguments about individual merit were, in the view of one industry consultant and expert, "strange."[58]

Not that the insurance industry did not endorse a version of merit. Rather, insurers and their lobbyists offered consumers a fundamentally competing notion of merit, one that took into account forces beyond a motorist's control. The problem, as Carmody explained, was that consumers devalued environmental and social forces. "For instance, should rural drivers pay more for insurance even though they cost far less to insure than drivers who live in congested cities where accidents and lawsuits are far more frequent? And should older people pay more so young people can pay less?"[59] The identity politics of postal codes, more than individualism, ultimately informed the industry's governing philosophy. Such typecasting resulted in the ghettoizing of policyholders. This was most likely an unintended consequence of the industry's desire for a less expensive, more cost-effective system of determining insurance policy rates that would yield higher profits and larger dividends for their stockholders.

Ghettoizing motorists in this way conformed to a wider contemporary trend, increasingly taking hold after the mid-1970s, toward openly appealing to and profiting from cultural segmentation among American consumers. This trend was characterized by a move away from mass marketing, and a two-decade color-blind approach, to isolating markets. Key to this shift, according to social and economic historian Lizabeth Cohen, was psychographics—a new technique introduced by marketers and social scientists who, building on earlier demographic variables of age, education, race, and gender, began applying newer profiles around the values, lifestyles, behavioral traits, and attitudes of targeted consumers. Psychographics worked from the assumption that it was sound science and business to charge consumers more because of the risks they posed and choices they made, such as the "choice" to live in an unsafe neighborhood, culture, or community. In these new isolated markets, neighborhood profiles or behavioral traits, as opposed to race, for example, took on greater explanatory power. Narrowcasting incorporated (or rein-corporated) disaffected groups into the commercial marketplace. This practice of targeting publics came of age amid the greatest period of lax regulation in the twentieth century.[60] This was particularly acute in the financial services industry, where women and Blacks, having equal legal access to auto insurance and equity lenders for the first time, nonetheless found themselves marketed and steered to high-cost loans and insurance.

Creating a cultural taxonomy enabled lobbyists to tap into another dominant motif of the 1980s and 1990s: the ostensible failing of society's undeserving, who, by making poor personal "decisions," perpetuated a collective culture of poverty. The system was already "unfair," wrote Carmody, in that it rewarded bad behavior. "It is bad enough that we have a major uninsured motorist problem in this state, which penalizes people who buy insurance with an additional financial burden. Now, Rosenfield [Prop 103's creator] is asking many of those same insured drivers to shoulder an even greater insurance cost so that bad drivers and others can pay less. . . . This is a matter of fairness. . . . Those who cost the system more should pay higher premiums. Those who cost the system less should pay lower rates."[61] Yet the solution the industry habitually turned to was based more on sociology than on individual drivers; the insurers' common refrain was that miles driven, years of experience, and driving record were insufficient factors for accurately judging insurance risk.[62]

As insurers saw it, the least deserving motorists were those who made bad life choices, such as the "choice" to live in poorer neigh-borhoods. The general counsel for the Association of California Insurance Companies, Jeff Fuller, echoing its president, told report-ers, "We do not discriminate on the basis of race, wealth, national origin." On the contrary, Fuller admonished media, it was risky per-sonal behavior that explained the rate gap. "Insurance is all about discrimination. It's all about discriminating between different risks."[63] Bias was built into insurance, Carmody acknowledged else-where: "Some subjectivity—business judgment—must be allowed in the business of insurance so long as that subjectivity is fairly applied by individual insurers."[64]

Beyond disputes concerning the likely victims and beneficiaries of Proposition 103, insurers' focus on "fairness" may have also delayed solving what the association president regarded as the major problem for motorists: uninsured drivers. By 2004, with 25 percent of the state's motorists lacking insurance, California had the second-highest rate of uninsured motorists in the United States and nearly double the national average of 14.6 percent.[65] Insured drivers generally stood to benefit from a lowering of the premium barrier for poorer motorists in poorer communities. Many in those communities could not afford the higher auto insurance premiums, so lower premiums would have translated into more insured drivers. This, in turn, would have had the broader effect of spreading risk by increasing the pool of the insured and thereby reducing premiums for all drivers—young and old, women and men, rural and urban. For policyholders at least, it is cheaper to cover 50 percent more drivers than none of the uninsured at all. "This issue . . . has serious economic implications," insisted Oakland's city attorney, Jayne W. Williams. Raising the bar to entry, she added, "push[ed] many residents of lower income neighborhoods in Oakland out of the automobile insurance market."[66]

Gender and Geography

Since the 1980s, the insurance business had lobbied hard to uphold gender as a factor in rating in the United States and Canada, charging that its elimination would unfairly hike rates for women drivers.[67] In 1983, when Congress debated antidiscrimination legislation to prohibit sex categorizations in insurance, the American Council of Life Insurance strongly objected to the presentations of politicians and the press. Gender-free categories were not only harmful to the industry, according to the council's president, but they would most likely have "a severe economic impact" on women, who "present very different risks," such as lower mortality.[68] "Women will suffer," another East Coast lobbyist predicted three years later when Pennsylvania looked at ending sex-based classification in auto insurance.[69] Yet groups such as the National Organization for Women and the League of Women Voters saw the continuation of gender-based pricing to be an insurance shell game—a hidden tax in which women, under the current system, had their rates lowered in one category of insurance only to pay a much steeper rate in another.

Ultimately, women actually paid more. They paid proportionally higher auto insurance premiums than they would have in a system based, for example, on miles driven each year, because they drove less than men. "The insurance industry's refusal to use mileage as a rating factor continues discrimination against all low-mileage drivers and costs women in Pennsylvania over $100 million per year in overcharges," the National Organization for Women's state chapter president asserted. Perhaps more significantly, gender-neutral laws would most likely be applied not just to auto rating but throughout the entire insurance pricing process, where classifications based on sex continued to be used for pensions, annuities, and healthcare. Insurers cared less about women-protectionist policies in these three areas of insurance practice, in which women generally paid more than men. The National Organization for Women and the League of Women Voters concluded that by over-charging low-mileage drivers, thereby penalizing most women, insurers preferred identity over merit because it was more profitable.[70] Billions might be lost if the insurance business ended gender categorization.

What also eluded industry experts was the correlation between gender and poverty.[71] Because more women than men live in poverty, particularly single mothers, more women stood to disproportionately benefit from the elimination of postal code profiling. Consider the Central California community of Huron (zip code 93234), where the median household income was reported to be $25,521. There, three out of four households in poverty were headed by women. Similarly, in Fresno (93701), where more than 90 percent of households earned $50,000 or less (and the median household income was $14,213), female householders with children under the age of eighteen accounted for 70.2 percent of families living below the poverty level. Poverty figures were consistently bleaker for women with young children, as was the case in Cutler (93615), another Central California town, where the median household income was just $26,694. Although less than one-half of female-headed households with children under eighteen lived below the poverty level, approximately two out of three households headed by women with children aged five or under lived in poverty.[72]

In contrast, America's most iconic zip code, Beverly Hills's 90210—where 44.9 percent of households in the 1990s made $200,000 or more and the median household income was $112,572, placing it in the top

1 percent in the state—had only 18.1 percent of households headed by females with children under eighteen living below the poverty level. In the wealthier 92067 San Diego suburb of Rancho Santa Fe, where the median household income was $196,298 and nearly one-half of the population made $200,000 or more, not a single female-headed household, with or without children, lived below the poverty level, according to the 2000 US Census.[73] Even in poor neighborhoods with sizable White populations, women suffered more. In Van Nuys, for instance, whose population was approximately one-half White and female, full coverage for women with twenty-two years of driving experience cost $943 more per year than full coverage for similar women drivers in Pasadena.[74] Nationally, women, who possessed less wealth and earned roughly eighty cents to the dollar paid to men, were also far less likely to live in better neighborhoods with lower territorially rated insurance premiums. This, combined with women's general lack of access to credit, limited their residential opportunities. More significantly, the language of Prop 103 never struck down the use of gender in the rate formula, allowing insurers to still use gender while minimizing territorial ratings.

The industry's gender argument belied the lived reality of motorists in Black or Latinx communities as well. For example, a twenty-two-year-old female driver with a perfect driving record—that is, no accidents, no tickets—who drove her 1996 Acura primarily to work paid, on average, 12.9 percent ($152) higher premiums to California's three largest insurers (State Farm, Farmers, and Allstate) if she lived in a predominantly Latinx zip code area. She paid 59.7 percent ($704) more in a predominantly Black zip code area than a woman with the same driving profile living in Huntington Beach.[75]

Beverly Hills 90210 versus Inglewood 90301

Although insurers typically regarded any government reform of postal code profiling as "artificial," few disputed the disparate racial impact of perpetuating it.[76] Poor Black and Latinx motorists paid more. But fearful of being accused of taking race into account in calculating premiums, the insurance industry insisted its process was color-blind. "Insurance companies don't use race as part of their rating criteria," said Carmody's successor as president of the Association of California Insurance Companies, Sam Sorich, in 2005, though he noted that "territory is a significant factor."[77] According to one former George H. W. Bush administration official turned independent insurance broker in San Antonio, Texas, agents were knowledgeable and practical field underwriters, unlike the "liberal social engineers who crafted 103 and who are now planning to implement a similar socialist medicine in Texas." He went on to accuse them of using the regulatory environment to overturn insurance's natural order.[78]

But zip codes, the most contentious tool used by insurance practitioners in determining rates, were anything but natural. The modern American zip code system was a foreign import. It was introduced in Germany in 1941 to expedite wartime communication and adopted domestically in the United States in the early 1960s by a federal regulator with the US Postal Service.[79] Once the coding was implemented by the government, direct marketing theoreticians adapted zip codes as a tool for market segmentation. Using the average demographics of each zip code, marketers, vendors, and salespersons "narrowcasted" specific commercial products, from music to auto insurance, to consumers.[80] In this way zip codes stood as the very instantiations of artificial, man-made creations, the socially conceived designs of town planners such as regulators and social scientists, and what suburban scholars such as Kenneth Jackson have called the "built environment."[81]

Although others agreed with the insurance industry that location should matter in setting premium rates, they contended that zip codes were an ineffectual predictor. Instead, the exhaustive findings of one expert risk-assessment firm, based on 15 million policyholders and 2 million claims, discovered that the best indicator of risk to carriers involved landmarks. Landmark theory contended that the most accurate determinant for insurers was what publics were served in a particular communal space. "While ZIP codes may be convenient and necessary for speedy mail delivery, they are not a particularly good predictor of property/casualty insurance losses," the study concluded.[82] Rather, car theft, vandalism, and auto accidents were far more likely to occur around landmarks like restaurants, bars, and banks. Conversely, the greater the number of houses of worship—mosques, synagogues, freestanding and storefront churches—in a neighborhood, the lower the likelihood of auto accidents (and thefts) in the area.[83]

Certainly urban Black America is rife with cheap restaurants and bars, and the prevalence of these establishments partially explains the inflated premiums. Few would deny this. That said, the Black and Latinx urban landscape is equally dotted with mosques, churches, and day care facilities that, according to place-based socioeconomic characteristics, should deflate pricing premiums. Even after we take into account neighborhood-based primary risk factors (claim and loss rates) and secondary risk factors (accident and crime location statistics), both typically used by insurers, traditional redlining (not place-based risk factors such as the presence of bars or churches) still "explain[s] more of the gap in auto insurance premiums between black (and Latinx) and white neighborhoods and between poor and nonpoor neighborhoods." As Paul Ong and Michael Stoll have demonstrated, race and income remain major determinants of what people pay for car insurance.[84] In sum, legitimate place-based factors may have played a role in pricing discrepancies, but so did race.

Years later, the California Department of Insurance revealed that in their efforts to stop Proposition 103, insurers misled the public by altering their evidence. They "had manipulated their own data calculations to make the claim" that some drivers would see massive rate hikes if postal code policies were abolished.[85] This truth could remain concealed, especially under Quackenbush, because insurers were not obligated to disclose pricing and other underwriting data—information essential to tracking auto insurance redlining. Without this evidence, it was virtually impossible to ascertain whether zip codes and other nonindividual factors played a role and to what extent. In not pressing for full disclosure from the insurance industry, Quackenbush failed to enforce another key provision of 103, which required that all information submitted by insurers to the commissioner be available for public inspection. Only after Quackenbush left office in 2000 would his successor press insurers to follow the law by releasing pricing and other data.[86]

The industry's foiling of 103 was, in no small measure, tied to its talents in branding the proposition with the hot-button cultural issues of the mid-1990s, particularly affirmative action. The industry embedded the insurance debate within a larger minority critique—at a time when affirmative action, immigration, and welfare dominated the political rhetoric. In the 1990s, critics charged that personal responsibility and merit were being subsumed under the principle of equality and that policies such as Proposition 103 were little more than social engineering projects disguised as regulation. Although equality was not as socially charged as race, insurers and their supporters invoked those familiar narratives of the 1980s and 1990s. Ironically, their insistence on postal code profiling and identity politics belied their argument for personal responsibility and merit. Relying on postal codes, education, gender, and other indirect measures threatened to distort what most mattered in a meritocracy of motorists: the quality of an individual's driving record.

What motivated insurers to adamantly support the continued use of social factors in determining insurance rates may never be completely known. They certainly feared that altering the calculus—by favoring an individual motorist's merit over broader social and environmental forces—would result in lower profits. It is also likely that insurers were motivated by the rhetoric and debates of the time. Whether by accident or design, insurers saw their struggle through the lens of the cultural-political debates of the 1980s and 1990s and the fight against "social engineering" and subsidizing the "undeserving poor," even though the territorial rating system itself was predicated on the theorizing of a different set of social engineers.

The dim prospects for cross-selling (or bundling) also partly explain why insurers maintained the use of social factors, fearing 103 might take a bite out of their business's bottom line. Like other consumer financial services, the insurance industry targeted motorists who would most likely renew policies or buy additional consumer financial products and services. On cross-sells, insurance agents were willing to assume or amortize front-end expenses like application, processing, or altering deductible costs over a longer period for the existing customer, since by cultivating loyalty they might persuade the client to buy a range of other products (home insurance, annuities, life insurance), which promised to yield lucrative, long-term financial rewards. For insurers, the industrywide perception was that future sales were far less likely to be made to urban, working-class, or minority insurance shoppers. Viewing these as one-off transactions, insurers often charged higher rates to postal code–profiled consumers out of a belief that the company would be unable to recoup its initial transaction and service costs through additional sales over time.[87]

Cross-sells grew exponentially more lucrative after 1999, when the landmark Gramm-Leach-Bliley Act freed insurers and other financial institutions to merge or create subsidiaries across the financial services sectors. For the first time since the Great Depression, banking and insurance companies could merge. This change permitted financial conglomerates to make cross-sells for a variety of financial products to their customers. An insurance agent could now sell existing customers a mortgage or home equity loan on top of their car insurance. But the one-stop shopping allowed by financial deregulation would further diminish the incentive for insurers to offer lower rates to postal code–profiled drivers looking to buy only auto insurance.[88]

Alternative Responses to Postal Code Profiling, Hyper-deregulation, and "Regulatory Capture"

Even after Quackenbush resigned in 2000 under threat of impeachment, Proposition 103 was never fully implemented. And its most contested goal—abolishing postal code profiling—was left largely intact. As the nation embraced a widespread laissez-faire approach to regulatory enforcement and unfettered capitalism, it grew harder to rein in the abuses of the free market even after consumers had overwhelmingly voted for regulators to do so. No branch of government was accountable for ensuring that the aims of the vote were realized. State lawmakers stood silent while many of the provisions of Prop 103 were rolled back. The chief enforcer of the state's law, California governor George Deukmejian, widely considered to be hostile to regulatory policy, refused to throw the weight of his office behind the new regulatory commissioner through either his enforcement powers or the bully pulpit. The courts lacked the enforcement powers to compel insurers or regulators to act. Disillusioned and overwhelmed, some consumers gave up on reforming the rating system altogether, and weariness set in relatively early. According to a 1989 poll, though a substantial majority of the 1,007 Californians questioned liked Prop 103 (62 percent, versus 20 percent who thought the law a bad idea), only 29 percent believed they would ever see rate changes.

Nationally the failure to implement 103 dampened optimism in other states that postal code–based pricing could be easily abolished. Whereas thirty states initially expressed interest in reforming the territorial rating system in November 1988, that number dwindled to a fraction of this figure once implementation of 103 stalled. Instead of fighting the rating system, consumers began finding ways to work within it. In Pennsylvania, for example, residents of one Pittsburgh neighborhood banded together and petitioned to be rezoned rather than demand that the rating system be changed. Meanwhile, better-off Coloradans, concerned about price hikes in auto and health insurance, fought against having their zip code folded into a neighboring one thought to be in a less desirable part of northwestern Denver.[89]

The epicenter of opposition to the territorial rating system, though, may well have been America's Motor City, where Detroit residents paid an average of $1,200 more each year for car insurance than the average Michigan motorist. Rather than attempt to reform the rating system, however, half of Detroit drivers engaged in individual acts of personal resistance, operating cars with no insurance. In comparison, roughly one in ten Michiganders outside of Detroit drove without insurance. Individual resisters included Detroit's embattled mayor Kwame Kilpatrick's press secretary, who was caught illegally registering his vehicle under a false suburban address.[90] "There is absolutely no benefit at this point for people [in Detroit] to purchase insurance," said Detroit state House member Nelson Saunders. "People are paying more just to live in Detroit," added Morris Hood III, the ranking member of Michigan's House Insurance Committee.[91] Although these and other actions resisted the disparate pricing, they also left them in place without confronting the structural inequality.

Opponents of 103 were also aided by a climate of hyper-deregulation. Corporate interests, in particular, couched their opposition to 103 as part of a wider struggle over the fundamental role of government in society. Specifically, insurers claimed that 103 signaled the latest example of "creeping socialism," in which the state actively sought to redistribute wealth from the deserving to the undeserving. (Such postulates ignored the initiative process, which gave consumers a direct say in the actions taken by government.) But fear of creeping socialism and wealth redistribution did not overshadow motorists' immediate concern over increasing costs. Eager to shift the argument, insurers gave in on one-time rate rollbacks and refunds to Californians. By doing so, insurers garnered greater support (or, at a minimum, less opposition) to keep their system of postal code–based pricing intact.

Immediate rate relief enabled insurers to capitalize on the imagined space of California's inner cities, which many at the time described as populated by society's least deserving citizens. Trade groups played on the unfounded perception that California's suburban and farm families were being forced to foot the bill for undeserving inner-city motorists. The Association of California Insurance Companies and other industry reps touted public opinion polls that showed "almost 7 out of 10 persons feel it is unfair to make suburban and rural residents pay higher auto insurance premiums to subsidize those living in urban areas" as yet further proof of the drain urban America was on the rest of society.[92] Such framing aimed to undo (or at least neuter) Proposition 103 by exploiting the perception of a predominantly White, suburban majority being made to subsidize an undeserving urban minority.[93]

Experts underestimated the increasing importance in the mid-1990s of corporate funding of political campaigns.[94] Charles Quackenbush's campaign and tenure as insurance commissioner personified "regulatory capture." A long-shot candidate to win the general election in 1994, Quackenbush was catapulted ahead of his rival by the infusion of insurance money. Indebted, Quackenbush spent his time in office defending insurance interests over those of consumers. In the rare instance when he did collect regulatory settlements, Quackenbush often applied the funds to public relations efforts, including paying for political polls and advertisements to further prop up his political career.[95] Ironically, experts had predicted in 1990 that changing the office of insurance commissioner to an elected post, rather than one appointed by the governor as it had been, would lessen the possibility of regulatory capture. In fact, it probably made candidates more beholden to the industry. As the story of Quackenbush showed, a financial services sector driven by a high-stakes interest in the outcome of social policy and possessing the means to capture a state regulator could easily overwhelm weak campaign finance laws.

The stymieing of Proposition 103 in California effectively shut down similar ballot initiatives elsewhere. Insurers nimbly elided the implementation of Prop 103 by offering token discounts and one-time rebates to consumers. As the industry ignored regulation, it also dropped rates for consumers in California more than in any other state. Acceding to a onetime rate rebate and modest price reduction enabled corporations to keep intact the far more lucrative territorial rating system. Auto insurance continues to be pegged primarily to where one lives rather than how one drives. As a result of this subsidy, the premiums of rural and suburban motorists are underwritten by central- and inner-city motorists. Over the driving span of the typical motorist, this subsidy costs urban motorists more than tens of thousands of dollars. Postal code profiling has continued to perpetuate one of the most surreptitious policies of wealth redistribution in our society. But postal code profiling may well suggest something beyond how wealth is perpetuated in contemporary American society. It may well be that the primacy of social factors and policies of identity over the ethos of individual merit is the nation's transcendent value, more interwoven into the fabric of American society than heretofore imagined.

Today, in Chicago, for example, the price of auto insurance consumes approximately 5 percent of the paychecks of people living in low- and moderate-income neighborhoods, compared with 1 percent or less of residents' paychecks in wealthier areas.[96] The fact that insurance premiums take up more of a worker's paycheck is not just symptomatic of a rating system predicated on neither merit nor mobility when it comes to insurance pricing. It may also equally reflect the ever-widening gap between income and expenses that has plagued US workers and has made mobility in this country more illusory today than perhaps at any other time in the lived experiences of most Americans. This very gap between income and expenses may be chiefly responsible for the rise of the most predatory of all the fee-driven consumer financial products—a product we will review next.

4

Shadow Bankers and the Great Wage Stagnation: The Story of Payday Lending

THERE APPEARED TO BE nothing wrong with the millennial economy in the Kansas City suburb of Overland Park right on the Missouri border. For decades CNN, *Money*, and *Businessweek* had consistently rated this suburb one of the top ten places in the United States to live, grow up, and raise a family. Overland Park boasted the best trappings of middle-class America. This included Fortune 500 companies, a per capita median income in the nation's upper quintile,[1] and only 3 percent of residents living below the poverty line—just a fraction of the national average during the decade beginning in 2000.[2] Its quintessential suburbanness made it the idyllic setting for the short-lived *The United States of Tara*, a 2008 Showtime cable series about the struggles of a less than perfect family living in a putatively perfect suburb.

Yet the stores synonymous with servicing America's down-and-out denizens, payday lenders, were busy setting up shop in Overland Park. Beginning in 2004, three payday loan stores sprang up in Overland Park in the span of thirty-six months, just blocks away from each other in the same shopping district. In Overland Park these stores were hardly servicing their traditional customer base—typically thought of as the working class and African Americans—given that the city's population was 90 percent White, and its largest racial minority, Asian Americans, boasted a larger annual household income than the average American in 2006. "Those are the kinds of stores that you see in parts of town you don't want to live in," said local resident Lori

Olson, who had watched paydays pop up in her middle-class enclave. "I don't believe it's the type of development that we want to see in Overland Park," city councilman Terry Goodman told the *Kansas City Star*. "It portrays an image of an area in decline."[3] The rising popularity of payday lenders in Overland Park mirrored the industry's increased presence and increasingly precarious family finances in satellite suburbs throughout the United States.

A payday lender is a short-term, high-interest, cash-advance store. To secure a payday loan, a cash-strapped borrower writes a postdated check for his or her next pay period (usually two weeks) and immediately receives the amount in cash, minus a transaction fee. Because the fee constitutes interest, the rates often range between 300 and 900 percent of the amount. The loan has to be repaid in full out of the borrower's next paycheck; otherwise the borrower must assume another loan plus interest or the amount of the transaction fee. A 2012 Pew study revealed how commonly borrowers wound up paying $895 in fees and interest for a $375 loan.[4] The final bill is so hefty largely because paying in full and on time is rare. One 2009 Nebraska study showed that 91 percent of borrowers rolled their loans over not once, but at least five times, and each time added a whole new set of fees.[5] Given the high risks involved, the remarkable rise of payday lenders is a troubling free-market response to the decline in real wages for middle- and working-class jobs.

In 1992, there were roughly three hundred paydays nationwide. By 2000, well over three thousand dotted the American landscape. By decade's end, the number of payday lenders and similar high-cost, check-cashing outlets had ballooned to more than twenty-four thousand, challenging the myth that they catered solely to the American working poor and those living on the fringes of the nation's financial system.[6] A 2012 Pew report indicated that each year 12 million payday borrowers were paying more than $7 billion on payday loans.[7] America's disappearing middle class might be found in the nation's payday lending storefronts; the number of these stores, by decade's end, would eclipse those most cherished cornerstones of middle-class consumerism: McDonald's and Starbucks.[8] The industry mushroomed despite the fact that nearly one in three states actually outlawed abusive lending terms.

Part One

A Cash-Poor Middle Class: Median Wages

The rapid rise of payday lenders beginning in the 1990s was, at bottom, the free market's response to the largely structural, generation-long problem of wage stagnation. The free-market cure has worsened the problem. In addition to helping drive America's working and middle classes deeper into debt, these household liabilities drain the overall national economy, as would-be consumers have fewer dollars to save, invest, and spend. Moreover, the short but significant history of payday loans offers a glimpse into high-risk lending and how a laissez-faire policy agenda contributed to the spread of arguably the most hazardous of all consumer loan products, with interest rates ten to twenty times higher than those charged by credit card companies and with a track record of two out of every three borrowers ending up in default on the eve of the Great Recession. Not only did a deregulatory environment pave the way for high-cost, high-risk consumer products, but by refusing to federally regulate payday lenders until after the 2008 financial meltdown, policymakers made sure that the buck stopped with the American taxpayer.

The growing demand for payday lending is not reducible to one cause or factor. Rather, it is linked to declining personal savings rates, inflation, the decrease in retail-oriented banking by mainstream financial institutions, and even shifts in personal choices. Those tendencies include profligate spending, a growing personal comfort with debt, and a decreased tendency to go to the boss for cash or to pawn personal items and instead to rely on a payday lender for emergency expenses. But no mechanism has been more central to this expansion than wage stagnation.

Since the 1970s, the median wages of American workers have either declined or remained stagnant. From 1970 to 2010, when adjusted for inflation (AFI), the median earnings of prime-aged working men, twenty-four to sixty-five years old, fell 4 percent,[9] and the annual incomes of the bottom 90 percent of US families have risen by only 10 percent since 1973.[10] While their incomes have risen faster than in the decades prior to the 1960s, women still earn significantly less than their male counterparts. Even worse, working women watched their

AFI wage fall by some 6 percent between 2000 and 2010.[11] Jobless recoveries following the economic recessions in 1990–91 and 2001 only placed more downward pressures on wages. The result was that while almost two-thirds of families have higher incomes (absolute mobility), a significant portion of Americans are not able to climb the income ladder relative to their peers (relative mobility).[12]

A payday loan correlates to employment and wages more closely than any other consumer financial product. As its very name intimates, a payday loan is virtually impossible to obtain without a job, which is not a requirement for almost any other form of short-term consumer credit. Unemployed children, life partners, and even pets have all been known to have access to credit; not so with payday loans, where a pay stub is a must for any borrower.

Once thought to service exclusively urban minorities and the working poor, payday loan stores have mushroomed within middle-class America since the early 1990s. By 2008, the average approved online payday borrower earned $47,260 annually, higher than the $46,242 median household income for the entire United States. According to the 2010 US Census Bureau's American Factfinder, 45.2 percent of payday borrowers owned their own homes.[13] Payday lending studies conducted by economic researchers since the early 2000s have shown that a critical part of the industry's customer base are middle-class consumers, with three out of four borrowers having a high school diploma or some college education.[14] And as economist Robert Frank noted in *Success and Luck*, even among college graduates, earnings growth over the past thirty years has been relatively nonexistent or small, a fact that too often gets obscured because of high earnings at the very top of the pay scale.[15] Payday lenders understand the boon that a generation of flat incomes provides to their business's bottom line. Darrin Anderson, president of the industry's largest trade association, the Community Financial Services Association, recognized, "Our customers represent a broad demographic segment and cannot be grouped based on race, sex, or religion." He added, "The only common denominator is that our customers [have] steady sources of income and bank accounts."[16]

Between 1998 and 2005, the money lent by paydays nationally increased tenfold, totaling more than $45 billion a year, according to the California Department of Corporations.[17] A 2012 Pew Center report on payday lending revealed that Americans relied heavily on these high-priced loans to cover everyday expenses. According to Pew, 69 percent of these payday customers took out short-term loans for recurring expenses such as food, rent, utilities, and credit card payments, while only 16 percent used them for emergency expenses such as auto repairs.[18] Wage stagnation has sapped middle-class consumers of the purchasing power once enjoyed by previous generations. "Payday lending is the least of middle-class problems," commented Peter Stone, lead contributor to PersonalMoneyStore.com, on the growing number of middle-class borrowers turning to alternative financial institutions. "Stagnating wages, combined with inflation, is a recipe for middle class disaster [and] the problem may be getting worse."[19]

Payday lending's dependence on wage stagnation reflects its nature as a "countercyclical" industry.[20] As such, it may best be understood as an inverse index to national economic well-being. Industry profits rise as the fortunes of the working consumer fall. Not coincidentally, then, the boom for payday lenders occurred in a period marked by elevated poverty, rising unemployment, falling income levels, and declining disposable income.[21] The industry's own cost structure is a microcosm of the broader economy. The increased profit margins for the average industry operator since the early 2000s appeared to result partly from decreasing wages of the payday employees themselves.[22] As a consequence, at the same time that overall payday industry revenue was growing, aggregate wages for payday employees as a percentage of total payday lending industry revenue declined, from 31.07 in 2005 to 30.76 in 2008.[23] The average wage of payday lending workers (adjusted for inflation 2014) decreased from $38,864.73 to $36,105.46, a pattern that appeared to continue well into at least 2014.[24]

Shadow Banking

"Shadow banking" (or "parallel banking") is an umbrella term for entities and activities that are involved in market-based, credit intermediation but that operate at least partly outside the regular banking system and are typically unregulated or lightly regulated. These range from entities such as insurance firms, hedge funds, and finance companies to instruments such as collateralized debt obligations, derivatives, and mortgage-backed securities. Like traditional banks or depository institutions, shadow banks function as intermediaries between the credit and real economies, gathering funds from those with money to invest (e.g., corporations, households, institutions, securities) and then pooling these monies to lend to other households or businesses.[25]

Shadow banks are different from traditional banks and depository institutions in some notable ways. Most important for consumers, unlike traditional banks' or depository institutions' funds, those raised by shadow banks are not explicitly guaranteed. However, many of the largest shadow banks have interlocking relationships with traditional banks, which effectively means that shadow bank activities can be indirectly guaranteed, or "backstopped," by institutions that do receive federal guarantees or have a public safety net.[26] When advantageous to them, industry allies use this indirect guarantee to make a case for emergency funding for payday lenders. It was this implied federal guarantee that appeared to prompt Tennessee senator and longtime defender of payday lending Bob Corker and other industry allies to reason that a bailout of big banks would also provide a much-needed backstop for payday lenders.[27] Despite this legal relationship, and while banks are comprehensively regulated, many shadow banks escape federal financial oversight or are only lightly regulated, if at all.[28] Because they tend to lack an explicit public safety net and operate outside banking regulation by conducting their activities outside the traditional banking system, shadow banks typically have no access to deposit insurance or the discount-lending window from the central bank that financially troubled traditional banks may use as a last resort to secure capital on short notice.[29] The central bank has used this quick and guaranteed access to extensions of credit during liquidity emergencies for traditional banks with collateral in order to avoid runs on banks by nervous customers and thus expects traditional banks to avoid excessive risk-taking.[30] With no access, however, shadow banks do not have the central bank's expectation of minimal risk-taking.[31]

Modern shadow banking began in earnest in the mid-1970s and 1980s, the beneficiary of financial innovations and technological advances that opened up new avenues of credit, as well as new deregulatory policies. By 1996, the total earnings, assets, and liabilities of shadow banks were nearly $1 trillion, exceeding those of traditional banks. The shadow banking sector continued its steady growth for more than a decade until the eve of the financial crisis in 2008, when shadow banking liabilities collectively topped $20 trillion, compared with approximately $11 trillion for traditional banking.[32] Its growing importance made shadow banking a primary factor in the subprime mortgage crisis of 2007–08 and the global recession that followed.[33]

The structures of shadow banks vary widely. The payday lending industry is but one of the fifteen or more entities and activities that help make up parallel or shadow banking.[34] Because the shadow banking system typically involves large-scale institutional transactions and actors, payday lending is sometimes an invisible sector of this system.[35] But the relationship between those large-scale institutions and payday loan shops is significant. Payday lenders are specialized sectoral financiers among shadow bankers that (along with leasing and real estate investment companies) provide a retail service to a targeted sector. The rise of payday lending could not have happened without the scale and speed of the capital flows within the shadow banking industry. Many players, including Wells Fargo, Bank of America, and J. P. Morgan Chase, were major financiers of paydays—even during and after the federal taxpayer bailouts these too-big-to-fail banks received.[36] Meanwhile, Wall Street and other global investment firms—Goldman Sachs, Bear Stearns, Morgan Stanley, and Credit Suisse, among others—sat on payday lender boards, extended lines of credit, or served as lead underwriters for initial offerings for payday loan companies looking to go public.[37] And leading up to the Great Recession, Fidelity Funds was the largest single stockholder in the payday loan company ACE Cash Express, according to University of Texas law scholars Ronald Mann and Jim Hawkins.[38]

There were high profits to be made with paydays. Corner-store payday lenders were unusually positioned to meet the demands of households experiencing limited wage expansion. Through the decade beginning in 2000, with median real wages shrinking, the profit margins of paydays remained consistently at 20–25 percent, among the highest yields of any business sector.[39] Costing very little to set up (approximately $120,000), paydays provided investment returns of 23.8 percent, while traditional lender returns earned between 13 and 18 percent.[40] These profits came primarily from the usurious lending terms stores charged those least able to afford them. Forty-eight states had rate caps that set a general usury limit for consumers of 30 percent or less. But by finding ways of getting around state usury laws, paydays regularly charged their customers ten to fifteen times as much.[41]

By the end of 2000, twenty-three states had legalized payday lending, and other paydays, like Advance America and Check Into Cash, were operating in eight more because no law forbade them from doing so. Nonetheless, the growth potential for payday lending was hampered largely because state usury laws prohibited charging exorbitant interest rates. Citizens and state officials—whether by employing class-action suits, passing statutory reform, or enforcing existing anti-usury laws—attempted to rein in the predatory practices. Some tried to cap rates; others, like Ohio, looked to restrict the practice by banning consecutive borrowing from the same lender. In all, one in three states passed reform laws or ratcheted up enforcement.[42]

By 1999, paydays had begun partnering with banks as a way to elude policing by local and state governments. As national or federally chartered institutions, banks operated under a separate set of laws, rules that allowed them to ignore state usury laws and escape rate caps. The first payday shop to arrange such a partnership was ACE Cash Express in September 1999. ACE had more than eight hundred outlet stores that offered a variety of services, including auto insurance, check cashing, and payment of utility bills. The company was prohibited, however, from offering payday lending services in many of its thirty states because of their respective usury laws. It could not even offer the service legally in its home state of Texas. That was all about to change. Rather than make the loans itself, ACE would now simply process the loan and let a bank located in California, where paydays and usury were legal, issue the actual loan. "If a California bank can issue credit-card loans across state lines and charge interest rates that lenders based in other states wouldn't be allowed to, then California should be able to do the same with payday loans," reasoned an ACE official to the *Wall Street Journal*. With this arrangement ACE received a $30 processing fee for every $200 lent. Meanwhile, Goleta Bank of California also collected fees of $4 or $5 on the same $200 loan. And after it was issued in the form of a debit-like pay card that borrowers might use at an ATM or retailer, Goleta would sell a part of the loan to ACE.[43]

A publicly traded company, ACE anticipated that the national roll-out of a consumer financial product that charged an interest rate of 391 percent or more to borrowers would provide a "big boost" to the company shareholders. The Main Street lender imagined Wall Street playing a central role. "What the stock has needed, analysts say, is a reason for investors to put their money into it. Now, bulls say they found one that Wall Street has overlooked," wrote *Wall Street Journal* reporter Jonathan Weil. Trading at $14 a share, analysts predicted the new payday–bank deal would help ACE's price reach $20 by the next year. "The stock lacked a catalyst for a while," observed one Dallas securities analyst, but now "people realize their earnings are going to be much higher."[44] In the wake of ACE's success, the rest of the payday industry adopted the practice. In just three short years during the late 1990s, paydays had become a multibillion-dollar industry—reaching as many as 10 million households, making about 65 million loans totaling $8 billion to $14 billion in loan value, and resulting in at least $2 billion in revenue.[45] With this growth came increased concerns from bank regulators about rollovers and other questionable lending practices that put customers into a huge amount of debt and infected the overall economy.[46]

Part Two

Rent-a-Banks and Regulators

By 2000, federal regulators were expressing major concerns about the systemic risk posed by payday lending. In the weeks between the controversial 2000 election and President George W. Bush's inauguration, the two primary bank regulators—the Office of the Comptroller of the Currency (OCC) and the Office of Thrift Supervision (OTS)—issued a joint advisory to regulators and policymakers. "The OCC and OTS . . . have learned that non-bank vendors seeking to avoid individual state laws are approaching federally-chartered banks and thrifts urging them to enter into agreements to fund payday [lenders]," explained John D. Hawke, Jr., of OCC and Ellen Seidman of OTS.[47]

According to the OCC, payday lending represented a growing threat to America's banking system. The problem, it said, was that banks were increasingly entering into arrangements with paydays, which often rented a bank's charter. Ace Cash Express and Goleta Bank of

California pioneered this "strategic alliance" or "rent-a-bank" partnership that soon became an industry standard in which a bank "rents" its name and government charter to a payday lender for an annual fee. In addition to this fee, the payday lender puts up "the capital, solicits borrowers, advertisements, servicing, and collection of the loans." The payday lender also agrees to protect the bank by covering or insuring all non-credit-related losses and liabilities that may result from the loan operation.[48] New York presented a textbook illustration of how these strategic alliances worked. Payday lenders Cashnet and TeleCash looked to bring their operations to New York but did not want to abide by the strict usury caps of the Empire State, where it was a civil offense to charge customers more than 16 percent interest and a criminal offense to charge more than 25 percent. For payday lenders, these low caps were far cries from the 370 percent or more that Cashnet and TeleCash sought to charge their customers. The only way Cashnet and TeleCash could charge this amount was to partner with banks with charters in states having less restrictive rate cap rules, like Delaware. Federal law then allowed banks to export their home state rates (which amounted to unlimited interest rates for a bank domiciled in Delaware as well as South Dakota) to customers in other states. So Cashnet and TeleCash partnered up with Delaware-based Rehoboth Bank and moved into New York before being sued by New York attorney general Eliot Spitzer.[49]

Reputable banks were in on this, too. Payday lenders turned to larger banks rather than simply partnering with banks in states with friendlier usury laws. In addition to seeking out federally chartered financial institutions as a means of avoiding individual state laws, payday lenders often operated under the assumption that federal regulators would defend banks and, by extension, payday lenders against the encroachment of state and local law enforcement.[50]

These partnerships were mutually beneficial. They gave banks access to the capital of extremely profitable payday lending businesses. Advertising in bank trade publications, national payday chains promised banks that these partnerships would bring them eye-popping returns on equity. As one Check 'n Go ad in the *American Banker* magazine proclaimed, "What would your bank consider to be a good ROE [return on equity]? Now double that. Your company could realize an annual

20+% return on equity through a strategic alliance with Check 'n Go."[51] By 2003, eleven of the largest thirteen payday lenders were partnering with banks.[52] But the profitability of paydays, which rested in large part on the borrowers' inability to make scheduled loan payoffs, resulted from a business model that violated the most fundamental practices of sound banking. While these so-called rent-a-bank arrangements may have helped high-cost lenders evade state laws, they also opened the door for federal regulation of the payday lending industry. At stake was the banking system's "safety and soundness," the primary concern of bank regulators from the Federal Deposit Insurance Commission (FDIC) to OTS, OCC, and the Federal Reserve.[53]

Warnings from OCC comptroller John D. Hawke, Jr., should have awakened the Treasury, the White House, and Congress to the gravity of the systemic risk posed by rent-a-bank deals, since within the universe of bank regulators the OCC had rarely displayed the institutional stomach to issue such alerts. In contrast to other safety and soundness regulators, the OCC had been so inattentive to enforcement that it had typically relied on more compliance-oriented agencies like the OTS and Federal Reserve Bank to provide greater financial supervision and compliance with laws. Instead, the Bush White House preferred to dismiss a messenger, forcing the resignation of OTS director Ellen Seidman. Rumors swirled that Seidman, appointed by President Bill Clinton in 1997, had been too harsh on payday lenders and others, so the Bush administration pressured her to resign well before her five-year term expired.[54] Seidman shared her reluctance to resign as well as her fear that any successor would be less than zealous about oversight. "I do this reluctantly . . . [and] I am concerned that the request to cut short the 5-year term calls into serious question the independence of the Office of Thrift Supervision."[55]

As for the OCC, it did not want to ban rent-a-banks. The OCC simply looked to minimize their abuses and reduce risks. They proposed a series of tighter regulatory measures that included limiting borrowers to one payday loan at a time, presenting borrowers with a one-day return policy to take back a loan without charge, and prohibiting payday lenders from imposing a check-cashing fee for the check written as part of the payday loan origination process. In addition, it wanted any third-party arrangement to comply with the Truth in Lending Act, which requires the disclosure of accurate finance charges and annual percent-age rates. Finally, comptrollers strongly encouraged restricting the pop-ular payday practice of rolling over loans: "As with all lending, a bank should not make a payday loan without a reasonable assurance that the loan will be repaid at maturity. . . . [T]here needs to be a reasonable expectation that additional income or other deposit will be received on a date certain and that such income or deposit will retire the loan." But rollovers, also known as loan flipping, were paydays' golden goose. Typical borrowers flipped their original payday loan a minimum of twice and as often as eight times.[56] In a monthly series called "Protect Your Pocketbook," published by the state of Indiana's securities divi-sion, Indiana secretary of state Todd Rokita noted that 90 percent of lenders turned their profits mostly through the fees generated from cus-tomers who rolled over their loan to the next pay period.[57] Arguably the industry's main revenue source, these embedded fees alone generated approximately $4.2 billion annually.[58]

But the primary concern of the OCC was the system, not the bor-rower. OCC experts feared that the safety and soundness of the finan-cial system itself were imperiled by an unregulated payday industry: "Such third-party arrangements significantly increase risks to the bank."[59] Unsurprisingly, none of the OCC's recommendations were followed voluntarily or mandated by Congress. Investment analysts anticipated that payday volume would triple over the next three years, exacerbating the vulnerability of the financial system.[60] The OCC and OTS came out with a joint statement conveying their shared alarm about the safety and soundness of federally chartered banks and thrifts that entered into contractual agreements to fund paydays and title loans: "We urge national banks and thrifts to think carefully about the risks involved in such relationships, which can pose not only safety and soundness threats, but also compliance and reputational risks."[61]

Despite the red flags raised in the 2000 OCC advisory letter, the Bush Treasury Department, which oversaw the OCC, left the rent-a-bank practices largely intact through the first Bush administration. In 2004, instead of a systemwide overhaul, the OCC opted to pursue only what it deemed "isolated incidences" of consumer abuse emanating from the third-party arrangements between paydays and banks. However, the OCC intervened in only five arrangements, and the OTS in only two banks.[62] Regulatory oversight was effectively returned to the status quo, as if the November 2000 warnings had never been made.

Faced with little oversight or intervention and intense demand from cash-strapped consumers, the payday industry flourished. Between 2000 and 2003, industry analysts reported a 50 percent spike in the number of payday loan outlets. The industry's expansion was largely attributed to these strategic alliances with banks. These arrangements owed their ongoing existence to the FDIC; while other state and federal bank regulators like the OCC and OTS were growing wary of these institutional relationships, the FDIC gladly stepped into the breach. In the span of a few short years, the FDIC became the regulator of choice for the payday loan industry because it was considered to have laxer oversight standards than other regulators. For example, when the Federal Reserve Bank of Philadelphia in the spring of 2003 increased its regulatory scrutiny of the First Bank of Delaware because of its rent-a-bank deals with payday lending operations, by October 2003 the Delaware bank had merely switched to a new regulator, the FDIC, which gave the bank permission to come under its regulation and continue federal insurance coverage.[63]

FDIC-supervised banks seemed unable or unwilling to keep track of the quantity of payday loan recipients or the quality of the loans. That was the story behind the unchecked risky business practices of the People's National Bank of Paris, Texas, where 60 percent or more of that bank's classified assets were delinquent payday loans, which the bank failed to classify as substandard.[64] More troubling was the FDIC's apparent naïveté when it came to its knowledge of and ability to oversee arrangements between paydays and banks. Led by Pete Garcia of Chicanos Por La Causa, an umbrella organization of some eighty community and consumer groups unearthed and documented how the FDIC was being lied to by banks such as the Republic Bank & Trust of Kentucky, which rented out its bank charter to payday chains in Arkansas, North Carolina, Pennsylvania, and Texas.[65] In an effort to conceal its exposure to paydays, the Louisville-based bank deliberately misled the FDIC. Republic grossly understated the number of payday customers and store transactions it handled, claiming to have only seventy thousand payday customers when the figure appeared to be much closer to four hundred thousand. Though it reported six hundred store locations, those lenders actually conducted approximately 4 million transactions annually through Republic's three main payday contractors, Advance America, National Cash Advance, and ACE Cash Express.[66] The FDIC would have remained in the dark had consumer groups not brought the bank's deception to the regulator's attention.

Such lax enforcement and inattention partially came from the perverse incentive structure of the federal financial regulatory system. Under the existing system, the more banks under a regulatory agency's purview, the more federal dollars flowed the regulator's way. The budget for the FDIC and other bank regulators was partly contingent on the number of institutions under their purview. The more financial institutions they oversaw, the more funds those regulatory bodies received from Congress. Not surprisingly, businesses shopped around for a regulator that offered as little oversight as possible, fostering a race to the bottom among competing institutions.

The rise of the FDIC in overseeing rent-a-banks had major implications for American taxpayers. In theory, taxpayer dollars were not to be used to insure banks. Rather, the FDIC was supposed to cover depository institutions and accountholders (up to $100,000 from 1974 to 2008, then $250,000 starting in 2008) by collecting insurance premiums from member banks. But such logic collapsed under the weight of recent history. In 1991, following the savings and loan scandal, taxpayers came to the rescue of FDIC-member banks as the FDIC tapped the Treasury Department for a line of credit. Instead of learning from their past failure, "grasstop" FDIC regulators seemed content to repeat it. Unlike the "grassroots" civil servants who populated regulatory agencies, spending much of their time as in-the-field investigators, grasstop regulators were mostly political appointees possessing little if any current field experience. Grasstop regulators were more susceptible to repeating mistakes because they rarely faced those directly affected by their decision-making and did not have a long-standing history with the agency. The FDIC's lax lending standards regarding rent-a-banks threatened to again put taxpayers on the hook for an industry that was supposed to be wholly privately insured. "I often kid that I did not know what 'moral hazard' meant until I came to Washington," joked FDIC chair Donald Powell, deflecting concerns raised by representatives Carolyn Maloney (D-NY) and Ron Paul (R-TX) that the "rent-a-bank" policy was unsafe and unsound and might ultimately cost taxpayers.[67] Despite his apparent stab at humor, it remains unclear whether Powell, who chaired the commission from 2001 to 2006, or his predecessors grasped their fiduciary responsibility to taxpayers regarding moral hazard, particularly in light of what unfolded on their watch from 1996 to 2006.[68]

Just a few short years after taxpayers paid $105 billion to resolve the savings and loan crisis, the FDIC allowed banks to skip out on making premium payments, depleting the FDIC insurance fund while enabling speculation to flourish. Why? The belief was that most banks were well capitalized and that widespread bank failures or panics were a thing of the nation's past. Not having to pay the premium freed up capital for the banks. This halt in collections occurred during a ten-year window (1996–2006) when lending standards—whether for mortgage or short-term payday loans—were lowered while speculation peaked.

Depleted reserve funds combined with risky loans raised the real possibility that if a large number of banks failed, the American taxpayer would wind up footing the bill.[69] The FDIC directly contributed to loosening lending standards and heightening wild speculation by supporting policies like third-party arrangements, and the FDIC was faced with the real possibility of once again being bailed out by the Treasury or, worse, going directly to Congress for more money. "It's unfortunate that we didn't have more time to build up the fund in the good times," remarked incoming FDIC chairwoman Sheila C. Bair in 2008.[70] However checkered their record of enforcement, regulators proved far more attentive to safety and soundness issues than the elected officials in charge of financial oversight.

The checks and balances of the political system failed American taxpayers at least as much as any financial regulator. Some concerned members of Congress weighed in against the FDIC. "Is the FDIC going to continue to allow paydays to rent bank charters?" Congresswoman Maloney quizzed Powell at the 2004 hearing. She continued, "I really do consider this a safety and soundness issue and certainly good management." The Republican-controlled Congress overrode the concerns of Maloney and other minority members.[71] The GOP also ignored the concerns of fellow Republican Ron Paul, who objected to the "rampant deregulation" and the trampling of state regulators that rent-a-banks symbolized.[72] Instead, by endorsing a policy of inaction on rent-a-banks and insurance premium nonpayments by FDIC banks, the GOP effectively left American taxpayers holding the bag.[73] As the OCC and OTS had done in the past, the FDIC issued, in 2005, a "cease and desist order" against one bank partnering with payday lenders.[74] But this was an isolated enforcement measure—a sort of symbolic payday perp walk. By making a high-profile example of reining in a rogue bank, the FDIC hoped to deter the most abusive practices.

Consumer groups pressed a reluctant GOP-controlled Congress for greater regulatory action, ultimately to no avail. While the focus of consumer groups was primarily consumer protection, a couple of their proposed initiatives would have, at minimum, drawn attention to the rampant pattern of unsafe and unsound lending practices created by the strategic alliances between banks and paydays; at most, exposing these alliances could have helped limit the contagion and economic damage.

Take, for example, the Gramm-Leach-Bliley Act of 1999, named after Senator Phil Gramm (R-TX) and Representatives Jim Leach (R-IA) and Thomas J. Bliley (R-VA). This act removed barriers between financial institutions put in place by the 1933 Glass-Steagall Act and thereby permitted institutions from across the financial markets (e.g., banking, securities, and insurance) to combine. Consumer advocates called for walling off payday lenders, thus preventing them from infecting the entire financial system, by limiting their financial relations with federally insured depository banks.[75] Testifying before the Senate Banking Committee in July 2004, consumer groups—the Consumer Federation of America, Consumers Union, and US Public Interest Research Group—expanded their critique of payday loans and echoed the alarms raised by previous regulators. Much like the federal regulators, they concluded that the problem was no longer simply a consumer protection issue; these contracts exposed federally insured banks to reputational and safety and soundness risks. In particular, they claimed that the Gramm-Leach-Bliley Act opened a Pandora's box of rent-a-bank loopholes. Travis Plunkett, speaking on behalf of the consumer groups, urged Senate Banking Committee chairman Richard Shelby of Alabama "to clarify that bank charters are not for rent and halt the misuse of bank charters by third-party lenders looking to make loans under terms prohibited by states."[76] Unlike typical lenders, payday lenders rarely did the underwriting diligence required of safe and sound consumer lending such as conducting background checks with credit bureaus, collateralizing debt, or addressing other considerations as to whether the borrower ever possessed the capacity to repay.[77] In allowing banks to go into business with payday lenders, the Gramm-Leach-Bliley Act swung open the door for banks to enter into the high-risk, high-reward world of payday lending.

Despite their efforts, consumer advocates and experts had little influence on regulatory choices. To understand just how little, one need only observe their failed efforts to extend the oversight established by the Community Reinvestment Act (CRA) to the payday lending industry.[78] While CRA opponents have long argued that the law has had an outsized role in encouraging lending decisions, this was certainly not the case when applied to rent-a-bank arrangements. Consumer advocates and scholars consistently argued that the CRA should be expanded to include payday lenders in order to protect consumers from discriminatory and predatory practices. Further, they argued that partnerships with payday lenders should lower the CRA rating of banks. A lower CRA rating would make it more difficult for banks looking to grow by merger, acquisition, or branching. But, in reality, the CRA had almost no deterrent effect when it came to rent-a-banks nationally. For example, in 2000 the OCC, responsible for regulating national banks, gave Eagle National Bank a "satisfactory" rating despite claims filed by national consumer groups that the bank's partnership with payday lender Dollar Financial warranted a failing CRA score. On the whole, partnerships with payday lending had little or no influence on a bank's CRA ratings, and, in the rare instances when they did, almost no penalties were imposed on the bank, whether financial or otherwise.[79]

Applying CRA's standards to payday lenders may have reduced systemic risk while improving safety and soundness by compelling banks to more closely scrutinize the borrower's financial ability to repay the loan, given that CRA-evaluated banks imposed stricter lending standards than non-CRA institutions. Higher loan standards resulted in fewer borrower defaults, which ultimately limited the negative impact of payday lending.[80]

Meanwhile, the Republican-controlled Congress opposed any active oversight of the payday issue. This laissez-faire posture toward rent-a-banks spread risk throughout the financial economy. Controlling the major subcommittees, congressional Republicans largely ignored both consumer group pleas and regulator requests. The Congressional Research Service, a nonpartisan research arm of Congress that provides private reports to senators and representatives, conducted a confidential study of regulatory and legislative initiatives. It concluded that while bills attempting to limit the hazards of paydays by regulating the involvement of banks and thrifts had been introduced, "no further action [had] been taken."[81] Each time a regulatory reform bill that would have provided consumer protections and limited the contagion was introduced, congressional Republicans blocked it. By blocking reform, Congress allowed rent-a-bank arrangements with mainstream financial institutions to spread exponentially. Rather than being quarantined to a few paydays, the problems of safety and soundness went viral. It appeared to matter little to Congress whether concerns and reform efforts came from consumer groups out to protect borrowers, the military looking out for national security, or regulators worried that payday practices posed a systemic risk to the entire financial system. Congress appeared more concerned about the moral behavior of individual borrowers than the moral hazard fostered by this deregulatory environment.

After Congress refused to take action for nearly a decade, regulators did eventually step in. In 2007, regulators banned all (future) rent-a-bank arrangements, but the ban may have been too little, too late. The law banning rent-a-banks left loopholes so large it allowed some of the nation's biggest banks to continue their lending relationships with payday lenders, even after they received federal bailout dollars. Despite the new restrictions, for example, Bank of America continued to own stakes in four of the top five publicly held payday operations.[82] In 2010, Bank of America also extended a $205 million line of credit to Advance America, the nation's largest payday lender.[83] It, along with Goldman Sachs, was also the leading initial public offering (IPO) for the prepaid debit card Netspend, a company owned by payday lender Ace Cash Express.[84]

Wells Fargo also went unchecked. As the largest funder of payday loans in the country, it provided tens of millions of dollars to at least eight payday lenders, totaling nearly six thousand storefronts. Nor did the taxpayer bailout of Wells Fargo in 2008 deter it from continuing to engage in risky investing. Just days after the government cut the bank a $75 billion bailout check, Wells Fargo extended a $25 million line of credit to a Mexican pawnshop, pursued a credit agreement with Check Into Cash, and financed EZ Corp's financial ventures. Despite the destructive role paydays had played in recent years in the very under-banked communities that the CRA was designed to serve, the pay-day financier Wells Fargo still received an outstanding CRA rating.[85] Kevin Connor, who coauthored a report on the role big banks played in the payday lending industry after the bailout, stated, "Not having financing would shut the big [payday] players down."[86] Rather than shrinking their presence, banks actually enlarged their roles in pay-day lending in the months after the Great Recession and bank bailout. After the 2008 bank bailout, big banks began to bypass payday lenders and became directly involved in the business of making these loans—though they rarely promoted or advertised this retail service, partly for fear that doing so might draw the attention of bank regulators (and partly to distance themselves publicly from the stigma associated with payday lenders). By 2010, big banks had provided $1.5 billion in credit to publicly held payday loan companies and an estimated $2.5 billion to $3 billion to the industry as a whole.[87]

Payday lenders have been incredibly successful in using the gov-ernment when they see fit but avoiding regulation almost completely. They successfully opposed federal oversight by claiming that the federal government had no business governing their industry, insisting instead that state regulations provided oversight even as paydays entered into arrangements with federally insured banks that allowed them to avoid those same state laws. At the same time, they lobbied to be under the shelter of Uncle Sam and ultimately won the right to sue individ-ual consumers in federal bankruptcy court. They fashioned a world of moral hazard in which they reaped the benefits of low regulation while suffering little of the concomitant exposure that accompanies high risk. Consumers were faced with potentially being dragged into federal bankruptcy courts because of these high interest rates while paydays were able to flout the national lending laws (e.g., federal inter-est rate caps) meant to protect them from these very situations in the first place. This lose-lose situation for consumers was allowed to happen thanks primarily to congressional leaders.

Democrats also played a role in the spread of payday loans. Particularly in the earlier years of the industry, Democratic members of minority caucuses, like the Congressional Black Caucus and the Hispanic Caucus, welcomed the access payday stores provided to underserved consumers. Similarly, groups often allied with the Democratic Party, such as the Southern Christian Leadership Conference, the National Conference of Black Mayors, and the National Black Caucus of State Legislators (the last of which awarded payday lender and subprime credit company CompuCredit its Corporate Partner of the Year award as recently as 2006), have frequently found common cause with shadow bankers.[88] Many conservative Arkansas Democrats such as former senator Mark Pryor and former House member Mike Ross received considerable contributions from payday lending lobbyists, as have other state Democrats in recent years. Yet while the role of some Democrats in fueling payday lending is unquestionable, only Democrats led the charge to repeal, reform, or oppose payday lending outright. Except for Ron Paul, no Republicans actively fought usury in Congress, as laws were debated and passed that enabled the spread of this high-cost, short-term retail lending.

In the House, payday lending reform legislation was introduced almost annually between 1999 and 2007. A bill to establish minimum national standards for short-term interest rates and prohibit rollover loans was sponsored every year, typically by either Bobby Rush of Chicago or John LaFalce of New York.[89] In each session payday reform was killed by Alabama congressman Spencer Bachus, whose gatekeeping role as House Committee on Financial Services chair, as well as Subcommittee for Banking and Consumer Credit chair, meant that he largely controlled which bills received hearings.

Part Three

Bankruptcy and Payday Lending

The problem of payday lending found its way to the Senate docket as the upper chamber debated another significant consumer financial problem, bankruptcy reform. By the late 1990s, more Americans were declaring bankruptcy each year than were graduating from college. By 2000, fully 1.3 million Americans had filed for bankruptcy, a 75 percent jump from 1990.[90] Between 1990 and 1999, consumer credit debt jumped 163 percent. In 1996, a record-setting 1 percent of all households filed for bankruptcy, with 5 percent of all families reporting delinquency in payments and nearly three out of four American families in debt.[91] The popular perception, reflected in expert opinion, attributed the boom in high debt and personal bankruptcies to reckless borrowing by consumers. Borrowers certainly deserved some blame. Poor personal choices—from one's marriage or partner choice, to opting out of health coverage, gambling, or simply, as one personal finance guru wrote, the refusal to distinguish "wants" from "needs"—certainly contributed to the record run-up in personal profligate spending.[92] Further, credit companies complained of consumers who simply elected not to repay their debts. They pointed to various industry reports at the time that between 3 and 15 percent of debtors filing for bankruptcy could actually afford to pay as much as 20 percent of their unsecured debts.[93] Not mincing words, Federal Reserve chairman Alan Greenspan set aside his characteristically indecipherable jargon for the rigid moral grammar of economic analysis. "Personal bankruptcies are soaring because Americans have lost their sense of shame," he counseled Congress during the 1997 debates over reforming the bankruptcy code.[94] Greenspan's assessment resonated with at least some members of the business press. Writing in the *Atlanta Journal Constitution*, business reporter Marilyn Geewax argued that it was "time we toughen our laws and attitudes." She went as far as demanding the criminalization of debt, as is done with shoplifting and writing bad checks.[95] Republicans and most Democrats looked to curb bankruptcies by getting tough on filers. They made it harder for people to seek court protection from payment of debts by establishing new income requirements on bankruptcy filers and shrank the loopholes that let individuals shield their homes from creditors.[96]

In the Senate, payday lending surfaced in a proposed amendment to the bankruptcy bill introduced by the late senator Paul Wellstone (D-MN) in June 1999. Wellstone, who died in 2002, pitched an amendment expressly targeting payday lenders. Specifically, the Wellstone Amendment called for prohibiting any lender that charged more than 100 percent annual interest from recovering debts from consumers in bankruptcy proceedings.[97] Through their connection to the banking system, payday lenders gained access to federal bankruptcy courts, enabling these usury lenders to collect debts that state courts might otherwise deny. As in the House, at the center of the bankruptcy debate were Senate Republicans, who emerged as the most reliable defenders of the payday industry.

The bankruptcy bill punished borrowers while rewarding high-cost lenders. Worse, according to Wellstone, the legislation never addressed the source of the problem (i.e., stagnant wages) or the supplier—payday lenders who used rent-a-bank deals to routinely sidestep their respective state's usury laws.[98] Concerned that the proposed bankruptcy legislation expanded legal protections and might possibly indemnify an industry built on unsound lending practices that now turned to Washington for aid in recovering risky personal loans, Wellstone and others asked that both borrower and lender be held more responsible.

The Senate majority balked at this balancing act of accountability. Twice the Senate voted for the amendment, first in February 2000 and later in March 2001. Each time it failed largely along party line votes, 53 to 44 and 58 to 41, respectively.[99] When bankruptcy legislation did pass in 2005, there was no Wellstone Amendment. Instead, the new law allowed usurious lenders to sue in federal court. Critics of payday lenders did not necessarily want lenient bankruptcy standards. Rather, opponents like Wellstone argued that the bill was tilted too far toward the titans of usury. Notably, the actions of heavily leveraged US consumers demonstrated this tilt. A record two hundred thousand debtors filed personal bankruptcies a week before the new and more punitive 2005 bankruptcy law took effect. This number was triple the previous record, which had been set just two weeks earlier.[100] Payday loans had real-world consequences. Bankruptcy would be tethered to payday lending in ways that Wellstone himself probably could scarcely have imagined. Years later, bankruptcy studies would show how just the act of taking out a payday loan made borrowers nearly twice as likely to fall behind in debts or file for bankruptcy as similarly financially situated would-be borrowers *denied* a payday loan.[101]

Still, more government wasn't the answer; it was the source of the problem, countered fellow Republican senator Orrin Hatch, whose home state of Utah had the highest bankruptcy filing rate in the

United States. The only institution in need of reform was government, not the loan industry, added Hatch. Rampant bankruptcy filings were a reflection of our more permissive culture enabled by the federal government. Through the last major reform bill in 1978, the government had set up a bankruptcy system that, in Hatch's view, rewarded consumers who were "devoid of personal responsibility . . . and mock[ed] the rule of law." It did so, Hatch explained, by enacting consumer-coddling bankruptcy laws like Chapter 7—a form of filing that allowed consumers to settle outstanding debts simply by paying out of existing assets—rather than, for example, Chapter 13, which required debtors to repay debts for three to five years. By insulating consumers from the full risk of their debts, the government was enabling immoral actions and discouraging personal responsibility and honesty; it too easily forgave spendthrift consumers who wantonly racked up large bills, Hatch argued.[102] Hatch's view of consumer corruption was consistent with the broader conservative critique during the 1990s that faulted individuals despite increasingly placing blame on impersonal structures and mechanisms, whether state policies, culture, or government agencies, for giving individuals perverse incentives to do the wrong thing.

Between the polar views of Wellstone and Hatch were the perspectives of bankruptcy lawyers like George W. Liebmann. Liebmann, who, as a US bankruptcy trustee for the Justice Department since 1981, had scrutinized countless bankruptcy files, described "a sick, symbiotic relationship between consumers hooked on credit and the companies that charge them enormous fees—at least, until they go bankrupt." "It's a fundamentally corrupt situation, corrupt for both debtors and creditors," he told a *New York Times* reporter.[103] Yet despite being complicit in the near killing of the credit system, the lender was allowed to walk and, in Hatch's system of moral justice, receive a pardon. Thus, while Hatch delivered homilies on the Senate floor about the collapse of consumer honesty, when the issue turned to the creditor and truth in lending, he and his colleagues did not express comparable concerns that laws enacted by Congress enabled predatory practices.

Coming to payday lenders' defense with equal fervor was Alabama senator Jefferson Sessions, then a senior member of the Judiciary Committee. On Tuesday, September 21, 1999, Sessions echoed Hatch in declaring bankruptcy "a moral question." Sessions insisted that Wellstone's amendment got it all wrong. Sessions declared his support for small-business owners and their employees, implying that they would benefit from the bankruptcy bill without the Wellstone Amendment, when the opposite was likely true: working families, in particular, were more likely to be harmed by the proposed bankruptcy bill. According to Sessions, excluding usurers from bankruptcy claims would allow the better-off to skip out on a debt they owed to other cash-strapped wage earners: "The man making $100,000, who owes $60,000 in debt—$2,000 of that may be to the mechanic who fixed his car—who ought to be paying that? Who ought to get the money? The man who did the work for him and fixed his car or fixed the roof on his house?" In this rhetorical sleight of hand, the morality was clear: "It is a simple question of justice and right and wrong." The evidence belies Sessions's rhetoric.[104] While his analogy could be used to expose the unfairness of the bankruptcy laws that applied to the unlucky working class as well as the profligate wealthy, Sessions made it seem as though mechanics or roofers would be first in line to receive bankruptcy payments, when in fact it would be corporate claimants and big banks taking the first bite of these assets. Sessions seemed to be speaking metaphorically, but his metaphor was entirely wrong, and these small-business owners and employees would be some of the last to be paid under the bankruptcy bill without the Wellstone Amendment.

As statistics during the 1990s bear out, the borrower Wellstone's amendment was intended to protect was far more likely to be a mechanic than a six-figure-salaried employee. A 1999 study by federal bankruptcy judges reported that the median income for Americans filing for bankruptcy was $22,000; as a point of comparison, that same year the poverty line was $17,000 for a family of four.[105] Given this, Wellstone's amendment, which stipulated that banks offer a low-cost alternative to customers, was far more likely to help a mechanic who had taken out a short-term loan from a payday store chain. Moreover, in the cosmology of culture and credit constructed by the Alabama senator, usury appeared to be a foreign concept, and usurious lenders, unlike borrowers, were not bound to any moral code. The concern that the new law, unless amended, would only bury borrowers deeper in debt was ignored by payday defenders in Congress.[106]

Senate Majority Leader Trent Lott also effectively protected the interests of payday lenders. The Mississippi senator throttled usury reform through the seemingly innocuous mechanism of parliamentary procedure. Lott filed cloture to guillotine debate when Senate Democrats brought amendments to lower interest rates. His tactics frustrated colleagues like Senator Wellstone, who complained on record that "when some of us say we want to bring . . . amendments to the floor that deal with exorbitant interest rates, we are told by the Senate Majority Leader that we are going to be shut out from being able to offer amendments, and therefore the majority leader files cloture" to end debate.[107] Nor did conservatives like Lott want to go public about defending usury—in the form of overriding the filibuster—at the expense of their state's working poor: "Apparently, a lot of my colleagues on the other side do not want to be on record . . . [with] an up-or-down vote on amendments that really do deal with these payday loans, with these exorbitant interest rates, making sure again that low-income people have access to banking services."[108] As a result, payday reform got nowhere. While Hatch, Sessions, and Lott expected individuals to behave morally and assume responsibility for their debts, creditors were not held to a similar moral standard.[109] Instead, officials looked the other way as these institutions continued to make rent-a-bank arrangements and individuals continued to rack up troubling debt.

Military, Congress, and Paydays

Despite its powerful defenders in Congress, the payday loan industry had a new vocal critic: by the early 2000s, payday lending abuses had become a growing problem for the military. One in five active-duty service members was a payday borrower. An enlistee was three times more likely than the average consumer to assume a payday loan.[110] Realizing this consumer base, short-term-loan stores sprouted near military bases across the country throughout the 1990s and early 2000s. A later study commissioned by the Defense Department produced maps showing that communities hosting military installations easily had the highest number of payday lenders, and lenders tended to concentrate in the counties and zip code areas in or adjacent to military bases. In Colorado, for example, military personnel made up 1.1 percent of the state's population but 4.6 percent of payday loan customers.[111]

This was no geographic coincidence—service members were ideal customers for payday lenders. Nearly three-quarters of active-duty military personnel never made more than $30,000 a year.[112] Young, strapped for cash, and inexperienced with money but guaranteed biweekly paychecks from the US government, military families proved a highly reliable source of steady revenue. Lenders also knew these borrowers could not afford to default on their loans. Failure to repay a debt was a violation of the Uniform Code of Military Justice, punishable by confinement, court martial, transfer to a different unit, discharge, or, most commonly, loss of security clearance.[113] By 2003, debt accounted for nearly two out of three losses of security clearance in the military.[114] For navy personnel the figure was even higher than that for the military as a whole; financial issues accounted for 80 percent of all security clearance personnel revocations and denials.[115] In 1999, "we had a little over 100 sailors lose their security clearance because of financial problems," recently retired petty officer Terry Scott told *ABC News*. "That number is almost 2,000 for fiscal year 2005. . . . All of this impacts our readiness, our mission capability." This indebtedness was a concern for all naval leadership.[116]

Despite the threat to military readiness posed by lenders, Congress dragged its feet in addressing the problem. Publicly, Congress expressed concerns about federal encroachment. Privately, however, most payday lender defenders in Congress "had strong ties with the industry back home" that likely made them reluctant to take on shadow bankers.[117] The Defense Department, the State Department, and several service associations, among them the Military Officers Association, the Air Force Sergeants Association, the National Association for the Uniformed Services, and the Enlisted Association of the National Guard, urged Congress to address the issue. These service associations sought to exempt soldiers from new bankruptcy reform legislation, known as the Sessions bill. But Jeff Sessions, a senior member of the Armed Services Committee, held fast to a zero-tolerance position. Soldiers were not spared his moral view of debtors. Their high rate of debt and bankruptcy was a failure of moral and personal responsibility. Sessions sought to persuade Senate skeptics by telling them, "It is not [lenders'] fault if someone does not pay it back. . . . It is the consumers'." Major figures in the party—Hatch, Shelby, and Bill Frist (R-TN)—lined up to support their colleague's bill, which had the backing of the payday, credit card, and banking lobbies, though Sessions explicitly distanced his bill from those in the industry lobbying on its behalf, claiming his was "not a bill written by credit card companies to meet their special interests."[118]

Undaunted by the spike in bankruptcies—sixteen thousand active-duty members, or 1.2 percent, filed for bankruptcy in 1999, which roughly mirrored the national average that year—the GOP leadership argued that the Servicemembers Civil Relief Act (SCRA) already existed to protect servicemen and -women and that Congress lacked jurisdiction at the time to reform the law covering the military.[119] The modern SCRA was passed in 1941, placing a moratorium on pre-service debt proceedings such as foreclosures, garnishments, and other credit collections for active-duty military personnel. The immediate aim was to protect on-duty service members against civil actions so those in uniform could clear their minds enough to defend the United States abroad and at home. But the current law was clearly inadequate, since it allowed American troops to fight for their country overseas while also fighting legal battles back home for lien enforcement on autos and other property taken by repossession, in which a creditor simply seizes collateral based on the terms of a contract rather than court order. Among SCRA's shortcomings was that it did not apply to debts incurred during military service nor was it automatic; service members still had to go to court and fight bankruptcy. Orrin Hatch urged, "If bad actors are preying on our military personnel through nefarious payday loans or other questionable practices, then I encourage Senators Shelby and Sarbanes, the head of our Banking Committee in the Senate, to look into the issue." However, Shelby had never demonstrated the political will to curb lending abuses. And as the ranking member for the minority party in the Banking Committee, Sarbanes had little chance of getting bills heard in committee. By ignoring the warnings and requests from the Defense Department, the State Department, and the full panoply of the uniformed service community, conservative Republicans placed lenders' interests over those of the military.

An amendment exempting service personnel from the 2005 bankruptcy bill failed. But payday lenders feared that future legislation might go further and cap interest rates for military families. In 2006, hoping to protect its highly lucrative military market, CompuCredit, a leading payday lender, turned to J. C. Watts, a former Oklahoma congressman. Having been the highest-ranking Black House Republican in the nation's history, Watts retired from Congress in 2002 and immediately set up a DC lobbying firm. The Watts Company was dedicated to issues he had championed during his eight years as a congressman. "I will have fewer restrictions, more leeway to operate," Watts told reporters when his firm opened its doors in January 2003.[120] With his newfound freedom, Watts worked to advance the cause of payday lending to service personnel, over the expressed concerns of the military about the harm such lending had on soldier readiness. CompuCredit paid the J. C. Watts Company $60,000 to lobby on the industry's behalf against curbing rates for military borrowers. Despite the best lobbying efforts of Watts, the Military Lending Act passed, capping rates lenders could charge military personnel at 36 percent, still above all state usury limits.

In the five years since the first federal payday oversight bill was introduced, industry receipts had more than doubled, totaling $40 billion plus another $6 billion in finance charge fees by 2005.[121] Through their deliberate, benign neglect of the industry's transgressions, Congress and the Bush-era executive branch effectively preempted state laws that looked to outlaw paydays. Consequently, in thirteen states that had actually outlawed the abusive lending practice in recent years, paydays were made possible only by the rent-a-bank arrangements. North Carolina was typical of these states. Despite its having banned the practice in 2001, the rent-a-bank mill persisted there. "All paydays have done is partnership with banks," said the frustrated state's attorney general. The volume of FDIC-bank loans in the Tar Heel State was thought to far exceed the $150 million figure cited by the FDIC.[122]

Democrats who proposed addressing these issues got nowhere, with Congress locked down by the GOP. New Mexico legislator Tom Udall introduced the Federal Payday Loan Consumer Protection Amendment in May 2006, which would have prohibited federally insured banks from partnering with payday lenders and affixed a "high-interest warning label" on any loan product charging a rate above 36 percent. Once more, however, conservatives led the charge in throttling the bill. It would be 2007 before banking regulators finally banned these chartered relationships without the help of Congress. But by then it was too late.

Money and Politics: Senator Bob Corker as a Case Study

By the late 2000s, Congress was increasingly on the defensive about whether its judgments about deregulation stemmed from the fact that they were often too neatly aligned with the financial interests of corporate campaign contributors. The payday industry had more than doubled its spending on lobbying and campaign contributions during the mid-2000s, according to a 2009 report by Citizens for Responsibility and Ethics in Washington, a nonpartisan watchdog group.[123] Its investment seemed to have paid off, as payday lenders continued to repel government oversight.[124] Within the financial services sector, only the banking industry had complained more vociferously and had perhaps been more effective in pushing back against federal regulation.

The uptick in spending helped foster several lawmakers' cozy relationships with the industry. Bob Corker (R-TN) was a leading, but by no means solitary, proponent of the payday industry and shared a hometown with Check Into Cash, headquarters of one of the nation's largest payday lender chains. Corker's policy positions closely followed those of the industry, which had regularly funded his political career since his first election as mayor of Chattanooga in 2001. Corker had become fast friends with local payday lender magnate W. Allan Jones, a relatively early entry into the business in 1993 when he founded Check Into Cash in nearby Cleveland, Tennessee. By the mid-2000s, Check Into Cash had grown into one of the largest payday lenders, with more than a thousand stores in the United States and Great Britain. Like Check Into Cash and other paydays, Corker had consistently opposed federal intervention in the payday lending industry until the 2007–08 global financial crisis. Thanks largely to Jones's financial backing, Corker raised more funds from the financial services industry than any other member of the Republican National Committee. The industry's close ties to Corker may have paid off in 2008, when paydays and others in the financial services sector needed someone in the Senate to make their case. Senator Corker argued that a government rescue was good for the general economy. "This is not a 'bail-out of Wall Street,'" he claimed, explaining the positive trickle-down effect that saving banks would have on retail creditors, "but an unprecedented effort to avert a catastrophe that would devastate Main Street."[125]

Two years later, in the spring of 2010, lenders flip-flopped on how intimately tied Wall Street was to Main Street consumer finance and so did Corker. When Federal Reserve chairman Ben Bernanke visited Capitol Hill, he was looking for greater oversight responsibilities of "Main Street, as well as Wall Street" so that financial regulators could have a more comprehensive understanding of what was happening in the entire banking system, but Corker again objected to expanding any oversight of payday practices. One reporter directly asked him if his efforts on behalf of paydays were linked to the substantial contributions the industry had made to his campaign over the years. Corker responded, "Categorically, absolutely not."[126] When pressing his case in 2008 for a federal backstop or bailout to protect the financial interests of payday lenders, Corker openly affirmed the connections between Wall Street and the payday lending industry. In 2010, however, he avoided acknowledging that any meaningful dealings between paydays and Wall Street existed.[127]

The Executive Branch: Financial Literacy, Payday Lenders, and Savings

Arguably, no regulator set the bar lower when it came to paydays than the Federal Trade Commission (FTC). The government agency had been set up in the later years of the Progressive Era by trustbusters within the Woodrow Wilson administration to safeguard consumers against unfair practices and deceptive financial products. This transparency was thought to be a key component of promoting a competitive business environment.[128] By the late 1970s, a growing chorus of FTC critics was claiming that the agency had become too powerful, dampening business growth and innovation.

Following a trend that began under Carter and accelerated under Reagan, the FTC leaned more heavily on libertarian-oriented economists, reduced its own budget, investigated fewer deceptive-practice cases, and moved toward encouraging voluntary or industry self-regulation while recommending that consumers become more knowledgeable about financial issues.[129] It more or less continued down this path after Reagan left office. From 2000 to 2008, the FTC made almost no mention of systemic abuse. While other regulators pushed for bans on the most excessive abuses of payday lending, the FTC instructed consumers to improve their financial literacy and saving habits. In a 2000 consumer alert, the FTC offered this self-help advice: "A savings plan—however modest—can help you avoid borrowing for emergencies. Saving the fee on a $300 payday loan for six months, for example, can help you create a buffer against financial emergencies."[130] Similarly, consumer groups and the Federal Reserve often cited a strong correlation between payday loans and declines in savings, producing a report showing that nonpayday borrowers were twice as likely to save than those assuming loans.[131] Yet even on these two very modest measures—improving financial literacy and encouraging savings—financial regulators seemed to be working at cross-purposes with America's first president with an MBA.

Financial literacy was a rare area of consensus in a Congress often riven by ideological strife and partisanship. Educating consumers about personal finances cost taxpayers relatively little, emphasized the value of individual accountability, and placed no additional burden on the business community. Thus, when Hawaiian Democratic senator Daniel Akaka introduced the Excellence in Economic Education Act in 2003, an amendment to No Child Left Behind, many conservative and moderate senators leapt to sign up as cosponsors. Seven Republicans originally cosponsored the Akaka bill, which looked to improve the quality of students' understanding of personal finances and economics in K–12 education. Despite the law's broad-based support, the program was placed on the chopping block by the George W. Bush administration, slated to be cut or eliminated completely in every budget the White House submitted to Congress beginning in 2005. While President Bush took to his bully pulpit to call for the reauthorization of No Child Left Behind, the White House decided to zero-out the budget of the Excellence in Economic Education Act altogether.[132] "The program needs a chance to work before it is arbitrarily terminated," Akaka told Bush.[133] Bush's budgetary priorities sent an unmistakable message on the eve of the Great Recession: the education of American consumers and their children about economic issues was not a government priority. In this way, the president did not merely oppose more robust financial regulation; his objections to funding financial literacy also countered fellow conservatives' efforts to inform the public about matters like payday lending, potentially consigning future generations to ignorance about the hidden costs of payday lending and other high-cost, fringe banking practices.

In the public school system, financial literacy had an undersized role in the curriculum. And what young people did know about finance strongly suggested that students were more familiar with managing investments than managing debt such as payday lending. According to a Harris poll, nearly every adult (97 percent) wanted economics or personal finance taught in high schools, yet only 50 percent of high school students surveyed reported having been taught either subject. The poll—commissioned and published in April 2005 by the National Council for Economic Education (NCEE), whose corporate underwriters included Allstate, Citigroup, and mega-publisher McGraw-Hill—confirmed that adults had a better understanding of the stock market than of interest rates (74 percent to 65 percent) despite their multiple daily interactions with credit transactions as compared with investment trading.[134] The future of financial literacy seemed at least as bleak. Students were largely unfamiliar with how interest rates worked. A majority of student respondents (61 percent) had no knowledge of how interest rates functioned, compared with those (38 percent) familiar with calculating interest rates. While students' grasp of the stock market and consumer borrowing at fixed rates had improved since 1999 when the last Harris poll was taken, students still knew nearly twice as much about the stock market (49 percent) as they did about consumer borrowing at fixed rates (27 percent).[135] The relative lack of knowledge regarding rates was especially unsettling given that a majority of eighteen-year-olds enrolling in college had at least one credit card and were likely to take out a student loan.[136] The National Council for Economic Education warned that the poll "indicates that teens do not have the basic knowledge they will need to make effective financial decisions." As the NCEE noted in its economic literacy campaign, "Each year the number of students who graduate from high school without a foundation of economic and financial literacy continues to grow."[137] Teachers were ill equipped to remedy the issue, according to surveys taken in 2007 and 2008. While 89 percent of teachers agreed or agreed strongly that high school students should be required to take a financial literacy course or pass a test on the subject to graduate, only 29.7 percent had actually taken a course themselves. Even fewer, 11.1 percent, had ever taken a workshop on teaching financial literacy.[138] Seemingly undisturbed by reports confirming the nation's persistent, if not growing, economic ineptitude, the Bush White House renewed its call for the Excellence in Economic Education Act's outright abolition in the 2007 budget.[139]

In a canny PR move, payday lenders filled the vacuum and created their own educational program. Down the street from the White House, the payday lenders' main trade group, the Consumer Financial Services Association, initiated a series of financial literacy workshops for Washington, DC, children on saving and spending. This was the financial equivalent of Joe Camel—the infamous cartoon camel for the tobacco industry—teaching America's kids about (not) smoking. Workshops designed to promote the value of savings and teach savings tips to inner-city children were sponsored and run by the very businesses benefiting from the high interest rates that put many of these kids' parents into debt. "Once it was brought to our attention, we immediately called the schools [to stop it]," said a spokesperson for DC school chancellor Michelle Rhee about the workshops at area high schools. "It was unacceptable."[140]

Not until the most serious financial collapse since the Great Depression was looming did Bush and Treasury Secretary Hank Paulson hastily launch a financial literacy council in the last year of the Bush administration. In prepared remarks delivered on January 22, 2008, President Bush told the media and America, "We want people to own assets; we want people to be able to manage their assets. We want people to understand basic financial concepts, and how credit cards work and how credit scores affect you, how you can benefit from a savings account or a bank account. That's what we want. And this group of citizens has taken the lead, and I really thank them—thank you a lot."[141] The council was too little and came too late from a lame-duck administration overseeing an economy more in triage than in prevention mode. The short-lived council produced only one "annual report" and was in operation for less than one year.[142] The White House's decision to name discount broker Charles Schwab as council chairman may have clouded the administration's message and further compromised its effectiveness.[143] The appointment of an industry insider as council chair—familiar to Americans for his company's "Talk to Chuck" promotional ads on television, on billboards, and in newspapers—instead of a financial literacy educator, consultant, or expert gave the council the feel of an infomercial, eager to sell a Wall Street–wary America on the patriotic virtues of investing.

The Last Place in America

Even in states where these rent-a-bank arrangements were not used, their mere specter moved state legislatures, with a critical assist almost always from conservatives, to accede to the industry. That was the story in Arkansas, the last place in America one might expect payday lender rates to be legal. Historically, no other state had taken a tougher stance against usurious practices than Arkansas, which in 1874 became the first and only state to constitutionally ban the practice, capping rates at 10 percent (before amending the cap, in 1982, to 5 percent above the federal discount rate).[144] But Arkansans' century-long opposition to usury proved no match for payday lenders and their conservative allies. During debates in 1999, state legislators were urged by the payday lending industry to legalize payday loans in order to keep out non-Arkansas banks, which could charge much higher rates. After the Arkansas legislature passed industry-friendly laws, some payday lenders still partnered with out-of-state banks to bypass newly raised limits set by the payday loan law.

Democrats played a role in facilitating the spread of paydays in Arkansas. Democrats, after all, controlled Arkansas's state legislature in 1999, when the law opening the doors to such lenders passed. The biggest Democratic recipients of lobbyist dollars—Pryor and Ross—were also among the party's most culturally conservative members.[145] (In the Congress, Senator Pryor and Representative Ross continued to be lead recipients of the payday lobby within the Arkansas congressional delegation.[146]) Although the role of Democrats in fueling payday lending is unquestionable, state Democrats Cliff Hoofman and Mike Beebe sought to repeal the state's 1999 Check Cashers Act in 2001, a law that effectively enabled payday lenders to violate state usury laws with impunity. On the opposite side of the aisle, the GOP provided no comparable voice on behalf of the consumer.

Governor and future presidential hopeful Mike Huckabee, the state's most powerful and charismatic Republican, was critical in facilitating the rise of the industry in the state. When Huckabee entered the governor's office in 1997, the number of payday lenders in Arkansas could be counted on two hands. By the time he left in 2007, there were 275 stores.[147] His office appointed (and reappointed) regulators to oversee the payday lending industry, but they were slow to regulate and had obvious conflicts of interest. Huckabee also promoted and signed the Check Cashers Act of 1999, state legislation that effectively eliminated the usury cap that had governed relations between consumers and creditors since the 1870s. Under Huckabee, 139 of the 275 payday operations were neither licensed nor regulated by the state's chief regulator, the Arkansas State Board of Collection Agencies (ASBCA).[148] Huckabee's approach to payday lenders was made evident by Gary Frala, the "public-at-large" representative for the ASBCA. Huckabee appointed Frala twice to the post—despite Frala's clear conflict of interest as treasurer and controller of a payday loan business, where he oversaw the operations of thirty-two state stores. He and another member of the ASBCA had personal financial connections to out-of-state paydays. Unsurprisingly, he repeatedly voted against regulating out-of-state lenders.[149]

Through 2000 and 2001, there were a series of challenges to the Arkansas Check Cashers Act. The Federal Reserve ruled that payday lenders in the state were charging their borrowers interest rates, not fees, as had been claimed by the industry and its defenders. On the heels of this ruling, state Democrat Cliff Hoofman introduced unsuccessful legislation to repeal payday lenders' exemption from usury. However, Huckabee continued to defend Arkansas's banking industry and on November 20, 2001, pressed for its expansion through the Gramm-Leach-Bliley Act, even if it meant sacrificing a bit of state sovereignty. He convinced Mike Ross, then the state's freshman Democratic House representative, that Washington should override the usury cap in Arkansas's constitution because it "has restricted economic growth and development, caused billions of dollars in investments to leave the state, and prohibited the extension of credit to many Arkansans. What was once a concern of discrimination is now a concern of credit availability. . . . We must take immediate action to include nonbank lending institutions to the override provisions contained in the [Gramm-Leach-Bliley] Act of 1999."[150] The act passed and empowered banks to rent their charters to payday lenders. "I was complicit," admitted Hoofman in his 2006 testimony before the Arkansas state legislature. In 1982, Hoofman had backed a state law that increased the usury cap to 17 percent but set no penalties on lenders for violating the ceiling. Now contrite, Hoofman acknowledged his role in opening the door to interest rates that were 400 percent or higher. Hoofman was explicitly trying to fix the problem he recognized he had helped create.[151] In contrast, Huckabee stayed silent despite his self-styling as a politician who spoke his mind.

In December 2005, as the debate raged over the "morality" of usury lending, Huckabee took a position that bore little resemblance to his national reputation as a "true maverick" who once said that "I've always believed leaders don't ask others to do what they're unwilling to do."[152] While Arkansans were driven deeper into consumer debt because of usurious rates, which had helped make Arkansas a leader in bankruptcy filings the year before, Huckabee declined to share his thoughts on payday lending abuses.[153] As a result of the vacuum created by Huckabee's silence, the payday lending issue was ceded to the state's ethically challenged Democratic attorney general, Mike Beebe. As a state senator from the late 1990s to 2002, Beebe had opposed the Check Cashers Act and later pushed for its repeal. As attorney general, however, Beebe (like his predecessor) would maintain a lax attitude toward usury enforcement, influenced by his political ambition for higher office and the requisite need to fill his campaign coffers with contributions from lending lobbyists. Actions like these prompted the publishers of the *Arkansas Leader* to ponder in an editorial, "Why aren't Gov. Huckabee and the gubernatorial candidates speaking out on this issue?"[154] With Huckabee's tenure coming to a close in 2006, more than three out of four Arkansas payday lenders escaped oversight.[155] These lenders continued to practice unchecked at an estimated cost of $68 million each year to Arkansans.[156] The industry continued to flourish until 2008, when threats by the state's attorney general against payday lenders for violating the state's constitutional ban on high interest rates and a sudden economic downturn forced several payday business closures in Arkansas.[157]

The Great Recession only heightened the indispensability of payday lending to middle-class America. Rather than receding, it actually became more widespread and more mainstream. Several big banks, including Wells Fargo, US Bank, Fifth-Third, and Regions, began or expanded their direct involvement in payday lending in the aftermath of the Great Recession, making short-term, high-interest, small dollar loans, often called "deposit advances," to their cash-strapped account-holders. According to the Consumer Financial Protection Bureau, banks charged a fee of $10 per $100 borrowed and repaid themselves, on average, twelve days after making the loan by automatically withdrawing the full amount plus fees directly from the borrower's account; this very short-term loan thus bore an astonishing 304 percent APR.[158] If repayment happened to result in an overdrawn bank account, the borrower was then charged an insufficient fund fee for subsequent transactions in addition to the fees that triggered the astronomical APRs.[159] For customers using this financial service, the median initial loan for a "deposit advance" was $180, yet the median average daily balance owed by a borrower was $343.[160] This median balance owed was almost double the median original advance amount and suggests that consumers were taking out multiple loans with these extraordinarily high APRs prior to repayment.[161] "Customers remained stuck in the loan cycle—meaning they owed money to the bank—for an average of 175 days per year," according to a 2014 Center for Responsible Lending report.[162] Though banks largely stopped making these payday loans euphemistically called "deposit advances" in 2014, they continued sharing their accountholders' data with payday lenders well into 2015.[163] Since customers in these usurious loan cycles took out multiple loans, these banks were actively victimizing their customers further by allowing payday lenders direct access to those already vulnerable to this type of debt.

As banks and credit card companies reduced or cut off credit altogether or charged high overdraft fees for bounced checks in the wake of the financial crisis, cash-strapped Americans turned to high-cost, short-term payday loan stores to pay for daily necessities. They used loans to buy groceries and, if they wished to maintain a good credit score, pay bills. As the stagnant economy affected more and more people, the number and kinds of borrowers grew. "Payday loans have increasingly become crutches for those higher up the economic scale," according to Elizabeth Warren's testimony to Congress in 2008.[164] Warren's brainchild, the Consumer Financial Protection Bureau, became the first federal agency to directly oversee the payday lending industry.

Recent reports suggest that paydays reduce households' disposable income, thereby reducing the money retained and circulated throughout the local economy. Omaha, Nebraska, provides a case in point. There, households with annual incomes of $40,000 to $100,000 showed *monthly deficits* after payday repayments were added to estimated essential monthly costs. Given the estimated amount Omahans borrow from payday lenders, they would pay $19 million in excess fees, with the payday industry reducing local economic output by $10 million each year while reducing local wage earnings by more than $3.2 million. (Paydays did, however, contribute to a slight gain in local employment.) These figures take into account any positive impact payday loans provide through local spending, employment, and reinvestment of business projects.[165] Payday loans produce a net drag on the local economy.

Conclusion

To be sure, a payday loan bubble won't bring down the economy. But it may well serve as a barometer of our general economic health. According to 2014 market projections, the payday lending industry will expand until at least 2019. "Household income and industry revenue are perfectly inversely correlated," IBISWorld, an international research firm specializing in long-range industry forecasts, explained in its annual report on the state of US payday loan services in February 2014.[166] "[The] industry benefits from falling income levels."[167] Since incomes are not predicted to increase in the near future, any decline in profitability would not be the result of rebounding wages, according to industry analysts.[168] Instead, the main threat to the industry is the possibility of greater regulatory strictures that might increase compliance costs, curtail access to would-be borrowers, and cap profits from fees, interest rates, and other transaction charges—though closer oversight is highly unlikely in the current Trump era.[169] For at least a decade, industry experts have documented how the rise of payday lending is inextricably linked to wage stagnation. As the free-market cure for stagnant and declining wages, payday lending has not simply exacerbated the plight of the working- and middle-class wage earners it targets. Lax regulatory policies and strategic alliances between paydays and banks have spread systemic risk throughout the financial economy.

The short but significant history of payday lending since the early 1990s offers a glimpse into high-risk lending and how a laissez-faire policy agenda contributed to the spread of arguably the most hazardous of all consumer loan products, with interest rates ten to twenty times higher than those charged by credit card companies and with a track record of two out of every three borrowers ending up in default. Not only did a deregulatory environment make high-cost, high-risk (predatory) consumer products possible, but by also refusing to regulate rent-a-bank arrangements between paydays and federally insured banks, policymakers made sure that the buck stopped with the American taxpayer. Payday lending sheds light on the world of shadow bankers and their ability to skirt regulations even when engaged in the most risky of financial transactions.

It's frequently argued that government and special interest groups from below pressured the private lending sector to lower lending standards. This argument has been especially commonplace in explaining the rise of subprime and subsequent mortgage market failure; consumer groups, civil rights organizations, and activists inside government have been blamed for spreading systemic risk by forcing lenders to make high-price, high-risk mortgage loans to unqualified borrowers for political rather than prudential reasons. But the story of a far more toxic financial product—the payday loan—shows that the financial services industry required little persuasion or encouragement from pressure groups, racial minorities, or federal regulators to make risky loans. In fact, when it came to payday lending, the vast majority of these stakeholders warned of the negative effect these unsafe and unsound consumer products would have on families, communities, and the financial system as a whole. Despite the risk it continued to pose, and despite mounting evidence of its deleterious impact on individuals' finances and the overall health of the nation's economy, payday lending continued to thrive because wage stagnation persists, as do lawmakers' protection and promotion of the industry.

Payday lending was supposed to be a credit salve for what ails workers and the middle class. Yet the runaway fees associated with payday lending have made the cure worse than the cause. Payday lending offers a window into how deregulation has contributed to exposing the nation's entire financial system to unsafe banking practices and systemic risk. The problem was not simply that deregulatory laws such as Gramm-Leach-Bliley invited strategic alliances with banks, which would exempt payday lenders from often tougher state anti-usury laws. By providing the implicit federal guarantee that went with the deals between payday lenders and federally insured banks, lawmakers and many federal regulators also ensured that the taxpayer would be the one held accountable for bank–payday lender agreements. The story of payday lending proliferation may be the best place to start for those wishing to understand how the profitability of fees served as a driver of reckless lending relations and spread throughout the economy, from Wall Street to Main Street.

Epilogue

IN A BOOK LIKE this, it is quite tempting to give a rundown of policy suggestions. And there certainly is no shortage of quality policy recommendations that I or others might offer. In housing, for example, one could propose reviewing key pieces of earlier mortgage deregulation legislation (e.g., DIDMCA, Garn-St Germain Act) to determine whether they have lived up to their purpose and goals. In higher education, federal expenditures could be geared toward eliminating tuition and fees at community colleges and four-year public universities for middle- and low-income households to make college more accessible.[1] In auto insurance, either the state or federal government could implement a merit-based system by abolishing the territorial ratings used in calculating premiums. In the payday loan industry, enforcing the guidelines of the Consumer Financial Protection Bureau would seem a reasonable first step.[2]

However, in the current hyper-deregulatory political climate, rather than making policy suggestions I might better spend my time writing utopian fiction. For both regulatory policy recommendations and utopian fiction amount to academic exercises at this historical juncture. My pessimism doesn't emanate from a specific concern over an issue, election, candidate, or officeholder. Any election can sweep a new party onto the Hill and a new agenda into the White House. Instead, it springs from recent history and a long-term calculus: any proposed policy or regulatory intervention that might improve consumer financial protections or ameliorate inequality seems unsustainable so long as the political party more likely to pursue these reform measures is not in leadership positions within government long enough for these policies to take root.

American capitalism's most celebrated period of success corresponded with the period, roughly from 1940 to the 1970s, when government was biggest and imposed the highest and most comprehensive regulatory standards on big business in our nation's history. A combination of these standards and strong unions contributed to high working-class wages. "The greatest generation was also the statist generation," wrote David Frum, a libertarian columnist and former George W. Bush speechwriter, acknowledging how midcentury liberalism's regulatory state and stimulus spending, despite any shortcomings, produced both a strong state and a strong middle class.[3] Since then, financial deregulation has coincided with a deteriorating economic situation for working- and middle-class Americans.

This is not a coincidence, according to scholars looking at the impact of deregulation on the incomes of Americans based on taxpayer filings. Deregulation and skill-biased technical change are the most influential determinants of today's income gap in the United States. David Jacobs and Jonathan Dirlam wrote in the *American Journal of Sociology* that, since the late 1970s, "national-level neoliberal political determinants best explain the extraordinary increase in U.S. income inequality."[4] An analysis across industries reveals that financial firms began to make money during a period of heightened deregulation and income inequality beginning largely under Reagan. His successors in both parties until 2009 or so would continue to support these policies. And yet while financial activity has certainly increased since the 1980s, scholars have noted that deregulation of both finance and labor has "led to the substantial acceleration in the growth of income inequality."[5] Although deregulatory policies received support from both parties, most of the electorate has been "substantially worse off" economically during Republican administrations than Democratic ones,[6] while the economy has performed better for most US households under Democratic administrations, writes Larry Bartels in *Unequal Democracy*.[7] Economic stratification, then, poses a dilemma for our political system.

But our political system, awash with outside money, has proved more responsive to the American donor class—and the lobbyists representing them—who want government to reduce regulatory protections, than to the needs of struggling citizens.[8] Money in politics has an outsized role in stymieing upward mobility, functioning as the common current running through housing, student loans, transportation, and payday lending. The donor class has a recurring role throughout this book— creating quid pro quos to codify mortgage instruments that became the basis for subprime lending; delaying the implementation of cheaper government-backed college loans, which proved costlier for students and taxpayers; neutralizing democratic measures passed to protect auto insurance consumers; and punishing lawmakers who advocated for consumer-friendly protections or who attempted to enforce existing usury laws already on the books. Moneyed interests have helped to erect laws to create, protect, or expand markets—all while increasing the costs of consumer financial products in housing, higher education, auto insurance, and short-term emergency lending.

Restrictions on lobbying and on donors, then, stand to produce useful reforms. Recent studies show that donors and nondonors of the same political affiliation possess quite divergent perspectives on policies, with the donor class generally tacking rightward on policies compared with the general population. When asked about five Obama-era policies (Affordable Care Act, Dodd-Frank, the Climate Action Plan, affordable child care, and the stimulus package), for example, Republican donors were 23 percentage points more conservative-leaning on these issues than nondonors of the same party. And independent donors were 33 percentage points more conservative on these issues than nondonors, according to researchers' analysis of Cooperative Congressional Election Studies of 2006, 2008, and 2010.[9] A split did appear among Democratic donors and nondonors, although it went in the other direction and was far less divergent: Democrats who gave $1,000 or more were 7 percentage points more liberal than Democratic nondonors.

Also, America's donor class is far wealthier, whiter, and more male than the general population.[10] Despite this divergence in policy preference and demography, regulations restricting money's influence in politics and other attendant reforms appear to be unrealistic so long as money makes a difference between winning and losing an election. The candidate who raises the most money wins more than 90 percent of the time.[11]

The evidence also shows that once elected, officeholders stay loyal to their financial backers, even at the expense of their own constituents. "Outside contributions decrease members' responsiveness to their districts" and *increase* the ideological extremism of the congressional member, according to research conducted by Anne E. Baker. In *Unequal Democracy*, Larry Bartels draws a similar conclusion: "Elected officials respond to the views of affluent constituents."[12] By comparison, the "preferences of the people in the bottom third of income distribution have no apparent impact on the behavior of their elected officials," he adds.[13]

While lobbyists and donors often work hand in hand, lobbying dollars mostly influence policy rather than elections.[14] Lobbyists spent more than $3 billion in 2016 seeking to influence Congress, the White House, and the other federal regulatory agencies, according to the Center for Responsive Politics.[15] Both total spending on lobbying and the number of registered lobbyists rose steadily between 2001 and 2009 during the George W. Bush years, while generally trending downward during the Obama years, from $3.51 billion (2009) to $3.12 billion (2016) and from 13,740 registered lobbyists (2009) to 11,143 (2016).[16]

The financial and political power of the donor class doesn't guarantee that it always wins in the policymaking process, though it does, by most accounts, shape the terms and direction of policy conversations. And that policy playing field is tilted in their favor. With significant money (i.e., donations of more than $1,000 per person) coming from just 1–3 percent of the population,[17] the best chance of regulatory reform lies with voters, especially the roughly 97–99 percent who don't give significant money to candidates. Exit polls on Election Day 2016 showed that 75 percent of voters wanted a candidate who could take back the country from the rich and powerful, while other polls since 2010 have consistently shown that most Americans want Wall Street regulations to remain as they are or become even stricter. Although Democrats are the party most identified with and much more likely to tackle regulatory policy while taking on the donor class, they lost gubernatorial mansions, Capitol Hill seats, and the White House in the 2016 election. Instead, the billionaire candidate who vowed to lower the regulatory bar won the election and filled his cabinet with an unprecedented number of wealthy individuals who had donated to him or his party.[18] Among these wealthy contributors-cum-cabinet-secretaries was Betsy DeVos. As she wrote in a 1997 *Roll Call* op-ed, when the billionaire heiress spent her "hard-earned American dollars" pushing a policy or candidate, she expected a quid pro quo from policymakers:

> My family is the largest contributor of soft money to the national Republican party. . . . I have decided, however, to stop taking offense at the suggestion that we are buying influence. Now I simply concede the point. They are right. We do expect some things in return. We expect to foster a conservative governing philosophy consisting of limited government and respect for traditional American virtues. We expect a return on our investment.[19]

Until the footprint of the donor class is significantly reduced, there is little hope of enacting lasting and meaningful regulatory reform in the face of expectations of a return on investment. Not only do donors influence elections, but their views also matter much more in policymaking even when they oppose what the majority of voters want, as Martin Gilens and Benjamin I. Page found in 2014.[20]

Public mobilization may well be the last best hope for our political system to push back against this imbalance of power between the superrich and the rest. Yet voting, too, seems fraught, because working- and middle-class White people appear to be unstable allies within the Democratic coalition. Too often, across income strata, White voters have backed candidates who embrace public policies that reduce mobility and increase inequity, further limiting the financial stability and futures of these voters. Real incomes—that is, incomes that take into consideration current purchasing power—typically rise twice as rapidly for middle-class voters under a Democratic president as they do under a Republican president.[21] For working-poor families, real incomes have increased six times as fast under Democratic presidents as they have under Republican presidents.[22] But these numbers have failed to translate into persistent Democratic electoral successes; the intensity of support by the working and middle classes hasn't matched how much they have benefited from Democratic policies. In fact, the share of Democratic voters has declined across all income classes since the 1960s. At the same time, the party has hemorrhaged voters in *and* outside of the South.[23] Why do Democrats get such a low electoral return on their policy investments that encourage economic prosperity in the White working and middle classes?

Critics suggest it is because of values and identity politics. Some, most notably Thomas Frank, argue that lapsed blue-collar Democrats have displaced their own economic interests to become values-voting Republicans (despite evidence indicating that working-class Americans are more likely to vote Democrat than Republican).[24] Others, notably Mark Lilla, point the finger not at ostensibly hoodwinked value voters but "narcissistic" liberal Democrats who expend "moral energy" on "African-American, Latino, LGBT, and women voters" at the expense of the White working class and those without college degrees, eight out of ten of whom voted for Trump.[25]

This backlash theory of resentment toward identity politics is a catchy sound-bite but tricky to prove. Blaming diversity advocates for "fixating on identity," as Lilla claims, seems misguided. After all, liberals, racial minorities, and many women vote with the party that has *both* found a way to historically do well by most US households and done the most good for vulnerable populations: boosting the household incomes of most White Americans while simultaneously supporting anti-homophobic, pro-immigrant, anti-racist, and anti-sexist laws. What Lilla seems to underestimate is the stickiness of the social identity and group attachment of the majority. If any demographic slice of America appears fixed on identity, it's that of the "shortsighted" independent voter. It's the demographic that feels collectively embattled by Democrats' embrace of diversity despite their own systemic racial advantages.[26]

A rich body of research continues to reveal the currency of group membership in policy and electoral politics. Earlier research, such as Michael Dawson's 1994 classic *Behind the Mule*, zeroed in on the racial group tethering of Black America. Dawson asks why the impressive growth of a Black middle class in postwar decades failed to produce greater voting diversity and a wider range of political beliefs within the Black electorate. His answer is simple: this racial electoral cohesion results from the forces of discrimination that bind African Americans together and helped cohere hundreds of distinct ethnic and tribal groups into a single subpopulation over the course of centuries. Their fates are linked regardless of where they find themselves on the income scale.[27] Indeed, studies show that the racial disparities between Black and White subprime mortgage borrowers actually grew *wider* the more Blacks earned; the more Black borrowers made, the more likely they were to be sold a subprime loan, compared with White borrowers with a similar income and credit score profile. Linked fate also trumps the skin colorism that has long been a potential wedge within Black America in what social scientists Jennifer Hochschild and Vesla Weaver dub the "skin color paradox." Dark-skinned Blacks are poorer, serve longer prison sentences, and are less likely to hold elective office than lighter-skinned Blacks. Yet despite both inter- and intra-racial discrimination, darker-skinned Blacks' voting behavior has, paradoxically, stayed remarkably similar to that of their lighter-skinned counterparts, Hochschild and Weaver write.[28] In effect, racism is class-blind and color-blind, and, as a consequence, so is Black cohesion at election time.

In recent years, researchers have extended and adapted this argument to identify Dawson's "linked-fate theory" operating within other racial and ethnic categories, most notably Whites and Asians (even as linked fate may be waning in political significance within Black America).[29] Findings in 2014 indicate that there is no statistical difference between African Americans and other racial groups in their views of linked fate: adherence to the theory among Blacks is neither particularly strong nor unique relative to the views of other racial groups. For example, 67 percent of Asians agree with the statement "What happens to Asians in this country will have something to do with what happens in your life." Similarly, 73 percent of Whites agree with the statement and 77 percent of Blacks do as well.[30] For Latinx, a nonracial category in the US census, though linked fate does exist,[31] it seems to be influenced more by class or national original group than by their pan-ethnic community.

While the relationship between linked-fate theory and political voting has not always been clear, nearly all voters cast their ballots on the basis of some social identity, not actual policy issues—whether they lean left or right, whether they are low-information voters or well-informed ones—as researchers of voter behavior Christopher Achen and Larry Bartels have recently identified.[32] "Group attachment" (e.g., parents' preferences, emotional connections by ethnicity, religion, social status, unionization, and race) based on *social identities* and party loyalties has been the driving force behind national electoral politics for more than a century. It can be suggested that, since the nineteenth century at least, linked-fate voters have tended to adjust their ideologies and perceptions to match their identity groups and partisan loyalties, not the other way around.[33]

This political moment, in which identity groups and political parties determine voters' ideologies and perceptions, might lead us to believe that voters can be swayed to vote against their interest if the political party aligns with their identity group. There are still large constituencies that vote for issues rather than on the basis of identity or political affiliation. Research into the growing population of independent and swing voters has largely assumed that they support policies against their material interest.[34]

This is not to suggest that independent or swing voters are linked-fate voters who cast ballots against their material interests, as Frank and others have implied. Rather, as Bartels shows, independents respond more favorably to short-term economic rewards (e.g., lower unemployment rates or tax cuts) in the months just before the election rather than to any economic gains realized during the full term of a governing administration. The presentist orientation of swing voters usually redounds to the benefit of Republicans, who are more likely than Democrats to produce greater income gains a few months in advance of an election. Democrats, in contrast, tend to produce income gains more often than Republicans and to prolong those gains, but earlier in the administration.[35]

Having such a reliably unreliable partner as today's independent or swing voter makes it difficult to create and sustain lasting economic and regulatory policies, as we saw in 2017 with the assault on the Affordable Care Act, the Dodd-Frank Act, and the Student Aid and Fiscal Responsibility Act. Each is in jeopardy of being rolled back or repealed entirely. Instead, having a reliable coalition partner would have resulted in keeping and possibly building on Obama's "New" New Deal, of which these acts would have been the cornerstones. Entrenching these policies, a "New" Fair Deal would have solidified and perhaps extended these policies if Obama had been followed by an Eisenhower-like moderate Republican who would have fundamentally left intact the decade-old legislation, even if trimming its assumed excesses to please the small-government rank and file.

It would be equally foolhardy and impractical for conservatives or liberals to assume, however, that demography itself will defeat deregulation (and the donor class that ceaselessly demands it). The fear of some and hope of others is that this nation is becoming less White and headed toward a "majority-minority" society—a demographic shift that promises to tug both the electorate and policymaking to the left. But as demographer Richard Alba and others have explained, the 2010 US Census system of "one-drop" categorization has likely overcounted the number of racial and ethnic minorities. The census counts an interracial person as a minority or non-White even if this person has only one minority ancestor. Possibly inflating numbers further, if there was "ambiguity about ethno-racial identity," the 2010 Census publicly counted the person as a minority.[36] If this one-drop rule applied in the opposite direction—one White ancestor made you officially White— then the percentage of Whites would be as high as 75 through approximately 2050, according to Alba.[37] Yet mixed-race people are counted as racial minorities even when they self-identify as White. Moreover, according to a 2015 Pew survey of 1,555 multiracial Americans eighteen and older, most multiracial adults with one White parent (e.g., one Asian parent and one White parent) feel more closely connected to Whites. Multiracial Black people are the exception to this connectedness rule, identifying more with other Blacks; however, there are fewer Black multiethnic or multiracial adults than Asian or Latinx ones.

This is all to say that we cannot dismiss linked-fate voters, but we also cannot assume that all those the census counts as a minority personally identify themselves solely in that way.

Multiracial Americans are more likely to have multiracial friends, more likely to marry a multiracial partner, and more likely to vote Democratic.[38] Multiracial Americans are also twice as young as Americans in the general public. Beyond this, one's self-expressed racial identity may change over time, or even from one situation to another.[39] In short, while the United States is growing more diverse, social identities around racial and ethnic identity and politics are highly fluid. Majority minorities, as defined by the 2010 Census and corrected in the analyses by Alba and others, should not be treated as Democratic locks. To paraphrase Alba: Just because this population is more likely to vote Democrat does not mean that it will. Democrats should treat members of this racially ambiguous and politically opaque multiracial population as the new independent or swing voters with an even more fluid, contingent social identity. Localities and states might prove the best starting grounds and laboratories for moving this new, amorphous swing population into a durable social movement, as Heather Gerken, an expert on democracy, has posited.[40]

Historical contingency tells us that our present and future politics is never "natural," "inexorable," or preordained—nor can it be understood in terms of any deterministic language used to describe or caricature the political and policy implications of having a majority-minority population. But the choices made by individuals, communities, and societies shape our present and future. These choices matter. Rather than simply assuming that a future of racial minorities making up the majority will automatically bring about effective regulatory policy, it is critical to build a pro-regulatory constituency that will buoy politicians and regulators who need public will to do their job.

As problematic, fluid, and uncertain as the future of majority-minority electoral politics appears to be, we *know* the dead-end history associated with so-called independent or swing voters and the candidates they support: they generally erode the financial regulatory framework while advocating for deregulatory policies—policies that have served to exacerbate economic inequalities in the past thirty years, as the financial services marketplace has become the lifeblood of the American economy.[41]

At almost no point in the lifetimes of the vast majority of Americans has the wealth gap between the rich and the rest been so wide by almost any measure. Estimates suggest that the share of total household wealth controlled by the top 1 percent of the nation's wealthiest families rose from 27 percent in 1992 to 41 percent in 2012.[42] The financial elite, especially the so-called working rich (e.g., hedge fund managers, Wall Street CEOs, and financial entrepreneurs), have been among the biggest beneficiaries of financial deregulation, even since the Great Recession of 2007–09. This group has been abetted not just by such deregulation, but also by a rollback in progressive taxation achieved through lower marginal rates and a spate of loopholes and deductions. These winners, ever in search of new markets, have forged new business models and approaches that have, whether by intent or impact, extracted wealth from working-poor and, increasingly, middle-income Americans.[43] Deregulating some businesses did yield cost-controlling benefits for consumers, if not necessarily workers, especially in the airline, trucking, and telecommunications industries.[44] Yet the net result of financial deregulation has been a rising tide that has sunk most American boats.

The fee economy has been central to this process. Amid America's gilded age of deregulation, fees took hold and have proved particularly destructive in areas vital to upward mobility in contemporary America. Spreading like kudzu in this deregulatory space, consumer financial fees have helped to choke off dreams of the middle class and middle-class aspirants alike.

Fees have become a key income and revenue generator over the past three decades as banks and other financial institutions have searched for new streams of revenue while keeping advertised prices low. From the early 1980s to 2004, fee income (also known as noninterest income) more than doubled as a share of retail banks' operating income, totaling almost half of all operating income generated by American banks by the mid-2000s.[45]

This has exacted a heavy price on consumers and citizens. As fee incomes helped profits soar to record highs, the typical American earner suffered a 72 percent drop in discretionary income from the early 1970s to the mid-2000s.[46] And it continues to be eaten away by a surfeit of fees and charges in areas central to upward mobility: housing, higher education, transportation, and employment. In the private realm, Wells Fargo made national headlines when bank customers signing up for free checking accounts that had been advertised as having "no strings attached" were being charged $5 to $14 per month when accounts were converted to fee-bearing ones.[47] Meanwhile at public universities, fees add as much as 20 percent to tuition. For lower- and moderate-income households, these fees further undermine upward mobility in the United States and widen the greatest wealth gap in American history. Yes, financial deregulation has been used by public-private partners to facilitate access to consumers, open up markets, and provide services and products to heretofore excluded or underserved communities: women, racial minorities, lower-income people, youth, immigrants. But this financial inclusion has come at ever-higher costs of entry—with more and more fees attached—affecting precisely those consumers who are least able to afford to pay them.

A report issued by the outgoing Obama administration's National Economic Council in late December 2016 sounded the alarm about "the growing trend and magnitude of fees in the U.S. economy." The report attributed the "systematic transfer of wealth" to fees and attendant costs in banking, education, transportation, and other industries.[48] Released on the eve of the next administration, the report was intended to be "a roadmap for policymakers, companies, advocates, and the research community to build on" in order to slow the generation-long "systematic transfer of wealth" that fees have facilitated.[49] But until the nation fixes its dead-end politics, fees will be our future—transferring wealth, choking off mobility, and raising barriers of entry to the American dream.

NOTES

———◆———

Introduction

1. Ray Boshara of the St. Louis Federal Reserve Bank, as quoted by Patricia Cohen, "Racial Wealth Gap Persists Despite Degree, Study Says," *New York Times*, August 16, 2015, http://www.nytimes.com/2015/08/17/business/racial-wealth-gap-persists-despite-degree-study-says.html?_r=0 (accessed August 16, 2016).

2. "Top Gripes: What Bugs America Most," *Consumer Reports Magazine*, January 2010, http://www.consumerreports.org/cro/magazine-archive/2010/january/shopping/what-bugs-america-most/overview/what-bugs-america-most-ov.htm (accessed August 16, 2016).

3. National Economic Council, "The Competition Initiative and Hidden Fees," December 2016, https://obamawhitehouse.archives.gov/sites/whitehouse.gov/files/documents/hiddenfeesreport_12282016.pdf

4. The figure cited in the text is based on the author's analysis of data from Equifax on housing, Brena Swanson, "Equifax: Subprime Mortgage Origination on the Rise," *Housing Wire*, February 1, 2016 https://www.housingwire.com/articles/36183-equifax-subprime-mortgage-origination-on-the-rise; Stephens, Inc.; John Hecht, "Alternative Financial Services: Innovating to Meet Customer Needs in an Evolving Regulatory Framework," Stephens, Inc., February 27, 2014, http://cfsaa.com/Portals/0/cfsa2014_conference/Presentations/CFSA2014_THURSDAY_GeneralSession_JohnHecht_Stephens.pdf; and Zack Friedman, "Student Loan Debt in 2017: A \$1.3 Trillion Crisis," *Forbes*, February 21, 2017, https://www.forbes.com/sites/zackfriedman/2017/02/21/

student-loan-debt-statistics-2017/. Note that this cumulative figure does not include an exact estimate for auto insurance, which obviously only increases the $1.46 trillion amount. For the 27 percent combined income, sales, and real estate taxes, see Sreekar Jasthi, "How Much Do Americans Really Pay in Taxes?," *NerdWallet*, April 8, 2015, https://www.nerdwallet.com/blog/taxes/how-much-do-americans-really-pay-taxes-2015/.

5. The 2015 median income is based on the author's analysis of https://fred.stlouisfed.org/series/MEPAINUSA672N. All of the analysis is based primarily on data collected between 2013 and 2016. The student loan yearly amount is based on the author's analysis of Friedman, "Student Loan Debt." The payday loan yearly amount is based on the author's analysis of http://files.consumerfinance.gov/f/201304_cfpb_payday-dap-whitepaper.pdf. The urban auto insurance annual premium is based on the author's cost comparison of Baltimore, Maryland, a fairly representative East Coast city with neither the highest nor lowest rate discrepancy, http://www.carinsurance.com/calculators/average-car-insurance-rates.aspx?zc=48154&submit=. Finally, the interest rate for a subprime mortgage is based on a 1.5 percent difference in prime and subprime rates, although this apparently varied a good bit, and variable rates were used. This was a conservative estimate. I estimated 3 percent as the median prime rate in 2015 (http://www.hsh.com/monthly-mortgage-rates.html). So our hypothetical person had a subprime mortgage of $162,500 with a 4.5 percent fixed interest rate.

6. Kelsey Oliver, "Check Cashing & Payday Loan Services in the US," IBISWorld Industry Report OD5408, December 2016, 6.

7. Robert Hiltonsmith, *The Retirement Savings Drain: The Hidden and Excessive Costs of 401(k)s* (New York: Demos, May 29, 2012), 2, http://www.demos.org/sites/default/files/publications/TheRetirementSavingsDrain-Demos_0.pdf (accessed August 16, 2016).

8. Mitchell Pacelle, "Putting Pinch on Credit Card Users," *Wall Street Journal*, July 12, 2004, as cited in statement of Senator Elizabeth Warren, *Regulatory Restructuring: Enhancing Consumer Financial Products Regulation: Hearing before the House Financial Services Committee*, 111th Cong., 1st sess., June 24, 2009, http://archives.financialservices.house.gov/media/file/hearings/111/warren_testimony.pdf (accessed August 16, 2016). Hereafter, Warren, *Regulatory Restructuring*.

9. Elizabeth Warren, "Making Credit Safer: The Case for Regulation," *Harvard Magazine*, May–June 2008, http://harvardmagazine.com/2008/05/making-credit-safer-html (accessed September 4, 2016).

10. Warren, *Regulatory Restructuring*.

11. Data from the Economic Policy Institute (EPI) in 2013 showed that from 1979 to 2007 the average worker put in 4.5 additional weeks per year. For EPI data, see Lawrence Mishel, "Vast Majority of Wage Earners Are Working Harder, and Not for Much More: Trends in US Work Hours

and Wages over 1979–2007," *EPI Issue Brief* 348 (January 30, 2013), http://www.epi.org/publication/ib348-trends-us-work-hours-wages-1979-2007/ (accessed August 16, 2016).

12. These extra work hours are the result of longer hours, second jobs, and working spouses, according to Juliet Schor, "The (Even More) Overworked American," in *Take Back Your Time: Fighting Overwork and Time Poverty in America*, ed. John de Graaf (Oakland, CA: Berrett-Koehler, 2003), 8; see also EPI data from 2013 in Mishel, "Vast Majority of Wage Earners."

13. Brian McKenzie and Melanie Rapino, *Commuting in the United States: 2009* (Washington, DC: US Census Bureau, September 2011), https://www.census.gov/prod/2011pubs/acs-15.pdf (accessed August 16, 2016).

14. See chap. 5, "Americans' Time at Paid Work, Housework, Child Care, 1965–2011," in Kim Parker and Wendy Wang, *Modern Parenthood: Roles of Moms and Dads Converge as They Balance Work and Family* (Washington, DC: Pew Research Center, March 14, 2013), http://www.pewsocialtrends.org/2013/03/14/modern-parenthood-roles-of-moms-and-dads-converge-as-they-balance-work-and-family/ (accessed April 17, 2016); for recent trends in play-date schooling, see Emma Jacobs, "The Serious Side of Child's Play," *Financial Times*, August 8, 2013, https://next.ft.com/content/ee988208-ff4b-11e2-aa15-00144feabdc0 (accessed April 17, 2016).

15. Alan Brinkley, *Franklin Delano Roosevelt* (Oxford: Oxford University Press, 2009), 61.

16. Barbara Alexander, "The Impact of the National Industrial Recovery Act on Cartel Formation and Maintenance Costs," *Review of Economics and Statistics* 76, no. 2 (May 1994): 254, 246; Robert Burns, "The First Phase of the National Industrial Recovery Act, 1933," *Political Science Quarterly* 49, no. 2 (Summer 1934): 161–94; James P. Johnson, "Drafting the NRA Code of Fair Competition for the Bituminous Coal Industry," *Journal of American History* 53, no. 3 (December 1966): 521–41; John Kennedy Ohl, *Hugh S. Johnson and the New Deal* (Dekalb, IL: Northern Illinois University Press, 1985), 114–15. Also see William Leuchtenburg, "Franklin D. Roosevelt: Domestic Affairs," University of Virginia, Miller Center https://millercenter.org/president/fdroosevelt/domestic-affairs (accessed October 29).

17. Brinkley, *New American History* (Philadelphia, PA: Temple University Press, 1997), 147–48.

18. Otis L. Graham, Jr., "The Broker State," *Wilson Quarterly* 8 (Winter 1984): 86–97.

19. Devin Fergus and Tim Boyd, "Banking Without Borders," *Kalfou* 1, no. 2 (Fall 2014): 9.

20. Jordan Weismann, "How Wall Street Devoured Corporate America," Atlantic.com, March 5, 2013, http://www.theatlantic.com/business/

archive/2013/03/how-wall-street-devoured-corporate-america/273732/ (accessed August 16, 2016).

21. Robin Greenwood and David Scharfstein, "The Growth of Finance," *Journal of Economic Perspectives* 27, no. 2 (Spring 2013): 4–5, http://www.people.hbs .edu/dscharfstein/Growth_of_Finance_JEP.pdf (accessed August 16, 2016).

22. Rick Brooks and Ruth Simon, "Subprime Debacle Traps Even Very Creditworthy," *Wall Street Journal*, December 3, 2007, http://www.wsj.com/ articles/SB119662974358911035 (accessed September 2, 2016).

23. David Gaffen, "We Are All Subprime Borrowers Now," *Wall Street Journal*, November 30, 2007, http://blogs.wsj.com/marketbeat/2007/11/ 30/we-are-all-subprime-borrowers-now/ (accessed September 2, 2016).

24. Greenwood and Scharfstein, "Growth of Finance," 5.

25. Bob Driehaus, "Some States Set Caps to Control Payday Loans," *New York Times*, September 8, 2008.

26. Greenwood and Scharfstein, "Growth of Finance."

27. Philip Leake, "Financials Is Fastest-Growing Area of Global Economy in December," *IHS Markit*, January 13, 2016, http://www.markit.com/ Commentary/Get/13012016-Economics-Financials-is-fastest-growing-area- of-global-economy-in-December (accessed August 16, 2016).

28. An acute example is Ferguson, Missouri, a suburb of St. Louis. In recent years, the city manager pressured courts and the police department to increase the cost and collection of fines and fees in order to close the municipal budget gap created by declining sales and property tax receipts following the Great Recession. US Department of Justice, Civil Rights Division, *Investigation of the Ferguson Police Department*, March 4, 2015, https://www.justice.gov/sites/default/files/opa/press-releases/attachments/ 2015/03/04/ferguson_police_department_report.pdf (accessed August 16, 2016).

29. Organization for Economic Co-operation and Development, "National Accounts at a Glance," http://stats.oecd.org/Index.aspx? DataSetCode=NAAG# (accessed August 16, 2016); see also Matt Bruenig, "Nontax Revenue Accounts for 92% of Growth in 'Taxpayer Money' since 1970," Mattbruenig.com, August 20, 2015, http://mattbruenig.com/ category/taxes/ (accessed August 16, 2016).

30. Saskia Scholtes and Francesco Guerrera, "Banks Make $38 Billion, *Financial Times*, August 9, 2009.

31. Thomas Hylands, "Student Loan Trends in the Third Federal Reserve District," *Cascade Focus* (Philadelphia: Federal Reserve Bank of Philadelphia, April 6, 2014), file:///Users/fergus24/Downloads/cascade- focus_3%20(1).pdf (accessed August 17, 2016).

32. For how much a BA degree holder will earn out of college in 2014, see "Executive Summary: Final Starting Salaries for Class of 2015—New College Graduates Data Reported by College Universities," in National Association of Colleges and Employers, *2016 Spring Salary Survey*

(Bethlehem, PA: National Association of Colleges and Employers, 2016), http://www.naceweb.org/uploadedfiles/content/static-assets/downloads/executive-summary/2016-spring-salary-survey-executive-summary.pdf (accessed August 17, 2016).

33. For TILA and credit cards, see Sean H. Vanatta, "Citibank, Credit Cards, and the Local Politics of National Consumer Finance, 1968–1991," *Business History Review* 90, no. 1 (Spring 2016): 57–80.

34. Andrea Ryan, Gunnar Trumbull, and Peter Trufano, "A Brief Postwar History of US Consumer Finance," Working Paper 11-058 (Cambridge, MA: Harvard Business School, December 2010), 26–27; see also Vanatta, "Citibank, Credit Cards."

35. Michael J. Migan, "Checking Out Bank Policies," *Orange Coast Magazine*, November 1985, 174.

36. Ibid.

37. Perdue's attorneys also argued that banks, by waiving fees of their favored customers, shifted the costs from one customer to another. For more on the case, see Perdue v. Crocker National Bank, 702 P.2d 503 (Cal. 1985), http://scocal.stanford.edu/opinion/perdue-v-crocker-national-bank-30701 (accessed August 16, 2016).

38. Dan Corian, "Court Bounces Rubber Check Charges," *California Courier*, July 21, 1985.

39. Raymond Bonner, "US Rule on Bank Fees Draws Fire," *New York Times*, December 19, 1983.

40. Valerie Block, "Supreme Court Upholds Nationwide Card Charges, Says States Can't Regulate Outside Issuers' Fees," *American Banker* 161, no. 106 (June 4, 1996): 1.

41. Ibid.

42. Smiley v. Citibank (S.D.), N. A. (95-860), 517 U.S. 735 (1996).

43. Ibid.

44. Sheyna Steiner, "Why We Pay Fees: The History of Fees," Bankrate.com, June 11, 2007, http://www.bankrate.com/brm/news/pf/20070611_fees_history_a1.asp (accessed April 17, 2016).

45. Karen Krebsbach, "Don't Stick a Fork in It Yet: OCC Debate Isn't Done," *US Banker* 114, no. 9 (September 2004): 50–51.

46. Scholtes and Guerrera, "Banks Make $38 Billion"; A. S. Pratt & Sons, *Clarks' Bank Deposits and Payment Monthly* 7, no. 19 (Washington, DC: A. S. Pratt & Sons, 2010); Corian, "Court Bounces Rubber Check Charges."

47. For borrowers who don't know a mortgage lender from a credit union, see the speech by Rajeev Date delivered at the National Constitution Center, Philadelphia, and reprinted by the Consumer Financial Protection Bureau, "Lessons Learned from the Financial Crisis: The Need for the CFPB," September 15, 2011, http://www.consumerfinance.gov/newsroom/lessons-learned-from-the-financial-crisis-the-need-for-the-cfpb/ (accessed

August 16, 2016). For borrowers' unpreparedness, see results from the survey conducted by Zillow's Mortgage Marketplace unit cited in Mary Umberger, "Survey Reveals Consumer Confusion on Mortgages," *Chicago Tribune*, May 13, 2011, http://articles.chicagotribune.com/2011-05-13/classified/sc-cons-0512-umberger-zillow-20110513_1_mortgages-home-loans-rate (accessed August 16, 2016). For accountholders' confusion over checking overdraft policies, see Pew Charitable Trusts, *Overdrawn: Persistent Confusion and Concern about Bank Overdraft Practices* (Washington, DC: Pew Charitable Trusts, 2014), http://www.pewtrusts.org/en/research-and-analysis/reports/2014/06/26/overdrawn-consumer-experiences-with-overdraft (accessed August 16, 2015). For borrowers' cavalier approach to mortgage shopping, see Patrick Barnard, "CFPB: Nearly Half of Borrowers Do Not Shop for a Mortgage," *Mortgage Orb*, January 13, 2015, http://mortgageorb.com/cfpb-nearly-half-of-borrowers-do-not-shop-for-a-mortgage (accessed August 16, 2016).

48. Aimee Picchi, "Rocket Mortgage Offers Speedier Mortgage Loans," *Consumer Reports*, March 25, 2016, http://www.consumerreports.org/money/rocket-mortgage-offers-speedier-mortgage-loans/ (accessed August 17, 2016).

49. Financial services was the fastest-growing sector in the economy. Since 1980, it has accounted for more than a quarter of the growth of the services sector as a whole and increased its share of the overall GDP from 4.9 percent to 8.3 percent between 1980 and 2006. Greenwood and Scharfstein, "Growth of Finance," 4–5. Before 1980, financial and nonfinancial profits grew at roughly the same rate. From 1980 until 2006, nonfinancial profits grew seven times, while financial profits grew sixteen times. Michael Konczal, "Frenzied Financialization," *Washington Monthly*, November–December 2014, http://www.washingtonmonthly.com/magazine/novemberdecember_2014/features/frenzied_financialization052714.php?page=all (accessed August 16, 2016).

50. Richard Bitner, *Confessions of a Subprime Lender: An Insider's Tale of Greed, Fraud, and Ignorance* (New York: Wiley, 2008), 24.

51. Brooks and Simon, "Subprime Debacle"; see also Financial Crisis Inquiry Commission, *Financial Crisis Inquiry Commission Report: Final Report of the National Commission on the Causes of the Financial and Economic Crisis of the United States* (Washington, DC: US Government Printing Office, January 25, 2011), 10.

52. Financial Crisis Inquiry Commission, *Financial Crisis Inquiry Commission Report*, 483.

53. "Federal Reserve Report Shows Home Equity Dipping Below 50 Percent, Lowest on Record," Associated Press, March 6, 2008.

54. Financial Crisis Inquiry Commission, *Financial Crisis Inquiry Commission Report*, 11.

55. Ibid.

56. Keith Ernst, Debbie Bocian, and Wei Li, *Steered Wrong: Brokers, Borrowers, and Subprime Loans* (Washington, DC: Center for Responsible Lending, April 8, 2008), http://www.responsiblelending.org/research-publication/steered-wrong-brokers-borrowers-and-subprime-l-oans (accessed August 16, 2016).

57. According to an analysis of Home Mortgage Disclosure data by the Housing Assistance Council, a borrower assuming a very modest subprime mortgage of $54,000 paid $125 per month more than he or she would have for an average prime loan.

58. David G. Wood, *Consumer Protection: Federal and State Agencies Face Challenges in Combating Predatory Lending* (Washington, DC: US General Accounting Office, January 30, 2014), http://www.gao.gov/assets/160/157512.html (accessed August 16, 2016).

59. Josh Nassar, *Overview of Mortgage Market: How We Got Here and Policy Responses* (Washington, DC: Center for Responsible Lending, July 23, 2008), http://www.responsiblelending.org (accessed August 16, 2016).

60. Ibid.

61. Center for Responsible Lending, *Soaring Spillover: Accelerating Foreclosures to Cost Neighbors $502 Billion in 2009 Alone; 69.5 Million Homes Lose $7,200 on Average* (Washington, DC: Center for Responsible Lending, May 7, 2009).

62. Kai-Yan Lee, "Foreclosures' Price-Depressing Spillover Effects on Local Properties: A Literature Review," *Federal Reserve Bank of Boston Public and Community Affairs Discussion Papers*, no. 1 (September 2008).

63. Ibid.

64. Center for Responsible Lending, *Soaring Spillover.*

65. Ibid.

66. Southern Rural Development Initiative cited by Associated Press, "Minorities, Poor Pay More for Home Borrowing," *Spartanburg Herald Journal*, February 23, 2000.

67. Karen Dynan, Kathleen Johnson, and Karen Pence, "Recent Changes to a Measure of U.S. Household Debt Service," *Federal Reserve Bulletin* 89, no. 10 (October 2003): 417–26.

68. National Association of Realtors, "First-time Buyers Fall Again in NAR Annual Buyer and Seller Survey," November 5, 2015, http://www.realtor.org/news-releases/2015/11/first-time-buyers-fall-again-in-nar-annual-buyer-and-seller-survey (accessed April 5, 2016).

69. Kelley Holland, "The High Economic and Social Costs of Student Loan Debt," *CNBC*, June 15, 2015, http://www.cnbc.com/2015/06/15/the-high-economic-and-social-costs-of-student-loan-debt.html (accessed August 16, 2016).

70. Stephan D. Whitaker, "Are Millennials with Student Loans Upwardly Mobile?" *Federal Reserve Bank of Cleveland Economic Commentary*, no. 12 (October 1, 2015), https://www.clevelandfed.org/newsroom-and-events/publications/economic-commentary/2015-economic-commentaries/

ec-201512-are-millennials-with-student-debt-upwardly-mobile.aspx (accessed August 16, 2016).

71. William Elliott and Melinda Lewis, *Student Loans Are Widening the Wealth Gap: Time to Focus on Equity* (Lawrence, KS: Assets and Education Initiative, November 7, 2013), https://aedi.ku.edu/sites/aedi.ku.edu/files/docs/publication/CD/reports/R1.pdf (accessed August 16, 2016).

72. Alvaro A. Mezza, Daniel R. Ringo, Shane M. Sherlund, and Kamila Sommer, "On the Effect of Student Loans on Access to Homeownership," *Board of Governors of the Federal Reserve Finance and Economics Discussion Series*, no. 10 (2016), https://www.fedinprint.org/items/fedgfe/2016-10.html (accessed April 29, 2016).

73. See especially fig. 3.6 of Ariane Hegewisch, Jeff Hayes, Jessica Milli, Elyse Shaw, and Heidi Hartmann, *Looking Back, Looking Ahead: Chartbook on Women's Progress* (Washington, DC: AARP Public Policy Institute, November 2015), http://www.aarp.org/content/dam/aarp/ppi/2015/Chartbook-On-Women's-Progress.pdf (accessed April 29, 2016).

74. Analysis and projection of 2010 Federal Reserve Survey of Consumer Finance done by Hiltonsmith, *At What Cost?* For the final budget of approximately $4 trillion submitted to Congress, see Angela Greiling Keane and Erik Wasson, "Obama Reaches for Relevance with $4.1 Trillion 2017 Budget," *Bloomberg News*, February 9, 2016, http://www.bloomberg.com/politics/articles/2016-02-09/obama-reaches-for-relevance-with-4-trillion-u-s-budget-plan (accessed August 17, 2016).

75. Elliott, Grinstein-Weiss, and Nam found that median assets in 2009 for a college-educated household without outstanding student debt are higher than those for a college-educated household with outstanding student debt (see their fig. 5); William Elliott III, Michal Grinstein-Weiss, and Illsung Nam, *Is Student Debt Compromising Homeownership as a Wealth-building Tool?*, Washington University Center for Social Development Working Paper No. 13-33 (2013), http://csd.wustl.edu/Publications/Documents/WP13-33.pdf. On the basis of its analysis of the 2007–09 Federal Reserve Survey of Consumer Finance, the Center for Assets, Education, and Inclusion at the University of Kansas indicates that living in a household with a four-year college graduate, outstanding student debt, and median assets in 2007 ($451,520) is associated with a loss of assets of about 36 percent compared to living in a household with a four-year college graduate, no outstanding debt, and similar assets. This translates into $163,637 (36 percent) less in assets in 2009 for borrowing households than households without student loan debt. William Elliott III and Melinda Lewis, *Student Loans Are Widening the Wealth Gap: Time to Focus on Equity*, University of Kansas, School of Social Welfare, Assets and Education Initiative (2013), https://aedi.ku.edu/sites/aedi.ku.edu/les/docs/publication/CD/reports/R1.pdf.

76. Holland, "High Economic and Social Costs."

77. Brent W. Ambrose, Larry Cordell, and Shuwei Ma, "The Impact of Student Loan Debt on Small Business Formation," *Federal Reserve Bank of Philadelphia Working Papers* 15, no. 26 (July 15, 2015), https://www .philadelphiafed.org/research-and-data/publications/working-papers/ 2015/wp15-26.pdf+&cd=1&hl=en&ct=clnk&gl=us (accessed September 2, 2016).

78. Ibid.

79. For the text of the Senate confirmation of Arne Duncan (2009), see US Senate, *Hearing of the Committee on Health, Education, Labor, and Pensions on Confirmation of Arne Duncan, of Illinois, to Be Secretary, U.S. Department of Education*, 111th Cong., 1st sess., January 13, 2009, https:// www.gpo.gov/fdsys/pkg/CHRG-111shrg46551/html/CHRG-111shrg46551.htm (accessed August 16, 2016).

80. The rising costs of college can be attributed to several factors, including the expansion of nonacademic personnel and support service staff, especially at higher administrative levels, increased capital expenditures, and declining government allocations.

81. Irving R. Levine, "Headline: Graduates' Debt," *NBC News*, December 29, 1986.

82. Meta Brown, Andrew Haughwout, Donghoon Lee, Joelle Scally, and Wilbert van der Klaauw, "Student Loan Landscape," *Liberty Street Economics*, February 18, 2015, http://libertystreeteconomics.newyorkfed .org/2015/02/the_student_loan-landscape.html (accessed April 5, 2016).

83. Raj Chetty, Nathaniel Hendren, Patrick Kline, and Emmanuel Saez, "Where Is the Land of Opportunity? The Geography of Intergenerational Mobility in the U.S.," *Quarterly Journal of Economics* 129, no. 4 (November 2014): 1553–1623.

84. Michael Mumper, "The Future of College Access: The Declining Role of Public Higher Education in Promoting Equal Opportunity," *Annals: American Academy of Political and Social Science* 585, no. 1 (2003): 97–117; Frank H. T. Rhodes, "After 40 Years of Growth and Change, Higher Education Faces New Challenges," *Chronicle of Higher Education*, November 24, 2006; Beckie Supiano, "Student Aid Is Up, but the Rise in College Costs Outpaces Family Growth," *Chronicle of Higher Education*, November 7, 2008.

85. Nelson D. Schwartz, "Interest Rates Have Nowhere to Go but Up," *New York Times*, April 11, 2010.

86. Erik Rauch, *Productivity and the Workweek* (Cambridge, MA: MIT Press, 2000); G. E. Miller "The U.S. Is the Most Overworked Developed Nation in the World—When Do We Draw the Line?," *20 Something Finance*, October 20, 2010.

87. David C. Johnston, "First Look at US Pay Data, It's Awful," Reuters, October 11, 2011.

88. James Heintz and Radhika Balakrishnan, "Debt, Power, and Crisis: Social Stratification and the Inequitable Governance of Financial Markets," *American Quarterly* 64, no. 3 (2012): 395. Also see Bureau of Labor Statistics (accessed September 4, 2016).

89. Demos analysis of National Center for Education Statistics, based on data from US Department of Commerce, Bureau of the Census, Current Population Survey, March Supplement, 1972–2003, as cited in *Paycheck Paralysis: Jobs and Income in Today's Labor Market*, Young Adult Economic Series (New York: Demos, Winter 2007), 2.

90. Rauch, *Productivity and the Workweek*; Miller, "U.S. Is the Most Overworked."

91. Rauch, *Productivity and the Workweek*; Miller "U.S. Is the Most Overworked."

92. Board of Governors of the Federal System, Division of Consumer and Community Affairs, *Report on the Economic Well-Being of U.S. Households in 2013* (Washington, DC: Board of Governors of the Federal Reserve System, July 2014), http://www.federalreserve.gov/econresdata/2013-report-economic-well-being-us-households-201407.pdf (accessed April 21, 2016); Neal Gabler, "The Secret Shame of Middle-Class Americans," *Atlantic*, May 2016, http://www.theatlantic.com/magazine/archive/2016/05/my-secret-shame/476415/ (accessed April 21, 2016).

93. Aaron Huckstep, "Payday Lending: Do Outrageous Prices Necessarily Mean Outrageous Profits?," *Fordham Journal of Corporate and Financial Law* 12, no. 1 (2007): 203–32; Uriah King and Leslie Parrish, *Payday Loans, Inc.: Short on Credit, Long on Debt* (Washington DC: Center for Responsible Lending, March 31, 2011); Nick Bourke, Alex Horowitz, and Tara Roche, *Payday Lending in America: Who Borrows, Where They Borrow, and Why* (Washington DC: Pew Charitable Trusts, 2012), http://www.pewtrusts.org/~/media/legacy/uploadedfiles/pcs_assets/2012/pewpaydaylendingreportpdf.pdf (accessed September 2, 2016).

94. Bourke, Horowitz, and Roche, *Payday Lending in America.*

95. The rise of online payday lenders has led to a trend of loosening these borrowing requirements in recent years.

96. PayDay Loan Advocate, "Working Americans Have Bigger Problems than Payday Loans," Personalmoneystore.com, October 28, 2010, https://personalmoneystore.com/moneyblog/working-payday-loans/ (accessed October 25, 2017).

97. Bourke, Horowitz, and Roche, *Payday Lending in America.*

98. Kathleen Burke, Jonathan Lanning, Jesse Leary, and Jialan Wang, *CFPB Data Point: Payday Lending* (Washington, DC: Consumer Financial Protection Bureau, March 2014), http://files.consumerfinance.gov/f/201403_cfpb_report_payday-lending.pdf (accessed August 2016).

99. Pew Charitable Trusts, *Pew Payday Lending Facts and the Consumer Financial Protection Bureau's Impact* (Washington, DC: Pew Charitable

Trusts, January 14, 2016), http://www.pewtrusts.org/~/media/assets/2016/
06/payday_loan_facts_and_the_cfpbs_impact.pdf (accessed September 2,
2016).

100. These two figures—seven times and 31 percent—are the difference
between what payday borrowers pay and what the research shows that
these borrowers can actually afford.

101. Susanna Montezemolo, *The State of Lending in America and Its Impact
on U.S. Households* (Washington, DC: Center for Responsible Lending,
September 2013).

102. Consumer Financial Protection Bureau, *Payday Lending and Deposit
Advances: A White Paper of Initial Data Findings* (Washington, DC:
Consumer Financial Protection Bureau, April 24, 2013), 44.

103. Paige Marta Skiba and Jeremy Tobacman, "Do Payday Loans Cause
Bankruptcy?," Vanderbilt Law and Economics Research Paper No. 11-13
(November 9, 2009), http://dx.doi.org/10.2139/ssrn.1266215 (accessed
September 2, 2016).

104. Brian T. Melzer, "The Real Costs of Credit Access: Evidence from the
Payday Lending Market," *Quarterly Journal of Economics* 126, no. 1
(2011): 517–55, http://qje.oxfordjournals.org/content/126/1/517.full.pdf+html
(accessed September 2, 2016).

105. Bourke, Horowitz, and Roche, *Payday Lending in America.*

106. This includes 87.9 percent of households whose members drove to work;
see Nancy McGuckin and Nanda Srinivasan, "Journey to Work Trends
in the United States and Its Major Metropolitan Areas," US Department
of Transportation, Office of Planning, Environment, and Realty, June 30,
2003, last modified April 4, 2008, https://ntl.bts.gov/DOCS/473.html
(accessed September 2, 2016).

107. Within the United States, forty-seven of fifty states have compulsory
vehicle insurance laws. De facto insurance liability coverage in the form
of proof of indemnification—via the uninsured paying an additional
motor vehicle fee (Virginia) or posting a special cash bond (Mississippi
and New Hampshire)—must be demonstrated by motorists in the three
states where it is legally permissible to drive without buying any auto
insurance.

108. David J. Cummins and Sharon Tennyson, "Controlling Automobile
Insurance Costs," *Journal of Economic Perspectives* 6, no. 2 (1992): 95–115.

109. John G. Lynch, Jr., "Introduction to the *Journal of Marketing Research*
Special Interdisciplinary Issue on Consumer Financial Decision Making,"
Journal of Marketing Research 48 (Special Issue 2011): Si–Sv.

110. Ibid.

111. Gregory D. Squires and Charis E. Kubrin, "Privileged Places: Race,
Uneven Development, and the Geography of Opportunity," *Urban
Studies* 42, no. 1 (January 2005): 47–68; Lawrence Vale, *From the Puritans
to the Projects* (Cambridge, MA: Harvard University Press, 2007); Xavier

de Sousa Briggs, ed., *The Geography of Opportunity: Race and Housing Choice in Metropolitan America* (Washington, DC: Brookings Institution, 2005); Brooks Jackson, "House Ethics Panel Clears St. Germain of Abusing Office Through Investments," *Wall Street Journal*, April 16, 1987; Steven Raphael and Lorien Rice, "Car Ownership, Employment, and Earnings," *Journal of Urban Economics* 52, no. 1 (July 2002): 118.

112. Raphael and Rice, "Car Ownership," 109, 130.

113. Ibid., 112.

114. William Julius Wilson, *When Work Disappears: The World of the New Urban Poor* (New York: Knopf, 1996), 40–41.

115. Mona Lewandoski, "The Bush Tax Cuts of 2001 and 2003: A Brief Legislative History," Briefing Paper no. 37 (Harvard Law School: Federal Budget Policy Seminar, May 6, 2008), 8, http://www.law.harvard.edu/faculty/hjackson/2001-2003TaxCuts_37.pdf (accessed September 2, 2016).

116. Nor is the $247 premium gap that far off from the Obama income tax cut in 2009, when 90 percent of working families and individuals received the "Making Work Pay" tax credit of $400, which was withheld from paychecks and spread over the entire year. Angie Drobnic Holan and Louis Jacobson, "Barack Obama Says He Cut Taxes for 'Middle-Class Families, Small Businesses,'" Politifact.com, September 9, 2012, http://www.politifact.com/truth-o-meter/statements/2012/sep/07/barack-obama/barack-obama-said-hes-cut-taxes-middle-class-famil/ (accessed September 2, 2016); see also Steve Wamhoff, "President Obama Cuts Taxes for 98% of Working Families in 2009," *Citizens for Tax Justice*, April 13, 2010, http://ctj.org/pdf/truthaboutobamataxcuts.pdf.

117. For a broader and clearer understanding of how the culture of pricing operates, see Frederick F. Wherry, *The Culture of Markets* (New York: Polity, 2012).

118. Wilson, *When Work Disappears*, 202.

119. Ibid., 39.

Chapter 1

1. Nancy L. Boss, "Lawsuits, Foreclosures Rise as 'Balloon' Notes Burst in California," *Washington Post*, October 31, 1982.

2. Ibid.

3. St Germain did not use a conventional period after the "St" in his surname because, according to him, he fell somewhat short of a saint. See Brooks Jackson and Tim Carrington, "Making a Fortune," *Wall Street Journal*, September 11, 1985, http://proxy.lib.ohio-state.edu/login?url=http://search.proquest.com/docview/135059491?accountid=9783; see also "Fernand St Germain, 1928–2014," *Providence (RI) Journal*, August 24, 2014, http://www.providencejournal.com/article/20140824/NEWS/308249952 (accessed July 13, 2016).

4. Office of the White House Press Secretary, "Remarks of the President at the Signing Ceremony for the Depository Institutions Deregulation and Monetary Control Act of 1980," March 31, 1980, Staff Offices, Speech Writers—Chronological File, Box 66, File "31 March 1980—Signing—Financial Reform Act [Depository Institutions Deregulation and Monetary Control Act of 1980 (H.R. 4086)] BR."

5. This act was added to the deregulation of the airline industry and, soon thereafter, of the rail, trucking, and communications industries.

6. Office of the White House Press Secretary, "Remarks of the President."

7. This effort culminated in the passage of the Gramm-Leach-Bliley Act in 1999. Yet by the end of the 1990s, most assumed financial deregulation was a fait accompli. Virtually no lawmaker contested deregulation.

8. US House of Representatives, *Home Mortgage Disclosure Act: Newly Collected Data and What It Means, Hearing Before the Subcomm. on Financial Institutions and Consumer Credit of the Comm. on Financial Services*, 109th Cong., 2d sess., June 13, 2006, H.R. Rep. No. 109-99, 149.

9. Statement of Sen. Dole, *Congressional Record* (1980), at 7,073.

10. FedPrimeRate.com, "History of Mortgage Rates," http://www .fedprimerate.com/mortgage_rates.htm.

11. Robert Carswell, "The Crisis in Thrift Institutions and Housing Finance," *University of Pennsylvania Journal of International Law* 4, no. 3 (1982): 281, http://scholarship.law.upenn.edu/jil/vol4/iss3/4.

12. For a history of income inequality and the role government policies have played in exacerbating wage stagnation, see James Kenneth Galbraith, *Created Unequal* (New York: Free Press, 1998).

13. Sheldon Garon, "Excerpt: From *Beyond Our Means*," February 2, 2012, www.berfrois.com (accessed July 31, 2016).

14. "U.S. to Sell 'Patriot Bonds' in Mid-December," *Wall Street Journal*, November 21, 2001.

15. Sheldon Garon, *Beyond Our Means: Why America Spends While the World Saves* (Princeton, NJ: Princeton University Press, 2011), 332; "U.S. to Sell 'Patriot Bonds'."

16. Garon, *Beyond Our Means*, 332.

17. Ibid.

18. Ibid., 337.

19. Hobart Rowen, "The Crusade of the Gray Panthers," *Washington Post*, September 13, 1979.

20. Statement of Sen. Morgan, *Congressional Record* (1980), 7,069.

21. For individual votes on this bill, see https://www.govtrack.us/congress/ votes/96-1979/h413. In addition to Regulation Q, Glass-Steagall established the Federal Deposit Insurance Corporation (FDIC) and prohibited bank holding companies from owning other financial companies (like investment banks). *Congressional Record* (1980), 7,070.

22. Cathy Lesser Mansfield, "The Road to Subprime 'HEL'* Was Paved with Good Congressional Intentions: Usury Deregulation and the Subprime Home Equity Market," *South Carolina Law Review* (Spring 2000): 511.
23. Ibid.
24. Other plaintiffs were Herbert and Annabelle Smith and John Coplin. See Laubach v. Fidelity Consumer Discount Co. (ca. 1986), http://www.leagle.com/decision/19881190686FSupp504_11096/LAUBACH%20v.%20FIDELITY%20CONSUMER%20DISCOUNT%20CO.
25. Mansfield, "Road to Subprime," 511.
26. Joseph Crespino, *In Search of Another Country* (Princeton, NJ: Princeton University Press, 2007), 1.
27. "Financial Institutions Bill Signed," *Washington Post*, October 16, 1982.
28. Rick Brooks and Ruth Simon, "Subprime Debacle Traps Even Very Credit-Worthy," *Wall Street Journal*, December 3, 2007, http://www.wsj.com/articles/SB119662974358911035 (accessed September 2, 2016).
29. Ibid.
30. Mansfield, "Road to Subprime."
31. Patricia McCoy, as paraphrased in *Fortune*, January 31, 2008.
32. Mark Zandi, *Financial Shock* (Upper Saddle River, NJ: Financial Times Press, 2008), 18.
33. Thus, in North Carolina, where aggressive anti-predatory laws were passed in 1999, "many brokers and lenders have continued to place prepayment penalties on NC home loans of $150,000 or less, even though state law clearly prohibit[s] it. They add these penalties to loans covered by AMTPA (loans that have balloon payments or adjustable interest rates (ARMs) and are therefore covered under the Alternative Mortgage Transaction Parity Act). These brokers and lenders claim that AMTPA, a federal law, preempts state law, an issue of continuing legal dispute. The prepayment penalty prohibition included in this new law applies only to brokered loans, and should not be subject to preemption since regulating brokers is a state function." See NC Mortgage Broker Licensing Law, "Frequently Asked Questions," http://www.responsiblelending.org/policy/state/north-carolina/NCbrokerfaq.html.
34. Standard & Poor's, "NIMS Analysis: Valuing Prepayment Penalty Fee Income," January 3, 2001; see also Standard & Poor's, "Legal Criteria Reaffirmed for the Securitization of Prepayment Penalties," May 29, 2002; and Standard & Poor's, "Prepayment Penalties Prove Their Merit for Subprime and 'A' Market Lenders," January 3, 2001.
35. Probably the most crucial lobbying efforts came from William O'Connell of the US League of Savings Association. O'Connell had several meetings with legislators and the treasury secretary, along with two meetings with President Reagan. Specifically, O'Connell singled out Treasury Secretary Donald Regan, Representatives Fernand St Germain and Frank Annunzio, and Senators Jake Garn and Donald Riegle (D-Michigan).

The total cost of the league's lobbying, estimated to be from $250,000 to $300,000, did not include the heavy staff time or campaign contributions of the league's political action committee (PAC), according to O'Connell. Nevertheless, the time and money were well spent, O'Connell added. "The bill . . . provide[s] that the industry doesn't get into this situation again." Janet Key, "Lobbying Pays Off in New S&L Aid Bill," *Chicago Tribune*, October 5, 1982.

36. Ibid.
37. Kathleen Day, "A Lobby's Decline and Fall: Bailout Erodes S&L Industry's Clout," *Washington Post*, July 28, 1989.
38. Ibid.
39. Howard Kurtz, "Draft Report Clears St Germain on Influence-Abuse Allegations," *Washington Post*, April 12, 1987.
40. Jackson and Carrington, "Making a Fortune"; Kurtz, "Draft Report Clears."
41. Jack Anderson and Michael Binstein, "Have PACs Turned Congress into Oligarchy?," *Desert News*, January 13, 1992; Jack Anderson and Michael Binstein, "PACs Call for Serious Reform Steps," *The Hour* (Norwalk, CT), January 13, 1992.
42. Jackson and Carrington, "Making a Fortune"; to adjust for inflation calculation in 2016, see the Bureau of Labor Statistics' Data Inflation Calculator, https://www.bls.gov/data/inflation_calculator.htm.
43. Citizens Against PACs, "What Is Rep St Germain Going to Do with $492,000 of Leftover Campaign Money?," protest ad, Box 27, Howard Gotlieb Archival Research Center, Boston University.
44. "St Germain's Fund Raising," n.d., Box 54, Howard Gotlieb Archival Research Center, Boston University.
45. Jack Maskell, "Expulsion, Censure, Reprimand, and Fine: Legislative Discipline in the House of Representatives," Congressional Research Service, May 2, 2013, 20–23, https://www.fas.org/sgp/crs/misc/RL31382.pdf (accessed April 23, 2016).
46. Jackson and Carrington, "Making a Fortune."
47. Kurtz, "Draft Report Clears."
48. Kevin Fox Gotham, "Creating Liquidity Out of Spatial Fixity: The Secondary Circuit of Capital and the Restructuring of the US Housing Finance System," in *Subprime Cities: The Political Economy of Mortgage Markets*, ed. Manuel B. Aalbers (New York: Wiley, 2012), 25–52.
49. Felicia Paik, "The Rich and Famous Use Trusts to Hide Ownership of Property," *Wall Street Journal*, November 27, 1998.
50. Jackson and Carrington, "Making a Fortune."
51. "Rice to FSG," August 24, 1986, Box 27, St Germain Papers, Howard Gotlieb Archival Research Center, Boston University.
52. US House of Representatives, Committee on Standards of Official Conduct, "Investigation of Financial Transactions Participated in and Gifts of Transportation Accepted by Representative Fernand St Germain,"

April 9, 1987, http://ethics.house.gov/sites/ethics.house.gov/files/documents/Hrpt100-46.pdf.

53. "The St Germain Embarrassment," *Washington Post*, August 9, 1987.

54. Jackson and Carrington, "Making a Fortune."

55. Stephen Chapman, "Congressional Ethics Shouldn't Remain Joke," *Chicago Tribune*, July 16, 1987.

56. "House Democrats Ensnared in Ethics Probe: St Germain Absolved," *CQ Almanac Online*, https://library.cqpress.com/cqalmanac/document.php?id=cqal87-1143728.

57. "House Democrats Ensnared in Ethics Probe."

58. Jack Maskell, "Expulsion, Censure, Reprimand, and Fine: Legislative Discipline in the House of Representatives," Congressional Research Service, May 2, 2013, 20–23, https://www.fas.org/sgp/crs/misc/RL31382.pdf (accessed April 23, 2016).

59. "Investigations That Might Have Been," *Wall Street Journal*, September 30, 1988.

60. George Lardner, Jr., "Charges of Favoritism, Tests of Credibility at House Ethics Panel," *Washington Post*, December 15, 1987.

61. "Panel Reviews New Evidence of Misconduct by Lawmaker," *New York Times*, November 1, 1988.

62. Sara Fritz, "Ex-Lawmaker Gets $248,000," *Los Angeles Times*, January 18, 1989.

63. Kathleen Day, "St Germain's Back on the Hill—As S&L Industry Lobbyist," *Washington Post*, June 15, 1989.

64. Jack Anderson and Dale Van Atta, "House Member Solicitous for S&L," *Washington Post*, October 21, 1985.

65. Kathleen Day, "A Lobby's Decline and Fall: Bailout Erodes S&L Industry's Clout," *Washington Post*, July 28, 1989; for the contribution amount, see "Review and Outlook: Paying for Ethics," *Wall Street Journal*, November 17, 1989.

66. Lawrence C. Soley, *Leasing the Ivory Tower: The Corporate Takeover of Academia* (Boston, MA: South End Press, 1995), 94–95.

67. McCoy, as paraphrased in *Fortune*.

68. Kirk White, "Marginal Tax Rates and the Tax Reform Act of 1986: The Long-Run Effect on the U.S. Wealth Distribution," US Census Bureau, January 29, 2004.

69. Denise Lamaute, "Gimme Shelter: Real Estate after Tax Reform," *Black Enterprise*, July 1, 1988, 33. For the tax breaks awarded to those buying a second home, see Gerald James Gallagher, "Investing in That Home Away from Home," *Black Enterprise*, September 1, 1989, 31.

70. Kent W. Colton and Kate Collignon, "Multifamily Rental Housing in the 21st Century," January 29, 2001, 13, http://www.jchs.harvard.edu/sites/jchs.harvard.edu/files/colton_w01-1.pdf; Richard K. Green, "Thoughts on Rental Housing and Rental Housing Assistance," *Cityscape:*

A Journal of Policy Development and Research 13, no. 2 (2011): 6–7, https://
www.huduser.gov/portal/icals/cityscpe/vol13num2/Cityscape_July2011_
thoughts_rentalhsg.pdf.

71. Andre F. Shashaty, "Realty Funds," *Financial World*, October 18, 1988, 48.

72. Securitization began in the 1930s, when the Depression-era government
created a secondary market to combat a shortage of residential loan funds.
In the 1980s, when agencies began rating privately issued mortgage-
backed securities, the first private-sector securitization arose. See
Benjamin Howell, "Exploiting Race and Place: Concentrated Subprime
Lending as Housing Discrimination," *California Law Review* 94, no. 1
(January 2006): 116–17; Elizabeth Laderman, "Subprime Mortgage
Lending and the Capital Markets," Federal Reserve Bank of San Francisco
Economics Letter, December 28, 2001.

73. Garon, *Beyond Our Means*, 349.

74. Ibid., chap. 11.

75. Advertisement, *New York Magazine*, December 22–29, 1986, 111.

76. Garon, *Beyond Our Means*, 351.

77. Souphala Chomsisengphet and Anthony Pennington-Cross, "The
Evolution of the Subprime Mortgage Market," *Federal Reserve Bank of St.
Louis Review* 88, no. 11 (January–February 2006): 37, https://files.stlouisfed
.org/files/htdocs/publications/review/06/01/ChomPennCross.pdf.

78. Zandi, *Financial Shock*, 10.

79. Ibid.

80. Chomsisengphet and Pennington-Cross, "Evolution of the Subprime
Mortgage Market," 38.

81. Robert Shiller, "Address a Growing Wealth Gap. What Now? Advice for
Obama on Economic Policy," *International Herald Tribune*, November
10, 2008.

Chapter 2

1. Institute for College Access and Success and Project on Student
Debt, *Student Debt and the Class of 2011* (Washington, DC: Project
on Student Debt, n.d.), http://projectonstudentdebt.org/files/pub/
classof2011.pdf.

2. This is up from one-third in 2007. Jesse Bricker, Arthur B. Kennickell,
Kevin B. Moore, and John Sabelhaus, "Changes in the U.S. Family
Finances from 2007 to 2010," *Federal Reserve Bulletin* 98, no. 2 (June
2012): 65, www.norc.org/PDFs/scf12.pdf.

3. Donghoon Lee, *Household Debt and Credit: Student Loan Debt*
(New York: Federal Reserve Bank of New York, 2013), 5,
www.newyorkfed.org/newsevents/mediaadvisory/2013/Lee022813.pdf.

4. William R. Emmons, "Don't Expect Consumer Spending to Be the
Engine of Economic Growth It Once Was," *Regional Economist*, January
2012, 2, http://www.stlouisfed.org/publications/re/articles/?id=2201.

5. While significant, the student loan sector is still roughly only one-tenth of the subprime housing market; see Cristian Deritis, "Student Lending's Failing Grade," *Moody's Analytics* (July 2011).

6. Consumer Financial Protection Bureau, *Student Loan Affordability: Analysis of Public Input on Impact and Solutions* (Washington, DC: Consumer Financial Protection Bureau, May 8, 2013), 10, http://files .consumerfinance.gov/f/201305_cfpb_rfi-report_student-loans.pdf. See also Walter Molony, "June Existing Home Sales Slip" (Washington, DC: National Association of Realtors, July 22, 2013), http://www.realtor.org/ news-releases/2013/07/june-existing-home-sales-slip-but-prices-continue-to-roll-at-double-digit-rates; Sam Lane, "First-Time Homebuyers Fighting for a Spot in an All-Cash World," *PBS NewsHour*, September 19, 2013, http://www.pbs.org/newshour/businessdesk/2013/09/first-time-homebuyers-fighting.html.

7. Loan debt may also have a disparate racial effect, helping to explain the declining percentages of Blacks entering medical school over the past decade or so, according to a report by Columbia University's Mailman School of Public Health, see Dugger, R. A., El-Sayed, A. M., Dogra, A., Messina, C., Bronson, R., and Galea, S. "The Color of Debt: Racial Disparities in Anticipated Medical Student Debt in the United States." *Public Library of Science (PLoS) ONE* 8(9) (2013): e74693. https://doi .org/10.1371/journal.pone.0074693. See Jamal Watson, "Hefty Debt Dissuades Blacks from Attending Med School," *Diverse Issues in Higher Education*, November 4, 2013, http://diverseeducation.com/article/57246/#.

8. http://files.consumerfinance.gov/f/201305_cfpb_rfi-report_student-loans .pdf. According to the American Medical Association (AMA), high debt burdens may play a significant role in the choice of practice area for medical students (e.g., geriatrics, family medicine, or more lucrative specialties) and where (e.g., rural, inner city, or urban) they pursue it. For more, see the AMA comments in Consumer Financial Protection Bureau, *Student Loan Affordability*.

9. Cathy Henderson, "College Debts of Recent Graduates," American Council on Education (Division of Policy Analysis and Research, Washington DC, December 1987), v.

10. Jacqueline E. King, "Student Borrowing: Is There a Crisis?," in *Student Loan Debt: Problems and Prospects*, ed. Institute for Higher Education Policy (Washington, DC: Institute for Higher Education Policy, 1997), 3.

11. Henderson, "College Debts of Recent Graduates," v.

12. John Hood, "How to Hold Down College Costs," *Consumers Research Magazine*, October 1993.

13. Scott Hollenbeck and Maureen Keenan Kahr, "Ninety Years of Individual Income and Tax Statistics, 1916-2005," *Statistics of Income Bulletin* (Winter 2008), https://www.irs.gov/pub/irs-soi/16-05intax.pdf.

14. University of Virginia, Miller Center of Public Affairs, "John F. Kennedy: Domestic Affairs," http://millercenter.org/president/biography/kennedy-domestic-affairs (accessed June 18, 2016).

15. Melvin Urofsky, *American Presidents: Critical Essays* (New York: Routledge, 2000), 554.

16. Barry J. McMillion, "Length of Time from Nomination to Confirmation for 'Uncontroversial' U.S. Circuit and District Court Nominees: Detailed Analysis," Congressional Research Service Report for Congress, September 18, 2012, http://www.fas.org/sgp/crs/misc/R42732.pdf; Sheldon Goldman, Elliot Slotnick, and Sara Schiavoni, "Obama's Judiciary at Midterm," *Judicature* 94, no. 6 (May–June 2011): 299–300.

17. Douglas Hibbs, *The American Political Economy: Macroeconomics and Electoral Politics* (Cambridge, MA: Harvard University Press, 1987), 312.

18. "A Chat with Dave Stockman," *Columbia Daily Spectator* 105, no. 146 (October 12, 1981): 1, http://spectatorarchive.library.columbia.edu/cgi-bin/columbia?a=d&d=cs19811012-01.2.5&srpos=&e=-------en-20--1--txt-txIN.

19. Ibid.

20. Terrel H. Bell, *The Thirteenth Man: A Reagan Cabinet Memoir* (New York: Free Press, 1988), 36.

21. Katherine A. Ozer, "Congress and the Politics of Financial Aid: A Student View," *Academe* 72, no. 6 (November–December 1986): 25–27.

22. Ibid.

23. Office of Management and Budget (OMB), "Director's Review," Box/file 20, Craig L. Fuller Files, Ronald Reagan Presidential Library, Simi Valley, CA.

24. "Mary Haldane, MASFAA President, to MASFAA Executive Council, January 6, 1982," Midwestern Association of Student Financial Aid Administrators Archive (henceforth MASFAA Archive), Bowling Green, Ohio.

25. Ibid.

26. OMB, "Director's Review," Fall 1984, Box/file 20, Craig L. Fuller Files, Ronald Reagan Presidential Library, Simi Valley, CA.

27. OMB, "Director's Review," Issue 6, Fall 1984, LVE, Box CFOA 178, Craig Fuller Files, Ronald Reagan Presidential Library, Simi Valley, CA.

28. C. A. Beier and Marcia D. Greenberger, "Federal Funding of Discrimination: The Impact of Grove City College v. Bell," Barnard Center for Research on Women Archives, Item 2443, http://www.bcrwarchives.org/collection/items/show/2443 (accessed December 12, 2013).

29. OMB, "Director's Review," Fall 1984.

30. "John Roberts to the Attorney General, December 8, 1981," RG60 DOJ, Box 26, Folder: Bob Jones-General, Series: Correspondence Files of Ken Starr, 1981–1983, Ronald Reagan Presidential Library, Simi Valley, CA; "Roberts to Tex Lezar, February 16, 1982," RG60 DOJ, Box 30,

Folder John Roberts Miscellaneous, National Archives and Records Administration, College Park, MD; "Clarence Thomas to Undersecretary of Education, April 14, 1982," RG441, General Records Office of the Secretary of Education, General Correspondence, Administration Files, 1979–1980, Folder CR01-02, Title IX-Sex 1982, National Archives and Records Administration; "John Roberts to Attorney General, July 1, 1982," RG60 DOJ, Box 30, Roberts Folders Miscellaneous, National Archives and Records Administration.

31. US Department of Labor, "Title IX, Education Amendments of 1972," https://www.dol.gov/oasam/regs/statutes/titleix.htm (accessed January 20, 2017).

32. "Kenneth Cribb to Craig Fuller, January 18, 1982," Edwin Meese, III, Files, 1981–1985, Ronald Reagan Presidential Library, Simi Valley, CA.

33. "John Roberts to the Attorney General, December 8, 1981," RG60 DOJ, Folder: Bob Jones-General, Series: Correspondence Files of Ken Starr, 1981–1983, Box 26, Ronald Reagan Presidential Library; "Roberts to Tex Lezar, February 16, 1982," RG60 DOJ, Box 30, Folder John Roberts Miscellaneous, National Archives and Records Administration, College Park, MD; "Clarence Thomas to Undersecretary of Education, April 14, 1982," RG441, General Records Office of the Secretary of Education, General Correspondence, Administration Files, 1979–1980, Folder CR01-02, Title IX-Sex 1982, National Archives and Records Administration; "John Roberts to Attorney General, July 1, 1982," RG60 DOJ, Box 30, Roberts Folders Miscellaneous, National Archives and Records Administration.

34. The Court decided that Title IX applied only to those programs receiving direct financial aid. Because Grove City was receiving assistance only in the financial aid program, that program alone had to be in compliance. The ruling in the Grove City case was a significant victory for those opposed to Title IX.

35. Michael D. Parsons, *Power and Politics: Federal Higher Education Policymaking in the 1990s* (Albany, NY: SUNY Press, 1997), 63.

36. Kenneth C. Green, "College Costs and Student Aid," *Viewpoints*, September 15, 1987, http://heri.ucla.edu/archives/b041.html.

37. Spencer Rich, "Reports Show Big Increase in Federal Student Loans, Drop in Grant Aid," *Washington Post*, December 29, 1986, http://digitalcollections.library.cmu.edu/awweb/awarchive?type=file&item=674081. See also Janet S. Hansen, *Student Loans: Are They Overburdening a Generation?* (New York: College Entrance Examination Board, 1987).

38. John B. Lee, *The Distribution of Student Financial Aid: Trends among the Postsecondary Sectors* (Washington, DC: American Council on Education, 1985), 9, table 1.

39. "Gene Sofer to Susan McGuire and Jack Jennings," January 14, 1985, Augustus Hawkins Papers, UCLA Collections, University of California-Los Angeles.

40. Timothy D. Naegele, "The Guaranteed Student Loan Program: Do Lenders' Risks Exceed Their Rewards?," *Hastings Law Journal* 34, no. 3 (January 1983): 599–633.

41. See Green, "College Costs and Student Aid."

42. Higher Education Research Institute, Inc., *Student Aid Down Dramatically since 1980: 1986 Freshman Survey Results* (Washington, DC: American Council on Education, 1986).

43. Johannah Cornblatt, "In Face of Reagan Cuts Low-Income Admissions Drop," *Harvard Crimson*, June 4, 2007, http://www.thecrimson.com/article/2007/6/4/in-face-of-reagan-cuts-low-income.

44. Ibid.

45. Ibid.

46. The Office of Management and Budget posited that less funding would translate into less federal intrusion. See OMB, "Director's Review," Fall 1984.

47. Bell, *Thirteenth Man*, 75.

48. Ibid.

49. Ibid., 75, 152.

50. Testimony of Clarence Pendleton, chairman of US Civil Rights Commission, *Civil Rights Restoration Act of 1985: Joint Hearings before the Comm. on Education and Labor and the Subcomm. on Civil and Constitutional Rights of the Comm. on the Judiciary,* US House of Representatives, 99th Cong., 1st sess. Statement of Mark R. Disler, deputy assistant attorney, Civil Rights Division, *Hearings before the Comm. on Labor and Human Resources Concerning Grove City Legislation,* April 1, 1987.

51. "John D. Skare to POTUS, June 11, 1987," Folder: June 1987, MASFAA Archive.

52. Norman C. Thomas, "The Development of Federal Activism in Education: A Contemporary Perspective," *Education and Urban Society* 15, no. 3 (1983): 271–90.

53. American Presidency Project, "Statement by the President upon Signing the National Defense Education Act," September 2, 1958, http://www.presidency.ucsb.edu/ws/?pid=11211#axzz2jJjPQtQa.

54. Janet Kerr-Tener, "Eisenhower and Federal Aid to Higher Education," *Presidential Studies Quarterly* 17, no. 3 (Summer 1987): 473–85.

55. Roger Roots, "The Student Loan Debt Crisis: A Lesson in Unintended Consequences," *Southwestern University Law Review* 29 (1999): 501; Wikispace Classroom, "National Defense Education Act," AP History, http://npaphistory.wikispaces.com/National+Defense+Education+Act. See also Charles Geisst, *Wall Street: A History* (Athens: Ohio University Press, 1997), 279.

56. William Spriggs, "Student Loans and American Skills: Different Times, Two Different Reactions," *Spring Observer*, July 12, 2013, http://www .yourhoustonnews.com/spring/opinion/william-spriggs-student-loans-and-american-skills-different-times-two/article_43487358-eb74-11e2-9fd5-0014bcf887a.html.

57. Stephen Engleberg, "Education Secretary Now Regrets Remarks during Stormy First Weeks," *Houston Chronicle*, May 5, 1985; Edward Fiske, "Reagan's Man for Education," *New York Times*, December 22, 1985.

58. Bell, *Thirteenth Man*, 56. These conservative crusaders took their cue from President Reagan, who bucked the party establishment in 1976 to become the first presidential candidate since 1952 to challenge (and beat in a primary) the sitting president of his own party and the first Republican to do so since at least 1924, when John W. Davis challenged Coolidge.

59. Ibid., 73; David Stockman, *The Triumph of Politics: The Inside Story of the Reagan Revolution* (New York: Avon, 1987), 404. Stockman, for example, would accuse Bell of submitting the largest education budget in history.

60. Stockman, *Triumph of Politics*, 123.

61. Kevin Kosar, *Ronald Reagan and Education Policy* (n.p.: Studies in Governance and Politics, 2011.)

62. National Commission on Excellence in Education, *A Nation at Risk: The Imperative for Educational Reform* (Washington, DC: U.S. Department of Education, 1983).

63. Bell, *Thirteenth Man*, 76.

64. Ibid., 155–56.

65. Ibid., 158.

66. Ibid., 160.

67. Ibid., 157–61.

68. Bob Hager, "Headline: Student Aid," *NBC Nightly News*, February 11, 1985.

69. Ibid.; emphasis added.

70. Fiske, "Reagan's Man for Education."

71. Ian Haney-Lopez, *Dog Whistle Politics: How Coded Racial Appeals Have Wrecked the Middle Class* (New York: Oxford University Press, 2014), 58.

72. "Marc L. Brenner to MASFAA Executive Council and Committee Chairs, September 2, 1972," Folder: August 1987, MASFAA Archive.

73. "Headline: Budget Proposal," *ABC News*, February 2, 1985; Jacqueline Adams, "Headline: Budget Proposal/Congressional Reaction," *CBS News*, February 3, 1985.

74. By April 15, 1985, Congress had risen the household income threshold to $60,000 and total aid to $8,000, minus expected family contributions.

75. Ozer, "Congress and Politics of Financial Aid."

76. Lawrence E. Gladieux, *Federal Student Aid Policy: A History and an Assessment* (Washington, DC: US Department of Education), http://www2.ed.gov/offices/OPE/PPI/FinPostSecEd/gladieux.html.

77. Edward P. St. John, "Untangling the Web: Using Price-Response Measures in Enrollment Projections," *Journal of Higher Education* 64, no. 6 (November–December 1993): 676.

78. Ibid.

79. National Center for Public Policy and Higher Education, *Measuring Up 2008: National Report Card in Higher Education* (Washington, DC: National Center for Public Policy and Higher Education), http://measuringup2008.highereducation.org/print/NCPPHEMUNationalRpt.pdf.

80. "Family Income and Educational Attainment, 1970–2009," *Postsecondary Education Opportunity* 221 (November 2010), http://www.postsecondary.org/last12/221_1110pg1_16.pdf (accessed December 6, 2013).

81. William T. O'Hara, Bryant College President, to Ronald Reagan, WHORM: Subject File, Ronald Reagan President Library, Simi Valley, CA.

82. John W. Chandler, Williams College President, to Ronald Reagan, May 2, 1985; Edward M. Elmendorf, Assistant Education Secretary, to Chandler, May 23, 1985, WHORM: Subject File, Ronald Reagan Presidential Library, Simi Valley, CA.

83. Lowell C. Smith, Nichols College President, to Martin Anderson, Executive Office of the President, White House, February 18, 1985, WHORM: Subject File, Ronald Reagan Presidential Library, Simi Valley, CA.

84. Kenneth P. LaValle to Ronald Reagan, February 25, 1985, WHORM: Subject File, Ronald Reagan Presidential Library, Simi Valley, CA.

85. See, e.g., Vassar College, "Taxation of Scholarship and Grants," https://admissions.vassar.edu/docs/finaid13-14/1314_taxation_of_scholarships_and_grants.pdf (accessed May 1, 2016).

86. Rich, "Reports Show Big Increase." See also Hansen, "Student Loans."

87. Levine, "Headline: Graduates' Debt."

88. Internal memo about 1988 fiscal year in "Issue Paper on Student Aid Policies," Ronald Reagan Presidential Library, Simi Valley, CA.

89. "Statement of the National Association of Student Financial Aid Administrators, before the Senate Subcommittee on Education, Arts, and the Humanities, Presented by A. Dallas Martin, Jr., President, December 11, 1987," Folder: December 1987, MASFAA Archive.

90. Parsons, *Power and Politics*, 63. A student loan default is defined as a payment in arrears for 120 days. Default rates were calculated by dividing the total amount disbursed to defaulted borrowers by the total amount that had entered repayment status.

91. "Brenner to MASFAA Executive Council."

92. James J. Kilpatrick, "Nail the Deadbeat Student," *Pittsburgh Press*, November 11, 1987, http://news.google.com/newspapers?nid=1144&

dat=19871111&id=FakcAAAAIBAJ&sjid=QWMEAAAAIBAJ&
pg=2747,2485474.

93. Allan Cromley, "Student Aid in Danger; Education Chief Cracking Down on 'Deadbeats,'" *NewsOK*, November 5, 1987, http://newsok.com/student-aid-in-danger-education-chief-cracking-down-on-deadbeats/article/2204334.

94. David G. Savage, "IRS Confiscates Tax Refunds to Cover Defaulted Loans," *Los Angeles Times*, June 5, 1986, http://articles.latimes.com/1986-06-05/news/mn-9747_1_federal-student-loan.

95. The troubled borrower was also far more likely to have dropped out of trade or technical school rather than be a Porsche-owning MD with a degree from Harvard Medical School, as Senator Charles Percy (R-IL) and others suspected. Roger Simon, "Only 1 Thing Worse than a Deadbeat," *Chicago Tribune*, November 9, 1987, http://articles.chicagotribune.com/1987-11-09/news/8703240203_1_schools-with-high-default-deadbeats-student-loan.

96. "Statement of the National Association of Student Financial Aid Administrators."

97. Ibid.

98. Lee A. Daniels, "Education; Government Delays Tougher Loan Default Rules," *New York Times*, September 28, 1988, http://www.nytimes.com/1988/09/28/us/education-government-delays-tougher-loan-default-rules.html.

99. Simon, "Only 1 Thing Worse."

100. OMB, Fuller Files, Ronald Reagan Presidential Library.

101. John Blackstone, "Headline: Education/Student Loans," *CBS Nightly News*, June 1, 1989.

102. Augustus Hawkins to William H. Natcher, April 15 1985, Hawkins Papers, UCLA Library.

103. Susan Boren, "The Pell Grant Program: Background and Issues," Congressional Research Service Report for Congress, June 26, 1989, 3, http://www.eric.ed.gov/PDFS/ED310646.pdf.

104. Ibid., 3, 12.

105. Ibid., 3, 16.

106. President Ronald Reagan, Address before a Joint Session of Congress on the State of the Union, January 25, 1988, http://www.presidency.ucsb.edu.

107. "Dallas Martin, MASFAA President, to National Council, Commission, Committee Chairs and State Presidents, President's Report for March, 1988," Folder: March 1988, MASFAA Archive.

108. "Budget Resolution, FY '89," statement by Education and Labor Committee Chairman Augustus Hawkins on President Reagan's educational budget, in August Hawkins Papers, UCLA Collections.

109. John D. Skare, College Board, to Lead.line Washington Report, January 22, 1988, Folder: January 1988, MASFAA Archive.

110. Gwendolyn Lewis, *Trends in Student Aid: 1980–1988* (Washington, DC: Office of the College Board, 1988), http://professionals.collegeboard .com/profdownload/trends-in-student-aid-2008.pdf.

111. John Quinterno, *The Great Cost Shift* (New York: Demos, March 2012), 17, http://www.demos.org/sites/default/files/publications/ TheGreatCostShift_Demos_0.pdf.

112. See Steven Gold's work on state responses to recession, "Losing Ground Report," http://www.highereducation.org/reports/losing_ground/ar2.shtml.

113. Quinterno, *Great Cost Shift*, 18–19.

114. Ibid.

115. The figure of $1,000 is in personal income. States invested less personal income in higher education despite the fact that personal income increased 66.2 percent over this period; see ibid., 2, 15.

116. Ibid., 15.

117. Ibid.

118. National Center for Public Policy and Higher Education, *Losing Ground: A National Status Report on the Affordability of American Higher Education* (2000), http://www.highereducation.org/reports/losing_ground/ affordability_report_final_bw.pdf.

119. It was the students who would pick up the slack, as the portion they covered went from 10 percent to approximately 50 percent between the 1970s and 2013. See Justin Draeger, Panel Remarks, Policy Summit on Housing, Human Capital, and Inequality, Cleveland Federal Reserve, September 19, 2013.

120. Ibid.

121. State Balanced Budgets Requirement, April 12, 1999, http://www.ncsl.org/ research/fiscal-policy/state-balanced-budget-requirements.aspx.

122. President Gerald Ford's declaration to New York to "drop dead," as the *New York Daily News* famously paraphrased it, in response to New York's request for financial assistance, is the exception that proves the rule of cities' and states' working assumptions of federal help during tough economic times. Within months, by early 1976, Ford did approve a loan to New York. Despite this, Ford has since maintained that just the perception a president would refuse federal assistance for a struggling local or state government was a major reason why he lost the 1976 election to Carter. Among the budget recommendations Ford suggested was that the City University of New York abolish its tuition-free policy. "Ford to City: Drop Dead," *New York Daily News*, October 30 1975; Sam Roberts, "Infamous 'Drop Dead' Was Never Said by Ford," *New York Times*, December 28, 2006.

123. Ronald G. Ehrenberg, "The Perfect Storm and the Privatization of Public Higher Education," *Change*, November 2005, http://digitalcommons.ilr .cornell.edu/cgi/viewcontent.cgi?article=1060&context=workingpapers.

124. Passed in 1965, Medicaid provided medical coverage for low-income households, children and their parents, and the elderly and disabled.

125. Adam Clymer, "Governors Oppose Reagan on Medicaid," *New York Times*, February 24, 1981.

126. Michael Feinsliber, "Democrats Dig for Quotes to Paint Dim Picture of Reagan," *Lakeland (FL) Ledger*, August 24, 1980.

127. Diane Rowland, Barbara Lyons, and Jennifer Edwards, "Medicaid: Health Care for the Poor in the Reagan Era," *Annual Review of Public Health* 9 (May 1988): 428.

128. Adam Clymer, "Governors Oppose Reagan on Medicaid," *New York Times*, February 24, 1981.

129. This cut was actually considered a compromise with the caps on Medicaid spending proposed by the White House, with Congress agreeing to a series of temporary reductions (between 3 and 4.5 percent) in the federal share of Medicaid expenditures in each state during the early and middle 1980s. See Rowland, Lyons, and Edwards, 431.

130. Ibid., 439.

131. Quoted in John Lee and Sue Clery, "Key Trends in Higher Education," *American Academic* 1, no. 1 (2004): 21–36.

132. Gold, "Losing Ground Report."

133. "For Professors, Phonathon Spells Raise," *New York Times*, September 20, 1995.

134. The incentive-laden system was modeled largely on Weisman's experiences as a Wall Street consultant. Fay Ellis, "Cuts in Federal Aid Cast Cloud over Semester," *New York Times*, September 17, 1995.

135. "Mercy College Ties Faculty Salaries to Enrollment," *Academe* 81 (September–October 1995): 6.

136. "For Mercy College Teachers: Recruit a Student, Get a Raise," *New York Times*, June 10, 1995.

137. Ibid.; "For Professors, Phonathon Spells Raise"; Eric Martone and Michael Perrota, *Mercy College: Yesterday and Today* (Charleston, SC: The History Press, 2013), 83.

138. "For Professors, Phonathon Spells Raise."

139. "For Mercy College Teachers."

140. Valerie Strauss and Rajiv Chandrasekaran, "Anger, Shock Greet Proposed Federal Cuts," *Washington Post*, May 12, 1995.

141. "Ivory Tower Budgets," *Washington Post*, August 13, 1994.

142. Echo Montgomery Garrett and Deborah Lohse, "Count on Big College Aid Changes under Bill Clinton," *Money*, April 1993, 14.

143. Ibid.

144. Clare McCann, "Student Loan Programs—History." New America EdCentral, http://www.edcentral.org/edcyclopedia/federal-student-loan-programs-history/.

145. Cong. Rec. S28419 (1995).

146. "President Clinton's College Loan Program Fails Students, Colleges and Taxpayers Through Early Dismissal of Private Enterprise, Says Hamm," *PR Newswire*, June 1, 1993.

147. In addition to offering this subsidy to private lenders, the federal government guaranteed the loan against default. If a borrower defaulted, the federal government guaranteed the bank a minimum return on investment, as much as 80 percent. If the borrower paid in full, a lender recouped the loan principal plus any additional profit in interest, plus fees and charges. Not only did a federally guaranteed loan promise lenders a minimum return on investment, it also allowed lenders and processing agencies—called state guarantee agencies—to add on expenses for originating, administering, managing, and collecting these loans.

148. For a recent primer on direct lending, see Sam Houston State University, http://www.shsu.edu/~fao_www/fa_intro/loans.html.

149. "President Clinton's College Loan Program Fails Students."

150. Ibid.

151. Ibid.

152. Hood, "How to Hold Down College"; Thomas Sowell, "Why College Tuition Costs So Much," *Consumers Research Magazine*, October 1993, 10.

153. Adam Clymer, "GOP Revises a Budget Rule to Help Banks," *New York Times*, August 20, 1995; see also "30 Year Terms on Student Loans," *New York Times*, July 3, 1994, http://www.nytimes.com/1995/08/20/us/gop-revises-a-budget-rule-to-help-banks.html.

154. James Popkin and Viva Hardigg, "The College Aid Face-off," *US News and World Report*, March 13, 1995, 64.

155. Ibid.

156. Clymer, "GOP Revises a Budget Rule."

157. Joyce Hall to MASFAA Executive Council, August 22, 1995, Folder: August 1995, MASFAA Archive.

158. Popkin and Hardigg, "College Aid Face-off."

159. Jeffrey Marshall, "Student Loan Mark: Incomplete," *American Banker*, December 1, 1995, http://www.americanbanker.com/magazine/105_12/-68028-1.html?zkPrintable=1&nopagination=1 (accessed August 12, 2016).

160. Alexander J. Basso, management analyst in Treasury Dept., to Gene Sperling et al., December 2, 1994, in *Congressional Record* 141 (150), 2.

161. Rene Sanchez, "Direct Student Lending Remains a Target," *Washington Post*, July 2, 1996; Karen DeWitt, "Student Loans Show Sharp Rise, Report Says," *New York Times*, September 22, 1995, http://www.nytimes.com/1995/09/22/us/student-loans-show-sharp-rise-report-says.html.

162. DeWitt, "Student Loans Show Sharp Rise."

163. "Student Loans: Number of Schools Using Direct Loans Is Growing, White House Report Says," *Bankruptcy Law Reporter* 31 (October 31, 1996).

164. OMB Director Alice Rivlin to Hon. William F. Goodling, September 19, 1995, in *Congressional Record* 141 (150).

165. "To Aid Banks, GOP Hobbling Student Loan Plan," *Chicago Tribune*, August 20,1995, http://articles.chicagotribune.com/1995-08-20/news/9508200203_1_direct-loan-program-direct-lending-direct-loans.

166. American Association of Collegiate Registrars and Admissions Officers, State PIRG Groups' Higher Education Project, US Student Association, *Easy Money*, May 2005, http://www.pirg.org/highered/easymoney.pdf.

167. Lawrence Lindsey to Spencer Abraham, June 9, 1995, in *Congressional Record*, 141 (150); Clymer, "GOP Revises a Budget Rule." Other Republicans who supported direct lending included Senators David Durenberger (MN) and Paula Hawkins (FL). Both had left the Senate by January 1995. See Cong. Rec. S28278(October 18, 1995).

168. Joyce Hall to MASFAA Executive Council, August 22, 1995.

169. "Student Loans: Student Default Rate Falls to Record Low of 8.8 Percent," *Bankruptcy Law Reporter* 11 (October 21, 1999).

170. Alexander J. Basso to Gene Sperling. Although borrowers might pay more in a direct loan income-contingent plan, which allowed them to amortize a loan over thirty years. However, such an extended payment term meant people paid interest on the principal for twenty additional years. "Student Loans: Student Default Rate Falls."

171. Stephanie Gallagher, "Stafford Loans Get Cheaper," *Kiplinger's Personal Finance Magazine*, December 1998, 62; Stephanie Gallagher, "Student Loans Are Cheaper than Ever," *Kiplinger's Personal Finance Magazine*, September 1999, 52.

172. McCann, "Student Loans Programs," 172; Megan Barnett, Julian E. Barnes, and Danielle Knight, "Big Money on Campus," *US News & World Report*, October 19, 2003, 30.

173. Office of the White House Press Secretary, Statement by the President on Direct College Loans, November 30, 1994, in *Congressional Record* 141 (150).

174. US Department of Education, Office of Student Financial Assistance, Federal Funds, 371, https://www.gpo.gov/fdsys/pkg/BUDGET-2006-APP/pdf/BUDGET-2006-APP-1-8.pdf (accessed February 3, 2017).

175. Office of the White House Press Secretary, Statement by the President on Direct College Loans, November 30, 1994.

176. William F. Goodling and Howard McKeon, "Making College Loans Fair," *Washington Post*, April 21 1995.

177. Clymer, "GOP Revises a Budget Rule."

178. Strauss and Chandrasekaran, "Anger, Shock Greet Proposed Federal Cuts."

179. McCann, "Student Loan Programs."

180. Highlights from 104th Cong., 1st sess., by Senator Paul Wellstone, *Native American Press / Ojibwe News*, December 28, 1995, http://proxy.lib.ohio-state.edu/login?url=http://search.proquest.com/docview/

368210387?accountid=9783 (accessed May 2, 2016); Madeleine M. Kunin, "A Math Lesson: College Loans," *New York Times*, June 13, 2007; Philip G. Schrag, "Federal Student Loan Repayment Assistance for Public Interest Lawyers and Other Employees of Governments and Nonprofit Organizations," *Hofstra Law Review* 36 (2007): 27, http://ssrn.com/abstract=1014622 (accessed May 2, 2016).

181. Barnett, Barnes, and Knight, "Big Money on Campus."
182. Popkin and Hardigg, "College Aid Face-Off."
183. Barnett, Barnes, and Knight, "Big Money on Campus."
184. Executive Council Meeting, May 5–6, 1996, Folder: May 1996, MASFAA Archive.
185. For example, see Executive Council Minutes, 1996, Folder: July 1996, MASFAA Archives.
186. Barnett, Barnes, and Knight, "Big Money on Campus."
187. Ibid.
188. Anne Marie Chaker, "More Schools Lend Directly to Students," *Wall Street Journal*, September 8, 2005, http://www.wsj.com/articles/SB112613816482334711.
189. Barnett, Barnes, and Knight, "Big Money on Campus."
190. Ibid.
191. "Student Loans: Congress Passes Temporary Solution to Student Loan Interest Problem," *Bankruptcy Law Reporter*, June 4, 1998.
192. Ibid.
193. "Student Loans: Lenders Get More Clarity in New Package of Guaranteed Student Loan Rule Proposals," *Banking Report*, August 23, 1999.
194. Administration officials also countered by claiming that competition from direct lending spurred the industry to offer better terms.
195. Barnett, Barnes, and Knight, "Big Money on Campus."
196. Ibid.
197. Candidate Clinton had spoken periodically since 1991 about a desire to have a "New Covenant" between government and citizens. President Clinton would return more consistently to the New Covenant theme in the aftermath of the Republican revolution in 1994. Clinton looked upon tuition tax credits as a cornerstone of his New Covenant agenda to target federal assistance to those Americans who were helping themselves, or an agenda the president described elsewhere as "more opportunity in return for more responsibility." President Clinton at the 77th Annual American Council on Education, San Francisco, February 14, 1995, in *Congressional Record* 141 (150).
198. Peter Applebome, "Clinton's College-Aid Plan Faces Doubt from Experts," *New York Times*, March 30, 1997, http://www.nytimes.com/1997/03/30/us/clinton-s-college-aid-plan-faces-doubt-from-experts.html.
199. Ibid.

200. Perhaps David W. Breneman, economist and dean of education at the University of Virginia, summed up the HOPE Credit best: "It's good politics but bad economics." Ibid.

201. Lawrence E. Gladieux and Robert D. Reischauer, "Higher Tuition, More Grade Inflation," *Washington Post*, September 4, 1996.

202. Karen Arenson, "Clinton Plan Could Push Tuition Up," *New York Times*, February 10, 1997.

203. Joseph Nocera, *A Piece of the Action: How the Middle Class Joined the Money Class* (New York: Simon & Schuster, 1994), 390–406. Eight in ten people polled by Gallup/CNN/*USA Today* in 1997 favored tax credits for postsecondary education. Gallup/CNN/*USA Today* Poll, May 1997, iPOLL Databank, University of Connecticut, Roper Center for Public Opinion Research, http://www.ropercenter.uconn.edu.proxy.lib .ohio-state.edu/data_access/ipoll/ipoll.html (accessed July 26, 2013). A similar survey commissioned by UBS at the time showed support among 79 percent of 1,006 Republicans polled (with investable assets above $10,000). UBS/Gallup Index of Investor Optimism Poll, May 1997, iPOLL Databank, University of Connecticut, Roper Center for Public Opinion Research, http://www.ropercenter.uconn.edu/data_access/ipoll/ ipoll.html (accessed July 28, 2013).

204. For information on the Taxpayer Relief Act, see http://en.wikipedia.org/ wiki/Taxpayer_Relief_Act_of_1997.

205. Recent data on the percentage changes in state spending since 2005 from the US Department of Education reveal that this great cost shift continues at the level of state governments. See US Department of Education, *Percentage Changes in State Spending Indicators: United States, Academic Years 2005–06 to 2010–11* (Washington, DC: Department of Education), http://collegecost.ed.gov/statespending.aspx.

206. "The Tactic: Playing the Inside Game," *US News and World Report*, October 27, 2003; Barnett, Barnes, and Knight, "Big Money on Campus."

207. US Department of Education, *Budget of the United States Government: Fiscal Year 2008* (Washington, DC: Government Printing Office, 2007), http://www.gpoaccess.gov/usbudget/fy08/sheets/28_6.xls.

208. Congressional Budget Office, "A CBO Study: Costs and Policy Options for Federal Student Loan Programs," March 2010, https://www.cbo.gov/ sites/default/files/111th-congress-2009-2010/reports/03-25-studentloans .pdf.

209. US Senate Healtj, Education, Labor and Pensions Committee, "Report on Marketing Practices in the Federal Family Education Loan Program," June 14, 2007, http://files.eric.ed.gov/fulltext/ED497127.pdf (accessed June 26, 2016).

210. Ibid.

211. Ibid.

212. US Attorney's Office Public Affairs, "Former Department of Education Official Pleads Guilty to Filing False Financial Disclosures and Violating Conflict of Interest Laws," October 29, 2009, http://www2.ed.gov/about/offices/list/oig/invtreports/dc102009.html.

213. US Senate Health, Education, Labor and Pensions Committee, "Report on Marketing Practices," 18.

214. Ibid.

215. Ibid., 19; New York Attorney General's Office, "Cuomo Announces Settlement with Student Loan Companies," December 11, 2007, http://www.ag.ny.gov/press-release/cuomo-announces-settlement-student-loan-company.

216. Doug Lederman, "The Cuomo Effect Spreads," *Inside Higher Education*, April 24, 2007, https://www.insidehighered.com/news/2007/04/24/loans.

217. New York Attorney General's Office, "Cuomo Announces Settlement with Student Loan Companies," December 11, 2007, http://www.ag.ny.gov/press-release/cuomo-announces-settlement-student-loan-company.

218. Ibid.

219. See interview with Andrew Cuomo by Doug Lederman, "Inside the Cuomo Probe," *Insider Higher Education*, July 30, 2007, https://www.insidehighered.com/news/2007/07/30/cuomo (accessed June 26, 2016).

220. Alfonso Serrano, "Fed Suspended in Student Loan Probe," *CBS News*, April 6, 2007, http://www.cbsnews.com/news/fed-suspended-in-student-loan-probe/ (accessed June 28, 2016).

221. Alan Collinge, *The Student Loan Scam: The Most Oppressive Debt in U.S. History and How We Can Fight Back* (Boston: Beacon Press, 2009), 73.

222. Ibid.

223. John Hechinger, "Former Education Official Pleads Guilty to False-Statement Charges," *Wall Street Journal*, November 2, 2009, http://www.wsj.com/articles/SB125720403027823983.

224. Kennedy to Education Secretary Margaret Spellings, April 25, 2007, https://votesmart.org/public-statement/254183/letter-to-department-of-education-secretary-margaret-spellings#.WfCoSEyZMyk; Amanda Ernst, "Lawmakers Ask DOE to Help in Student Loan Probe," April 27, 2007, http://www.law360.com/articles/23576/lawmakers-ask-doe-to-help-in-student-loan-probe (accessed June 28, 2016).

225. U.S. Attorney's Office Public Affairs, "Former Department of Education Official"; Ernst, "Lawmakers Ask DOE To."

226. New York Attorney General's Office, "Cuomo Announces Settlement"; Collinge, *Student Loan Scam*, chap. 6.

227. Cristian deRitis, "Student Lending's Failing Grade," *Moody's Analytics* (July 2011), 59.

228. William Bennett to Terry Branstad, July 3, 1985, WHORM: Subject File, Ronald Reagan Presidential Library, Simi Valley, CA.

229. Lewis, *Trends in Student Aid*, 11.

230. Ian Shapira, "Bush Signs Sweeping Student Loan Bill into Law, Adding an Asterisk," *Washington Post*, September 28, 2007, http://proxy.lib.ohio-state.edu/login?url=http://search.proquest.com.proxy.lib.ohio-state.edu/docview/410168759?accountid=9783.

231. See Rohit Chopra interview by Chris Morran, "The Trump Administration Eases Restriction on Student Loan Debt Collectors," *Consumerist*, March 17, 2017.

Chapter 3

1. Consumers Union, "Consumers Union Applauds California for Ending ZIP Code–Based Auto Insurance Rates," *Consumer Reports*, July 14, 2006, http://consumersunion.org/news/cu-applauds-california-for-ending-zip-code-based-auto-insurance-rates/ (accessed September 3, 2016).

2. *ABC Evening News*, October 13, 1988; *NBC Evening News*, November 9, 1988; *CBS Evening News*, November 10, 1988.

3. Ibid.

4. A coalition of community and low-income organizations had actually unsuccessfully challenged California's mandatory auto insurance law, claiming it was unconstitutional to require the purchase of auto insurance without also protecting consumers from territorial rating, which made the insurance unaffordable to many poor consumers. Although it was sympathetic to the plaintiffs' claim, the court, conscious not to legislate from the bench, stated that it was a matter for the California State Assembly. See King v. Meese, 43 Cal.3d 1217 (1987).

5. David Shribman, "State Legislatures Move to Bring Big Increases in Auto Insurance Rates to a Screeching Halt," *Wall Street Journal*, July 10, 1989.

6. The populists are "gang[ing] up on big interest groups who own state legislatures," commented the initiative expert Thomas Cronin, a Colorado College political scientist and the author of a book on the modern proposition movement. Robert Reinhold, "The Nation: California Has 29 on the Ballot—With Proliferation of Ballot Initiatives, Suddenly Everyone's Interest Is Special," *New York Times*, November 6, 1988.

7. Michael Smolens, "Insurance Industry Fears 103 More than Any Other," *San Diego Union*, October 20, 1988.

8. *National Underwriter*, 1992–93.

9. Benjamin Zycher, "Insurance Fraud," *Wall Street Journal*, October 9, 1989.

10. D. C. Carson, "Insurers Smash Their Own Record on Spending in Proposition War," *San Diego Union*, October 8, 1988.

11. Zycher, "Insurance Fraud."

12. Stephen Sugarman, "Why Prop 103 Will Fail," *San Diego Union*, May 14, 1989.

13. James V. Grimaldi and Jeff Weit, "Car Insurance Sparks 'Initiative Warfare': 5 Measures on November Ballot Threaten California's

77-Year-Old Petition Process," *Orange County Register*, September 18, 1988.

14. Carson, "Insurers Smash Their Own Record."

15. Smolens, "Insurance Industry Fears 103."

16. Sonja Steptoe, "Policy Dispute: Auto Insurers Face Drive Consumers for Rate Reductions—Rollback Voted in California Spurs Activists Elsewhere; Some Firms Drop Lines," *Wall Street Journal*, November 22, 1989; LaBarbara Bowman, "Group Pushes Insurance Reform in 14 States," *USA Today*, January 11, 1989; Nora Lockwood Tooher, "California Leads Charge in Auto Insurance Rate Revolt," *Providence (RI) Journal*, January 22, 1989; Erik Ingram, "Insurers Buying National Ads to Stem Revolt," *San Francisco Chronicle*, February 20, 1989.

17. Mark Green, "How Minorities Are Sold Short," *New York Times*, June 18, 1990. Even between predominantly Black communities a discrepancy often existed, as was the case in Maryland, where Landover drivers paid $570, compared with the more affluent Mitchellville drivers, who paid $390. See David Montgomery, "For Some, It's All in the Numbers," *Washington Post*, October 4, 1993.

18. Carson, "Insurers Smash Their Own Record."

19. Ballotpedia, "California Proposition 103, Insurance Rates and Regulation" (1988), https://ballotpedia.org/California_Proposition_103,_Insurance_Rates_and_Regulation_(1988)).

20. Richard B. Schmitt and Sonja Steptoe, "California's Voters Shake Up Insurers," *Wall Street Journal*, November 10, 1988.

21. Vlae Kershner and Sabin Russell, "Prop. 103 Wins; Insurers Halt New Policies—State Turmoil," *San Francisco Chronicle*, November 10, 1988; Sabin Russell, "Insurers Panic over Prop. 103," *San Francisco Chronicle*, November 10, 1988.

22. Vlae Kershner, "Insurance Industry Accused of False TV Ads about Prop. 103," *San Francisco Chronicle*, September 30, 1988.

23. Schmitt and Steptoe, "California's Voters Shake Up Insurers"; see also Historical Data for New York Stock Exchange Composite Index, http://www.nyse.com/about/listed/nya_resources.shtml (accessed November 2012).

24. Shribman, "State Legislatures Move."

25. Kershner and Russell, "Prop. 103 Wins"; Russell, "Insurers Panic over Prop. 103"; Ron Roach, "Voters Revolt, Pass 103," *San Diego Evening Tribune*, November 9, 1988.

26. Jeff Weir, "State Farm Ordered to Hearing on Rate Discrimination," *Orange County Register*, January 27, 1989.

27. Vlae Kershner and William Carlsen, "New Moves in Battle over Prop. 103," *San Francisco Chronicle*, November 15, 1988.

28. Carriers' campaign of nullification and interposition was successful in part because of an apparent loss of will among motorists. For

example, one major stipulation of Proposition 103 required insurers to grant rebates to motorists. Yet five years later, most insurers remained in noncompliance with the court-ordered rebate. Among the most recalcitrant were California's two largest insurers, State Farm Insurance Group and Farmers Insurance Group. Combined, they controlled 40 percent of the California market, and others followed their lead. Many individuals responded just as Vincenza Scarpaci, a typical policyholder, did. Recounting his failed attempts with his insurer, State Farm, Scarpaci told his local newspaper editor that it was futile to hold out hope that insurers would comply. Not even the state supreme court's decision to uphold the refund made a difference, for auto carriers "refuse[d] to accept the ruling." The Petaluma, California, resident went on: "I wrote to State Farm to protest its behavior [withholding the rebate]. I received no reply. Instead, this same company that has no profits to refund to policyholders spent another untold amount of money to lobby against Prop 186 this fall. My conclusion: Neither the welfare of the policyholder nor their legitimate concerns are as important to this company as its control over the insurance market and unrestricted profits." Disillusioned, Scarpaci gave up and switched carriers. But having individual consumers switch carriers because insurers selected which laws to obey was no more a solution to auto insurance in California than asking parents of the Little Rock Nine, in 1957, to move from Arkansas to a state up North with a desegregated school system was the answer to Jim Crow. Whether in Little Rock or Petaluma, such selective compliance with the courts, by Orval Faubus or State Farm, was an assault on the principle of law and order. Edmund Sanders, "Quackenbush: Rebates May Be Small; Insurance Commissioner Backs away from Pledge to Give Prop. 103 Rollbacks Early," *Los Angeles Daily News*, March 17, 1995.

29. Robert Reinhold, "Apathy and Disaffection on the Rise among California Voters," *New York Times*, June 12, 1990.

30. Ibid.

31. Leslie Espinoza and Angela P. Harris, "Embracing the Tar-Baby: LatCrit Theory and the Sticky Mess of Race," *California Law Review* 85, no. 5 (1997): 1585–1645.

32. Quackenbush political ads, "Chuck Quackenbush," ID 60441-60444 (1994), Julian P. Kanter Political Commercial Archive, University of Oklahoma. For more on the use of the phrase "special interests" and how it is often coded racially, see Haney-Lopez, *Dog Whistle Politics*, 153.

33. George Lipsitz, *The Possessive Investment in Whiteness: How White People Profit from Identity Politics* (Philadelphia, PA: Temple University Press, 1998), 47–55.

34. Evan Thomas, "Decline and Fall," *Newsweek*, November 20, 2006.

35. Jack Skinner, a Texas insurance broker and former G. H. W. Bush official, celebrated the loss of House leadership by Democrats in Washington. Skinner expected the turnover of Democrat-controlled chairmanships—such as those of Henry Gonzalez, chair of the Banking Committee; Jack Brooks, state supreme court justice, and Daniel Rostenkowski, member of Ways and Means—to "have a dramatic impact on the way insurance is conducted in the state of Texas." Jim Skinner, "Election Results May Help Texas Insurance Market," *San Antonio Express*, November 20, 1994.

36. "Martinez for Insurance Commissioner, Incumbent Commissioner Bankrolled by Industry," *Sacramento Bee*, October 17, 1998.

37. Quackenbush claimed that $46 million was owed in refunds to insurers but reserved the right to seek an additional refund of $32 million, depending on 20th Century's losses from the recent Northridge earthquake—an issue that had nothing to do with Proposition 103 and auto insurance. See also Alfred G. Haggerty, "Quackenbush Cuts a Deal on Prop 103," *National Underwriter*, February 6, 1995.

38. Quackenbush's evasion of Proposition 103 gave consumer groups and other plaintiffs no choice: "If he won't implement the will of the people, the courts should force him to," a 103 Enforcement Project spokesperson told the press. Rick Orlov, "City Joins Call to End Insurance Redlining," *Los Angeles Daily News*, March 27, 1998.

39. "Auto Insurance," *Los Angeles Sentinel*, April 15, 1998; Proposition 103 Enforcement Project v. Quackenbush, Supreme Court of California (1998 Cal. LEXIS 6090); Spanish Speaking Citizens' Foundation v. Lowroman (2001 Cal. App. LEXIS 39).

40. Consumers Union, "CU Applauds California.

41. California Insurance Code, sec. 1861.02

42. Orlov, "City Joins Call."

43. Quackenbush essentially shared State Farm's and the industry's view that pricing and other underwriting data were trade secrets. Both Quackenbush's replacement and the courts fundamentally disagreed, however. State Farm sued Quackenbush's successor, John Garamendi, to block him from releasing the data. State Farm lost in the lower, appellate, and highest state courts. It brought the California Supreme Court a straightforward suit, which the court later dispatched of by unanimously affirming voters' and prior judges' decisions: insurers "may not invoke the trade secret privilege to prevent disclosure." "Court Upholds Insurance Redlining Suit," *Los Angeles Sentinel*, April 29–May 5, 2004.

44. Eric Young, "Insurance Contest," *Sacramento Bee*, October 19, 1998.

45. "Candidates Accept Insurance Donations," *Monterey County (CA) Herald*, October 17, 2002.

46. Kenneth Reich, "Insurers—Quackenbush's Victims, or His Allies?," *Los Angeles Times*, May 4, 2000, http://articles.latimes.com/2000/may/04/local/me-26487.

47. Scott Lindlaw, "Campaign-Finance Reform," *San Diego Union-Tribune*, April 21, 2000.

48. James P. Sweeney, "Candidates Fight over Insurance Industry Aid," *San Diego Union-Tribune*, September 20, 1994.

49. "United States: Quacking in His Boots." *Economist*, June 20, 2000.

50. J. C. Howard, "California State Auditor Hammers Quackenbush," *National Underwriter*, October 30, 2000.

51. Steve Lawrence, "State Decides Not to Indict Quackenbush," *San Diego Union-Tribune*, February 6, 2002.

52. "California Insurers Blast Anti-Redlining Proposal," *National Underwriter*, December 11, 1995.

53. Barry Carmody, "Sacramento—Proposition 103," *San Francisco Chronicle*, September 8, 1995.

54. Barry Carmody, "Fairness Drives Current Insurance System," *San Jose Mercury News*, September 13, 1995.

55. Barry Carmody, "Change in Auto Rates Could Hurt," *Fresno Bee*, May 1, 1995.

56. George Wallace, "Dangling Propositions," *Declarations and Propositions*, February 6, 2006.

57. Jessica Guynn, "Advocates Seek Reforms on Insurance," *Contra Costa (CA) Times*, December 5, 2003, http://www.consumerwatchdog.org/story/advocates-seek-reforms-insurance.

58. Wallace, "Dangling Propositions."

59. Barry Carmody, "Redistributing Car Insurance Rates," *Sacramento Bee*, April 19, 1995.

60. Lizabeth Cohen, *A Consumers' Republic: The Politics of Mass Consumption in Postwar America* (New York: Vintage Books, 2003), 292–328.

61. Carmody, "Redistributing Car Insurance Rates."

62. Carmody, "Proposed Rate Changes Hit Good Drivers with Bad News," *Sacramento Bee*, May 21, 1995.

63. Guynn, "Advocates Seek Reforms on Insurance."

64. J. C. Howard, "California Regulations Decried as Jim Crow," *National Underwriter*, October 22, 1997.

65. The Insurance Research Council calculates the uninsured driver proportion using the ratio of claims made by individuals who were injured by uninsured drivers (uninsured motorists coverage) to claims made by individuals injured by insured drivers (bodily injury liability coverage). Colorado's estimate is inflated because bodily injury claims are subject to a $2,500 threshold and uninsured motorists claims are not. In other states, the thresholds are the same. Insurance Research Council, "Uninsured Drivers Increasing; Vary by State; Miss. Highest, Maine Lowest," *Insurance Journal*, June 28, 2006, http://www.insurancejournal.com/news/national/2006/06/28/69919.htm (accessed February 3, 2013).

66. "Suits Filed Against ZIP Coded Auto Insurance Rates," *Oakland Post*, April 8, 1998.

67. Similarly, during the late 1980s in Canada, where auto insurance rates jumped 40 percent in only two years, a public outcry prompted Premier David Peterson to set up an Ontario provincial insurance board, hoping to keep insurance out of the hands of government and primarily a free-market enterprise. The board banned insurance companies from considering age, sex, marital status, and physical disability in calculating rates. Women were "losers," according to the board's chair, as they bore the major cost of any readjustment in order to subsidize young male drivers. The Canadian system still allowed non-driving-related factors such as conviction rate and region to be used. Robert Brehl, "Young Women to Pay Higher Car Insurance," *Toronto Star*, September 2, 1988.

68. Richard Schweiker, "Defective New Insurance Legislation," *New York Times*, November 16, 1983, http://www.nytimes.com/1983/11/16/opinion/l-defective-new-insurance-legislation-044983.html.

69. Stephen Drachler, "Gender-Based Auto Insurance Rates Vetoed by Thornburgh," *Allentown (PA) Morning Call*, February 22, 1986, http://articles.mcall.com/1986-02-22/news/2511207_1_auto-insurance-rates-dick-thornburgh-s-decision-powerful-insurance-lobby.

70. "Insure Against Sex Discrimination," *New York Times*, November 2, 1983.

71. For example, Carmody frequently asked, particularly in op-eds, "Should young female drivers, who tend to have fewer accidents, pay more even though young males tend to have the greater number of tickets and accidents?" Carmody, "Redistributing Car Insurance Rates."

72. Based on author's analysis of census data; see https://factfinder.census.gov/faces/tableservices/jsf/pages/productview.xhtml?pid=DEC_00_SF3_DP3&prodType=table (accessed January 28, 2017).

73. US Bureau of the Census, 2000. Unfortunately, similar characteristics are not available for earlier censuses.

74. "Where You Live Determines What You Pay." In Auto Insurance Premiums Vary Widely by Zip Code for Good Drivers in California. Insurance Commissioner John Garamendi's Public Hearing on Automobile Insurance Premiums, San Francisco, California, February 24, 2006. Consumers Union 2006., page 5.

75. Statistics demonstrating how those who could afford it least were made to pay more, regardless of their driving skills, were not new. Auto insurance redlining had been going on for years, wrote one opponent. Nor did those defending the insurers deny it; as one claimed, historically, there was just no way to get around geographical boundaries. But where the ghetto tax turned out to be the highest was in Black communities. One major insurer, for example, hiked up rates 83 percent, an average of $974, in some Black-majority communities. See Consumers Union, "California Insurers Charge as Much as $974 per Year More to Good Drivers Living

in Predominantly Black, Latino ZIP Codes," December 20, 2005, http://
www.consumersunion.org/pub/core_financial_services/002991.html
(accessed February 2, 2013); and Mark Savage, "Insurance Industry
Mounts Last-Ditch Effort to Block Proposal to End Discriminatory
'Zip Code Profiling,'" Consumers Union, April 6, 2006, http://
consumersunion.org/news/insurance-industry-mounts-last-ditch-effort-
to-block-proposal-to-end-discriminatory-zip-code-profiling/.

76. John Howard, "Rules Would Bar Address as Factor in Car Insurance," *Los
Angeles Daily News*, May 24, 1996.

77. Sorich replaced Carmody in 2002. Michael Liedtke, "Car Insurance Costs
Higher in Hispanic, Black Neighborhoods," *Daily Journal* (San Mateo,
CA), December 20, 2005, http://archives.smdailyjournal.com/article_
preview.php?id=52461 (accessed March 19, 2013).

78. Skinner, "Election Results May Help Texas."

79. US Postal Service Office of Inspector General, "The Untold Story of
the ZIP Code," Report RARC-WP-13-006, April 1, 2013, 4, http://
postalmuseum.si.edu/research/pdfs/ZIP_Code_rarc-wp-13-006.pdf.

80. The direct marketing theoretician Martin Baier, whose name
grew to be "synonymous with segmentation" (Terry C.
Williams, "Practitioners: Dogs that Climb Tree," *Direct Marketing*, May 1988),
published the first article in 1967 on market segmentation using zip
codes in the *Harvard Business Review* and wrote a college textbook on
direct marketing. He then founded the nation's first direct marketing
center at the University of Missouri, Kansas City, where he built
the discipline by refining the segmentation techniques of sampling,
customer valuation, and multivariate and regression analyses. See
Martin Baier, "Zip Code—New Tool for Marketers," *Harvard Business
Review* 45, no. 1 (January–February 1967): 136–40.

81. In 1944, Robert Moon proposed using a three-digit code, which described
generally a sectional facility of a region for mail sorting and distributing
(e.g., 554 for part of Minnesota); two later digits, for larger cities, were
added to the three-digit code (e.g., 55416 for Minneapolis, Minnesota).
Douglas Martin, "Robert Moon, an Inventor of the ZIP Code, Dies at
83," *New York Times*, April 14, 2001. For an overview of theories exploring
the nexus of race, the built environment, and suburbia, see Wendell
Pritchett, "Which Urban Crisis: Regionalism, Race and Urban Policy,
1960–1974," *Journal of Urban History* 34(2) (2008): 266–286.

82. Quality Planning Corporation, "Why People Who Live Close to
Restaurants Are More Likely to Have an Accident and Pay More for Auto
Insurance," December 6, 2005, https://www.qualityplanning.com/qpc_
resources_public/news/051206%20QPC%20Locations_F.htm (accessed
October 29, 2017).

83. Liedtke, "Car Insurance Costs Higher"; Quality Planning Corporation,
"Why People"; Paul D. Winston, "Study There Goes the Neighborhood,"

Business Insurance, December 18, 2005, http://www.businessinsurance.com/article/20051218/ISSUE04/100018075/study-there-goes-the-neighborhood (accessed January 28, 2017).

84. Paul M. Ong and Michael A. Stoll, "Why Do Inner City Residents Pay Higher Premiums? The Determinants of Automobile Insurance Premiums," Working Paper 1467276, University of California Transportation Center (January 2008), http://escholarship.org/uc/item/6zp0z9cj#page-1.

85. US Newswire, "Consumers Union Applaud CA Rules Barring ZIP-Code based Auto Insurance," July 14, 2006.

86. "Court Upholds Insurance Redlining Lawsuit," *Los Angeles Sentinel*, April 29, 2004.

87. For a slightly different interpretation of cross-sells and racial discrimination in the realm of auto insurance, see Scott Harrington and Gregory Niehaus, "Race, Redlining, and Automobile Insurance Pricing," *Journal of Business* 71, no. 3 (1998): 449, 467.

88. Jean F. Wells and William D. Jackson, "Major Financial Services Legislation, Gramm-Leach-Bliley Act: An Overview," Congressional Research Service Report for Congress, December 16, 1999, 2, 5, 8.

89. George Lane, "Denver ZIP Code Plan Stirs Concerns," *Denver Post*, March 11, 2002.

90. The insurance industry actually put the overall number of uninsured Michigan motorists during this period (1999–2004) slightly higher, at 17 percent. See Insurance Research Council, "Uninsured Drivers Increasing"; David Josar, "Police Detain Detroit Mayor's Press Secretary," *Detroit News*, November 3, 2007; Shareef Wright, "Redlining: Detroit Pays More," *Michigan Citizen*, July 5, 2003.

91. Associated Press, "Insurance Law Changes Are Sent to Governor; The Measure Would Permit Insurers to Charge Based on Neighborhood Criteria and Not the Broader Regional Data," *Grand Rapids (MI) Press*, February 7, 1996; "Plan to Lower Insurance Rates Gains Momentum," *Michigan Chronicle*, August 17–23, 2005.

92. Devin Fergus, "The Ghetto Tax: Auto Insurance, Postal Code Profiling, and the Hidden History of Wealth Transfer," in *Beyond Discrimination: Racial Inequality in a Postracist Era*, ed. Fredrick C. Harris and Robert Lieberman (New York: Russell Sage Foundation, 2013), 277–316.

93. Cognitive and psychological mechanisms often operate at the individual level, unlike environmental and relational mechanisms.

94. Joseph Fields et al., "Wealth Effects of Regulatory Reform: The Reaction of California's Proposition 103," *Journal of Financial Economics* 28, nos. 1–2 (1990): 233–50.

95. Douglas Heller, "The 'Quack Quake' Is Over," *Santa Monica Mirror*, July 23, 2000, http://cwd.grassroots.com/insurance/nw/?postId=1371 &pageTitle=The+%22QuackQuake%22+is+Over%2C+Now+the+Cl ean-Up+Must+Begin.

96. ValuePenguin. "Income Inequality in Chicago Extends to Auto Insurance Costs," 2015, https://www.valuepenguin.com/income-inequality-chicago-extends-how-much-residents-pay-auto-insurance.

Chapter 4

1. The upper income quintile was $62,000 in 2000 and $70,000 in 2007.
2. Nationally, between 2000 and 2012, the percentage of people in poverty increased from 12.2 percent to 15.9 percent; see US Census data at https://www.census.gov/prod/2013pubs/acsbr12-01.pdf (accessed January 27, 2017).
3. Brad Cooper, "Loan Shops Cash in on the Suburbs: More of the Businesses Are Popping up in Moderate-Income Areas," *Kansas City (MO) Star*, September 5, 2006.
4. Pew Charitable Trusts, *Payday Lending in America: Who Borrows, Where They Borrow, and Why* (Washington, DC: Pew Charitable Trusts, July 19, 2012), http://www.pewtrusts.org/en/research-and-analysis/reports/2012/07/19/who-borrows-where-they-borrow-and-why.
5. See Liz Rea, "League of Women's Voters of Nebraska Study of Payday Lending: A Progress Report," January 2011, http://lwvne.typepad.com/files/PayDay%20Lending%20Report--Rea%20011511.pdf.
6. Luis Gutierrez, *Hearing before the Subcomm. on Financial Institutions and Consumer Credit, Comm. on Financial Services*, 111th Cong., 1st sess., April 2, 2009.
7. Pew Charitable Trusts, *Payday Lending in America*.
8. Will Dobbie and Paige Skiba, "Information Asymmetries in Consumer Credit Markets: Evidence from Payday Lending," *American Economics Journal: Applied Economics* 5, no. 4 (October 2013): 256–82.
9. Michael Greenstone and Adam Looney, "The Uncomfortable Truth about American Wages," *New York Times*, October 22, 2012, http://economix.blogs.nytimes.com/2012/10/22/the-uncomfortable-truth-about-american-wages/?_r=0.
10. Edward Luce, "The Crisis of Middle-Class America," *Financial Times*, July 30, 2010, http://www.ft.com/cms/s/2/1a8a5cb2-9ab2-11df-87e6-00144feab49a.html#axzz19Xza5Slj.
11. Greenstone and Looney, "Uncomfortable Truth."
12. Pew Charitable Trusts, *Renewing the American Dream, Economic Mobility Project: A Road Map to Enhancing Economic Mobility* (Washington, DC: Pew Charitable Trusts, November 6, 2009), 3, http://www.pewtrusts.org/en/research-and-analysis/reports/2009/11/06/renewing-the-american-dream-a-road-map-to-enhancing-economic-mobility-in-america.
13. Based on a study of 736,369 individuals who applied online between June 10 and July 11, 2010. The yearly salary of these applicants was $41,753, and nearly 50 percent were homeowners. "Payday Loan Industry Report: 2010 Statistical Analysis of Pros and Cons," PersonalMoneyStore.com, September

2010, 5, http://personalmoneystore.com/wp-content/uploads/2010/09/2010PaydayIndustryReport.pdf.

14. "There are some low-income customers, but they're disproportionately middle income," stated Dr. Gregory Elliehausen of Georgetown's Credit Research Center, coauthor of an industry-commissioned study. According to Elliehausen, 75 percent have either a high school diploma or some college education. See also Linda A. Moore, "Study Finds Many in Middle Class Tap Payday Loans," *Commercial Appeal* (Memphis), May 25, 2001; US Newswire, "Claremont McKenna Professor Responds to Federal Agency's Payday Lending Study," April 13, 2005.

15. Robert H. Frank, *Success and Luck: Good Fortune and the Myth of Meritocracy* (Princeton, NJ: University Press, 2016), 53–54.

16. "Community Financial Services Association; News Flash: Payday Lending Industry Apparently Targets Everyone," *Business Week*, February 25, 2008.

17. California Department of Corporations, *Report to the Governor and Legislature, California Deferred Deposit Transaction Law*, December 2007, http://www.corp.ca.gov/pub/pdf/CDDTL07_Report.pdf; see also Department of Corporations, Payday Loan Study, 2007 (updated June 2008), http://www.dbo.ca.gov/Licensees/Payday_Lenders/Archives/pdfs/PDLStudy07.pdf.

18. Pew Charitable Trusts, *Payday Lending in America*.

19. Peter Stone, "Working Americans Have Bigger Problems than Payday Loans," Personal Money Store.com/money (blog), October 28, 2010; "Payday Loan Industry Report." The impact of wage stagnation on paydays is also acknowledged by business journalists like Peter Stone.

20. Income stagnation was listed as a chief factor in the growth of paydays in Canada as well, according to a study funded and published by Canada's Office of the Superintendent of Bankruptcy. See Ruth Berry and Karen Duncan, "The Importance of Payday Loans in Canadian Consumer Insolvency," October 31, 2007.

21. IBISWorld, "Check Cashing and Payday Loan Services," Industry Report OD5408, February 2014, 26.

22. Ibid., 18.

23. Ibid., 29.

24. Ibid.

25. David Luttrell, Harvey Rosenblum, and Jackson Thies, "Staff Papers: Understanding the Risks Inherent in Shadow Banking—A Primer and Practical Lessons Learned," Federal Reserve Bank of Dallas, no. 18, November 2012, 5; "From Out of the Shadows: Regulation for the Non-Banking Financial Sector," Salzburg Global Seminars, Salzburg, Austria, August 19–22, 2013; Zoltan Pozsar, Tobias Adrian, Adam Ashcraft, and Hayley Boesky, "Staff Reports: Shadow Banking," Federal Reserve Bank of New York, Staff Report No. 458, July 2010, 8–20; GPO Financial Crisis Inquiry Commission, "Financial Crisis Inquiry Report: Final Report

of National Commission on the Causes of the Financial and Economic Crisis in the United States," February 25, 2011.

26. Luttrell, Rosenblum, and Thies, "Understanding the Risks," 10; "From Out of the Shadows."

27. Bob Corker, " 'Wall St. Bailout' Is Really for Main St," *Tennessean*, September 27, 2008, http://www.tennessean.com/apps/pbcs.dll/article?AID=/20080927/NEWS02/809270380/1006/NEWS01.

28. Adam Schneider, "Growth and Evolution of the U.S. Shadow Banking System," Deloitte Center for Financial Services, April 2013, 3–4, http://richmondfed.org/conferences_and_events/banking/2013/pdf/cms_2013_deloitte.pdf.

29. Ibid.

30. Federal Reserve Bank of New York, "The Discount Window," July 2015, http://www.newyorkfed.org/aboutthefed/fedpoint/fed18.html.

31. While "shadow banking" is a common industry term, some bristle at its negative connotations or feel that it understates the significance of the sector. The adjective "shadow" minimizes shadow banking's actual role and impact on the real economy, according to the New York Federal Reserve. A term often preferred is "parallel banking," which suggests both greater transparency and systemic legitimacy. See Zoltan Pozsar, Tobias Adrian, Adam Ashcraft, Hayley Boesky, "Shadow Banking," Federal Reserve Bank of New York Staff Reports, Staff Report No. 458, July 2010, revised February 2012, https://www.newyorkfed.org/medialibrary/media/research/staff_reports/sr458.pdf.

32. Luttrell, Rosenblum, and Thies, "Understanding the Risks," 6–8; "From Out of the Shadows." See also GPO Financial Crisis Inquiry Commission, "Financial Crisis Inquiry Report."

33. GPO Financial Crisis Inquiry Commission, "Financial Crisis Inquiry Report," xviii.

34. Schneider, "Growth and Evolution," 5.

35. Payday lending is a sometimes invisible sector of the shadow banking system, largely because shadow banks are often large-scale institutional actors.

36. Albert Erisman and David Gautschi, *The Purpose of Business: Contemporary Perspectives from Different Walks of Life* (New York: Springer, 2015), 188.

37. Rick Jurgens, "Big Banks Help Payday Lenders Offer Quick Cash at Steep Prices," *SF Public Press*, December 15, 2011, http://sfpublicpress.org/news/2011-12/big-banks-help-payday-lenders-offer-quick-cash-at-steep-prices.

38. Ronald J. Mann and Jim Hawkins, "Just Until Payday," *UCLA Law Review* 54, no. 4 (April 2007), https://law.utexas.edu/wp-content/uploads/sites/25/hawkins_just_until_payday.pdf.

39. Gary Rivlin, interviewed on NPR's *Fresh Air*, June 2010. In the same interview, Rivlin, a business journalist, commented on the role of wage

stagnation in creating the payday market: "To me, the real reason payday has grown like it has is more of an economic reason than a geographic reason. There's been stagnating wages among the lowest 40 percent [of wage earners] in this country, and so they're not earning any more real dollars. At the same time, rent is going up, health care is going up [and] other expenses are going up, and it just becomes harder and harder and harder for these people who are making $20,000 [or] $25,000 [or] $30,000 a year to make ends meet. And the pay lenders are really convenient. Between going home from work and going shopping, you can stop at one of these stores and get instant cash in five minutes." Interview with Gary Rivlin, "Turning Poverty into A Multibillion-Dollar Industry," *Fresh Air*, June 7, 2010, http://www.npr.org/templates/story/story.php?storyId=127236038 (Accessed October 21, 2017).

40.   "How Paydays Became Big Business," *MSN Money*, June 3, 2010, http://articles.moneycentral.msn.com/Banking/BetterBanking/how-payday-loans-became-big-business.aspx?page=3.

41.   States with the highest general usury limits were New Jersey (30 percent), Florida (25 percent), Washington, DC (>24 percent), Maryland (24 percent), Tennessee (24 percent), and Rhode Island (21 percent). The two states without general usury limits for consumers were Delaware and South Dakota. See http://www.lectlaw.com/files/ban02.htm (accessed January 27, 2017).

42.   "How Paydays Became Big Business"; "Ace Cash Forewarns of Lowered Earnings in Fiscal Fourth Quarter," *Wall Street Journal*, June 12, 2000.

43.   Jonathan Weil, "Ace Cash's Payday Loan Venture Could Be Catalyst for Stock Growth," *Wall Street Journal*, September 29, 1999.

44.   Ibid.

45.   Stuart I. Greenbaum, Anjan V. Thakor, and Arnoud Boot, *Contemporary Financial Intermediation*, 3d ed. (Cambridge, MA: Academic Press, 2015), 50.

46.   "Payday Loan Stores Accused of Preying on America's Poor," *Financial Times*, February 23, 2000, http://find.galegroup.com.proxy.lib.ohio-state.edu/ftha/infomark.do?&source=gale&prodId=FTHA&userGroupName=colu44332&tabID=T003&docPage=article&docId=HS2304720685&type=multipage&contentSet=LTO&version=1.0.

47.   Office of Thrift Supervision (OTS) and Office of the Comptroller of the Currency (OCC), "Agencies Urge Banks and Thrifts to Evaluate Risks with Vendors Engaged in Practices Viewed as Abusive to Consumers," November 27, 2000, http://www.occ.gov/static/news-issuances/memos-advisory-letters/2000/advisory-letter-2000-11.pdf.

48.   People of New York v. County Bank of Rehoboth Beach, Delaware, Cashnet, Inc., and TC Services Corporation, d/b/a Telecash, complaint filed in the Supreme Court, County of Albany, September 23, 2003, at 4.

49. Ibid.; see also Consumer Federation of America, "Unsafe and Unsound: Payday Lenders Hide Behind FDIC Bank Charters to Peddle Usury," March 2004, http://www.consumerfed.org/pdfs/pdlrentabankreport.pdf.

50. OTS and OCC, "Agencies Urge Banks and Thrifts."

51. *American Banker*, March 21, 2001, 7.

52. Stephens Inc., "Update on the Payday Loan Industry: Observations on Recent Industry Developments," September 26, 2003, 15.

53. For federal regulators, safety and soundness generally entails an examination asking such questions as: Is a bank in compliance with banking laws and regulations? What level of risk is involved in a bank's transactions and activities? And how much risk or stress might the bank's transactions and activities pose to the overall health of the banking system?

54. "Seidman Reluctantly Resigns from Regulatory Post," *National Mortgage News* 25, no. 40 (July 9, 2001).

55. Ellen Seidman to George W. Bush, July 3, 2001, https://www.occ.gov/static/news-issuances/ots/press-releases/ots-pr-2001-43a.pdf.

56. See Indiana secretary of state Todd Rokita, "Protect Your Pocket Series—Understanding the Pit Falls of Payday Lending," Securities Division, Indiana State Government, Center for Responsible Lending Issue Briefing, http://www.americanprogress.org/issues/2009/04/caution_payday_loans.html. See also the comments of Rae-Ann Miller, special advisor on consumer issues in the FDIC's research division, in "Special Edition: 51 Ways to Save Hundreds on Loans and Credit Cards," *FDIC Consumer News*, Summer 2007; Kim Christensen, "Payday Loans Mushroom among Middle Class," *Los Angeles Times*, January 11, 2009. Recent findings have also called into question the effectiveness of banning rollovers: "When rollovers are banned, industry simply replaces them with back-to-back loan flips that continue to ensnare people in long-term debt carrying an annual percentage rate of 400 percent," said Leslie Parrish, senior researcher at the Center for Responsible Lending. "Payday lenders know this and that's why they support rollover bans."

57. Rokita, "Protect Your Pocket Series."

58. Uriah King, Leslie Parrish, and Ozlem Tanik, "Payday Lending Sinks Borrowers in Debt with $4.2 Billion in Predatory Fees Every Year," Center for Responsible Lending, November 30, 2006, http://www.responsiblelending.org/payday-lending/research-analysis/rr012-Financial_Quicksand-1106.pdf.

59. Julie L. Williams and Emory W. Rushton, OCC Advisory Letter, to Banks, Department and Division Heads, and Examining Personnel, November 27, 2000, https://www.occ.gov/static/news-issuances/memos-advisory-letters/2000/advisory-letter-2000-11.pdf.

60. Office of Public Affairs, Treasury Deputy Assistant Secretary Michael S. Barr, Remarks to the National Association of Attorneys General, Predatory Lending Summit, Portland, ME, November 15, 2000.

61. Office of the Comptroller of the Currency and Office of Thrift Supervision, "Agencies Urge Banks and Thrifts to Evaluate Risks with Vendors Engaged in Practices Viewed as Abusive to Consumers," November 27, 2000, NR 2000-88, http://www.occ.gov/static/news-issuances/news-releases/2000/nr-ia-2000-88.pdf.

62. For OCC and OTS statistics, see Pauline Smale, "Payday Loans: Federal Regulatory Initiatives," Congressional Research Service Report to Congress, Order Code RS21728, updated May 23, 2005, 5; see also Department of Treasury, OCC, "Bank Activities and Operations; Real Estate Lending and Appraisals," January 13, 2004, Docket No. 04-04, in *Federal Register* 69, no. 8, Rules and Regulations.

63. Consumer Federation of America, "Unsafe and Unsound: Payday Lenders Hide Behind FDIC Bank Charters to Peddle Usury," March 2004, http://www.consumerfed.org/pdfs/pdlrentabankreport.pdf.

64. Ibid.

65. Pete Garcia, Chicanos Por La Causa, to Donald E. Powell, FDIC Chairman, "FDIC: Stop Insuring Payday Loan Banks," May 20, 2003, http://www.consumerfed.org/pdfs/fdicrepublicbank052003.pdf.

66. FDIC, "To Whom It May Concern," November 18, 2003, http://www.woodstockinst.org/sites/default/files/documents/republicB%26T_nov2003_payday.pdf.

67. US House of Representatives, *Oversight of the Federal Deposit Insurance Corporation Hearing Before the Subcommittee on Oversight and Investigations of the Committee on Financial Services*, 108th Cong., 1st sess., March 4, 2004, 15.

68. Though she did not offer guidelines for banning the practice, Powell's immediate predecessor, Donna Tanoue, was circumspect about third-party deals, as evidenced by her June 13, 2000, speech to the annual greenlining economic development summit: "I do not believe the Congress contemplated that banks would be able to use this principle [exportation of interest rates] to take advantage of consumers. The practice of renting a charter merely to collect a fee to allow a high-cost payday lender to collect a fee to allow a high-cost payday lender to circumvent state law is inappropriate"; Consumer Federation of America and US PIRG, "Rent-A-Bank Payday Lending, 2001: Payday Lender Survey and Report," November 2001.

69. Eric Dash, "Deposit Plan Will Cost Banks More," *New York Times*, October 2, 2008.

70. Ibid.

71. Ron Paul was the rare, if not only, Republican who addressed concerns about the impact of "rampant deregulation" and paydays on the financial system, especially the safety and soundness of banks. The Federal Reserve Bank had no banks that contracted with paydays; see US House of Representatives, *Oversight of the Federal Deposit*, 10.

72. Ibid.

73. Ibid., 10.
74. Pauline Smale, "CRS Report for Congress," CRS Web, Library of Congress, updated May 23, 2005.
75. Ibid.
76. US Senate Committee on Banking, Housing, & Urban Affairs, http://www.banking.senate.gov/public/index.cfm?FuseAction=Files .View&FileStore_id=2bc1cb46-5dbb-405d-9b1b-76dc0fa9c8c3.
77. Smale, "CRS Report for Congress."
78. Passed originally in 1977 and amended several times since, the Community Reinvestment Act was designed to reduce discriminatory credit practices and require the appropriate federal financial supervisory agency to encourage banks to help meet the needs of creditworthy borrowers in the neighborhoods in which their local branches operated.
79. A notable exception occurred in 2000, "when OTS gave Crusader Bank a 'needs to improve' CRA rating . . . in part because of its payday lending operations; Crusader abandoned its payday lending relationship [shortly thereafter]." See http://archives.financialservices.house.gov/hearing110/ barr021308.pdf.
80. Pearl Chin, "Payday Loans: The Case for Federal Intervention," *University of Illinois Law Review* 4, no. 3 (January 3, 2004): 723–54.
81. Smale, "CRS Report for Congress."
82. Connor and Skomarovsky, "Predators' Creditors"; Adam Rust, "Connecting the Dots: How Wall Street Brings Fringe Lending to Main Street," Reinvestment Partners (2015), https://www.reinvestmentpartners. org/wp-content/uploads/2015/10/Report_Connecting_the_Dots_How_ Wall_Street_Brings_Fringe_Lending_to_Main_Street.pdf; Minnesotans for a Fair Economy, "Predatory Payday Lending in Minnesota: How U.S. Bank and Wells Fargo Hurt Consumers with 'Fast Cash' Loans," n.d., http://stmedia.startribune.com/documents/payday.pdf.
83. Bank of America and Wells Fargo, "Showdown in America," November 18, 2010, http://www.showdowninchicago.org/; Connor and Skomarovsky, "Predators' Creditors."
84. Ibid.
85. Ibid.
86. Connor and Skomarovsky, "Predators' Creditors."
87. Ibid.; Nathaniel Popper, "Big Banks Play Key Role in Financing Payday Lenders," *Los Angeles Times*, September 15, 2010.
88. CompuCredit founders Frank and David Hanna have donated heavily to Republican and Christian conservative causes. "Credit Executive Is SCLC Presidential Award Winner," *Cleveland Call & Post*, February 20–26, 2008; Stephanie Mencimer, "Civil Rights Groups Defending Predatory Lenders: Priceless," *Mother Jones*, July 31, 2008.
89. Rush, acknowledging that payday lenders have a role to play in his Chicago congressional district, did not call for their abolition—only

minimum national standards, such as a 36 percent interest rate cap and the prohibition of rollover loans, which tended to drive consumers deeper into debt and, according to several studies, contributed to the spike in bankruptcies.

90. Philip Shenon, "How Bill in Senate Would Add Hurdles to Erasing of Debt," *New York Times*, March 14, 2001, http://www.nytimes.com/2001/03/14/us/how-bill-in-senate-would-add-hurdles-to-erasing-of-debt.html.

91. Alan P. Murray, "Debt and 'the Consumer,' " *Business Economics*, April 1997.

92. Ibid.; Michelle Singletary, "Drawing a Line Between 'Need' and 'Want,' " *Washington Post*, February 25, 2001.

93. "New Study Finds Some Bankrupts Could Repay Debts," *Consumer Trends*, January 1999.

94. Quoted in Julie Kosterlitz, "Over the Edge," *National Journal* 29 (1997): 870, 871.

95. Marilyn Geewax, "Lax Attitudes at Root of Consumer Debt," *Atlanta Journal Constitution*, September 22, 1996.

96. Bankruptcy Reform Act of 2000, H.R. 833, 106th Cong., 1990–2000, Sec. 219.

97. "States Urged to Curb 'Payday' Loan Gouging: Short-Term Borrowers Pay Rates Averaging Nearly 500%, Consumer Groups Say," *Los Angeles Times*, February 2, 2000.

98. Wellstone's amendment looked to remedy the flaws in the lender-friendly bill by holding the most abusive lenders accountable. The amendment attempted to do so, for example, by preventing high-cost lenders (like paydays, car title companies, and other practitioners engaged in credit extension over 100 percent per annum) from filing claims of bankruptcy in federal court.

99. "States Urged to Curb 'Payday' Loan Gouging"; "Senate Close to Passage of Bankruptcy-Overhaul Bill," *Deseret News*, March 15, 2001, http://www.deseretnews.com/article/831258/Senate-close-to-passage-of-bankruptcy-overhaul-bill.html?pg=all.

100. Jeanne Sahadi, "The New Bankruptcy Law and You," CNNMoney.com, October 17, 2005, http://money.cnn.com/2005/10/17/pf/debt/bankruptcy_law/ (accessed June 26, 2017).

101. Paige Marta Skiba and Jeremy Tobacman, "Do Payday Loans Cause Bankruptcy?," Vanderbilt Law and Economics Research Paper No. 11-13, November 9, 2009, http://ssrn.com/abstract=1266215 or http://dx.doi.org/10.2139/ssrn.1266215.

102. Philip Shenon, "Senate Panel Approves Bill for Overhauling Bankruptcy Laws," *New York Times*, March 1, 2001.

103. Leslie Eaton, "Bankruptcy, the American Morality Tale," *New York Times*, March 13, 2005.

104. Bankruptcy Reform Act of 1999, *Congressional Record* S11088–S11094 (September 21, 1999), https://www.gpo.gov/fdsys/pkg/CREC-1999-09-21/html/CREC-1999-09-21-pt1-PgS11088.htm.

105. Shenon, "How Bill in Senate."

106. Ibid.

107. *Congressional Record* 21998 (September 21, 1999).

108. Ibid.

109. Since the nineteenth century, institutions have increasingly been understood legally and politically to be persons, but these "metaphysical" persons are often not held to the same moral standard as "human" persons. The most commonly cited example of the individual or moral rights of corporations is Santa Clara County v. Southern Pacific Railroad, 1886. The Supreme Court decision "effectively recognized corporations as persons and extend[ed] constitutional protections to corporations," though the actual assertion of the personhood rights (in the form of the equal protection clause of the Fourteenth Amendment) of corporations appears only in the introductory summary of the court's formal ruling. Robert W. Kolb, "Corporate Rights and Personhood," *Encyclopedia of Business Ethics and Society* 1 (2008): 500–501. For a discussion of the false equivalence between metaphysical and human persons, see Lynn Mie Itagaki, "United States, Inc.: *Citizens United* and the Shareholder Citizen," *Kalfou: A Journal of Comparative and Relational Ethnic Studies* 1, no. 2 (Fall 2014): 116–18.

110. Ozlem Tanik, "Payday Lenders Target the Military: Evidence Lives in Industry's Own Data," Center for Responsible Lending Issue Paper No. 1, September 29, 2005.

111. US Department of Defense, "Report on Predatory Lending Practices Directed at Members of the Armed Forces and Their Dependents," August 9, 2006, esp. 10–11, http://www.defense.gov/pubs/pdfs/report_to_congress_final.pdf; http://www.usa4militaryfamilies.dod.mil/dav/lsn/LSN/BINARY_RESOURCE/BINARY_CONTENT/2141721.pdf.

112. National Consumer Law Center, "In Harm's Way – At Home: Consumer Scams and the Direct Targeting of American's Military and Veterans," May 2003, 8.

113. Consumers Union Report, "Payday Lenders Burden Working Families and the U.S. Armed Forces," July 2003.

114. Ibid.

115. US Department of Defense, "Report on Predatory Lending."

116. "A Closer Look (Cycle of Debt)," *ABC Evening News,* August 22, 2006; G.V. 'Sonny' Montgomery National Defense Authorization Act for Fiscal Year 2007, page S6406, https://www.gpo.gov/fdsys/pkg/CREC-2006-06-22/html/CREC-2006-06-22-pt1-PgS6405.htm.

117. Joyce Raezer, "Interview," National Military Family Association, December 8, 2009.

118. Bankruptcy Abuse Prevention and Consumer Protection Act of 2005, *Congressional Record* –Senate (March 1, 2005), S1834–S1857, https://www .congress.gov/crec/2005/03/01/CREC-2005-03-01-pt1-PgS1834.pdf.

119. Derek B. Stewart, General Accounting Office, to Senator Richard J. Durbin, February 27, 2004, http://www.gao.gov/new.items/d04465r .pdf (accessed August 14, 2016).

120. "Politics and the Economy: Former Rep. Watts Opens Consulting Firm," *New York Times*, January 8, 2003.

121. "Payday Lending a Big-Growth Business, *Kiplinger Letter* 82, no. 3 (January 21, 2005); Erick Eckholm, " 'Seductively Easy' Payday Loans Often Snowball," *New York Times,* December 23, 2005, http://www .nytimes.com/2006/12/23/us/23payday.html; testimony of Jean Ann Fox, director of Consumer Protection Consumer Federation of America, "Financial Services Issues: A Consumer's Perspective," House Committee on Finance, Subcommittee on Financial Institutions and Consumer Credit, September 15, 2004, http://archives.financialservices.house .gov/media/pdf/091504jf.pdf; US Department of Defense, "Report on Predatory Lending Practices," 11; Darrin Andersen, "Viewpoint: 'Quicksand' and Demand,"*American Banker*, December 8, 2006, 8, http://proxy.mul.missouri.edu/login?url=https://search.proquest.com/ docview/249845076?accountid=14576?accountid=14576.

122. "FDIC Understates Bank Role in Payday," *American Banker*, June 3, 2005; see also *60 Minutes* segment on payday lending, May 23, 2005.

123. "CREW Releases Payday Lenders Pay Up—the First Ever Study on the Payday Loan Industry's Efforts to Gain Influence in Washington," *Business Wire*, April 23, 2009, http://www.businesswire.com/news/home/ 20090423006074/en/CREW-Releases-Payday-Lenders-Pay-%E2%80%93- Study. For a more recent report, see Citizens for Responsibility and Ethics in Washington, "2011 Update Payday Lenders Pay More," http://www .consumerfed.org/pdfs/PDL-CREW-Payday-Lenders-Report-2011.pdf.

124. Sewell Chan, "Consumer Bill Gives Exemption on Payday Loans," *New York Times*, March 9, 2010, http://www.nytimes.com/2010/03/10/ business/10regulate.html.

125. Corker, " 'Wall St. Bailout.' "

126. Chan, "Consumer Bill Gives Exemption." To see how Corker and the payday loan industry effectively blocked the industry's regulation at this juncture, see Robert Kaiser, *Act of Congress: How America's Essential Institution Works, and How It Doesn't* (New York: Vintage, 2013), 257–59.

127. Not surprisingly, payday CEO Allan Jones and friends have been the most reliable financial backers of Corker, giving the Tennessee senator $31,000 since 2001. Moreover, Corker had raised more money than any other Republican committee member.

128. Elizabeth K. MacLean, "Joseph E. Davies: The Wisconsin Idea and the Origins of the Federal Trade Commission," *Journal of the Gilded Age and*

Progressive Era 6 (July 2007): 248–84, esp. 257, 272, 281; G. Cullom Davis, "The Transformation of the Federal Trade Commission, 1914–1929," *Mississippi Valley Historical Review* 49 (December 1962): 437–55, esp. 451.

129. James C. Cooper, ed., *The Regulatory Revolution at the FTC: A Thirty Year Perspective on Competition and Consumer Protection* (New York: Oxford University Press, 2013); Gary T. Ford and John E. Calfee, "Recent Developments in FTC Policy on Deception," *Journal of Marketing* 50, no. 3 (1986): 82–103; W. MacLeod and R. Rogowsky, "Consumer Protection at the FTC during the Reagan Administration," in *Regulation and the Reagan Era: Politics, Bureaucracy and the Public Interest*, ed. R. E. Meiners and B. Yandle (New York: Holmes and Meier, 1989); Marc Davis, "History of the U.S. Federal Trade Commission," http://www.investopedia.com/articles/financial-theory/10/the-us-federal-trade-commission.asp (accessed March 19, 2016).

130. Federal Trade Commission, Bureau of Consumer Protection, "FTC Consumer Alert: Payday Loans Equal Costly Cash: Consumers Urged to Consider Alternatives," March 2008. Even when the FTC did go after the industry, as in the case against three internet payday ads in early 2008, aggrieved consumers received no recompense and the industry paid no penalty, agreeing only to disclose the APRs, which, among these three lenders, ranged between 460 and 782 percent; see http://www.ftc.gov/opa/2008/02/amercash.shtm. For the FTC lecture on self-help, see http://www.ftc.gov/bcp/edu/pubs/consumer/credit/cre19.shtm.

131. See Jean Ann Fox testimony before the US House Committee on Finance, April 2, 2009, quoting the Federal Reserve Bank.

132. *Congressional Record*, March 9, 2004, 3744.

133. Daniel Akaka, Support of the Bingaman Amendment to S. Con. Res. 18, March 14, 2005, http://akaka.senate.gov/public/index.cfm?FuseAction=speeches.home&month=3&year=2005&release_id=411.

134. National Council on Economic Education, "What American Teens & Adults Know about Economics," April 26, 2005, http://www.councilforeconed.org/cel/WhatAmericansKnowAboutEconomics_042605-3.pdf.

135. Ibid.

136. "Undergraduate Students and Credit Cards in 2004: An Analysis of Usage Rates and Trends," nelliemae.com.

137. National Council on Economic Education, "What American Teens and Adults."

138. Council for Economic Education, "CEL Quiz: About the CEL Quiz," http://www.councilforeconed.org/cel/ (accessed October 26, 2017).

139. U.S. Department of Education, "Fiscal Year 2007 Budget Summary," February 6, 2006, http://www.ed.gov/about/overview/budget/budget07/summary/edlite-section3.html.

140. Nikita Stewart, "DC Payday Lenders Unbowed Ahead of Vote," *Washington Post*, September 18, 2007.

141. White House, "President Bush Announces President's Advisory Council on Financial Literacy," January 22, 2008, http://georgewbush-whitehouse .archives.gov/news/releases/2008/01/20080122-7.html.

142. US Treasury Department, "President's Advisory Council on Financial Literacy 2008: Annual Report to the President," https://www.treasury .gov/about/organizational-structure/offices/Domestic-Finance/Documents/ exec_sum.pdf.

143. Ibid.

144. Statement of Sen. Blanche Lincoln of Arkansas, *Hearing before the Committee on Banking, Housing, and Urban Affairs*, 108th Cong., 2d sess., June 22, 2004. Arkansas is also instructive because it augurs the road not taken. It was in Arkansas in the early 1980s that an obscure but erudite southern governor turned to an even more unknown South Asian sociologist for advice on providing access to capital and credit by making short-term loans to the state's working poor. While Bill Clinton and Muhammad Yunus would reach the highest levels of success in their respective fields, as president and Nobel Prize laureate, respectively, they were a combined failure in Arkansas, as the microlending program they launched jointly failed to expand as they had hoped. The soon-forgotten alternative of microlending was replaced by the familiar payday industry, which squeezed out Clinton and Yunus's experiment. Amanda Fairbanks, "Lending Plan Won Prize, But Will It Work Here?," *New York Times*, April 1, 2008.

145. For more on the interplay between religious or cultural conservatives and payday lending, see Steve Graves and Christopher Lewis Peterson, "Usury Law and the Christian Right: Faith Based Political Power and the Geography of the American Payday Loan Regulation," *Catholic University Law Review* 57 (2008): 637–700.

146. See Paul Barton, "Lobbyists Pile It on for State Interests," Ark Against Abusive Payday Lending, July 5, 2006, http://stoppaydaypredatorsarkansas .org/pdfs2/06_0704_lobbyists_pile.pdf. Senator Pryor received $31,000 from 2004 to 2015, when he left the Senate, while Representative Ross received over $70,000 from 2004 to 2010, when he left the House, according to OpenSecrets.org. See "Payday Lending" in OpenSecrets.org at https://www.opensecrets.org/industries/summary.php?ind=F1420&recip detail=S&sortorder=S&mem=Y&cycle=2016.

147. Uriah King, Leslie Parrish, and Ozlem Tanik, "Financial Quicksand: Payday Lending Sinks Borrowers in Debt with $4.2 Billion in Predatory Fees Every Year," Center for Responsible Lending, November 30, 2006, http://www.responsiblelending.org/payday-lending/research-analysis/ rr012-Financial_Quicksand-1106.pdf.

148. Wesley Brown, "Report: Payday Lenders Cost State's Poor Millions," Arkansas News Bureau, March 9, 2006. See also Payday Lender Study in "Landmark Settlement," Arkansas News Bureau, March 11, 2006, http:// archives.arkansasnews.com/search/level+2+trauma+center+for+arkansas/

page/2011/02/09/arkansas-looking-to-snap-slide-in-starkville/page/1485/
void(0);/*1253280053599*/page/3385/.

149. "Governor's Appointments," *Arkansas Democrat-Gazette*, March
6, 2004, http://infoweb.newsbank.com/resources/doc/nb/news/
13C9B93EB2173248?p=AWNB; "State Should Be Set Free from Payday
Lenders," *Arkansas Business Leader*, March 20, 2006, http://www
.arkansasbusiness.com/article/48980/state-should-be-set-free-from-
payday-lenders-editorial.

150. The Ross Amendment did not exempt payday lenders from the state
constitutional ban. That said, it was likely if not inevitable that, had
the amendment passed, the payday lending industry would ultimately
have been protected by this proposed federal legislation. Gwen Moritz,
"More Lenders Look to Congress for Relief from Usury Limit," *Arkansas
Business*, July 15, 2002, http://www.arkansasbusiness.com/print/article/
58204.

151. Garrick Feldman, "How Did We Go from 10 Percent to 3,000 Percent
on Loans?," TheLeader.com, March 22, 2006, http://www.arkansasleader
.com/2006/03/from-publisher-how-did-we-go-from-10.html.

152. Kathy Kiely, "Health and Behavior," *USA Today*, July 11, 2004, https://
usatoday30.usatoday.com/news/health/2004-07-11-arkansas-governor_
x.htm.

153. See US Congress, "Providing for Consideration of S. 256, Bankruptcy
Abuse Prevention and Consumer Protection Act of 2005," April 14, 2005,
https://www.congress.gov/bill/109th-congress/senate-bill/256.

154. "Sad Sight in Front of Check Cashers," *Arkansas Leader*, April 5, 2006.

155. By "escaped oversight" I mean they were neither licensed nor regulated.

156. Brown, "Payday Lenders Cost State's Poor."

157. "Arkansas Attorney General Targets Payday Lenders," *Wall Street Journal*,
March 19, 2008; Trevor Anderson, "Advance America Reports Lower
Profits in '08," *Spartanburg (SC) Herald-Journal*, February 20, 2009.

158. Consumer Financial Protection Bureau, "Payday Loans and Deposit
Advance Products: A White Paper of Initial Data Findings," April 24,
2013, 28, http://files.consumerfinance.gov/f/201304_cfpb_payday-dap-
whitepaper.pdf.

159. Rebecca Borne and Peter Smith, "Bank Payday Lending: The State of
Lending in America and Its Impact on US. Households," Center for
Responsible Lending, September 2013, 4, http://files.consumerfinance
.gov/f/201304_cfpb_payday-dap-whitepaper.pdf.

160. Consumer Financial Protection Bureau, "Payday Loans."

161. Ibid.

162. Rebecca Borne, Joshua Frank, Peter Smith, and Ellen Schloemer, "Big
Bank Payday Loans: High-Interest Loans Through Checking Accounts
Keep Customers in Long-Term Debt," Center for Responsible Lending,
July 2011.

163. Zeke Faux, "Banks Stop Selling Account Data to Payday Lenders," *Bloomberg News*, January 21, 2015.

164. Kim Christensen, "A Middle-Class Move to Payday Lenders Critics Call the Short-Term Loans Costly Traps," *Los Angeles Times*, December 24, 2008.

165. George Oamek, "Payday Lending's Economic Impact on the Omaha Metro-Area Financial Stability Partnership," Honey Creek Resources, Inc. Honey Creek, Iowa, January 2009. In Author's Possession.

166. Stephen Hoopes, "Fast Cash: Consumers' Recessionary Struggles Proved Beneficial to Industry Services" IBISWorld Industry Report OD5408, February 2014: 8, 14; Stephen Hoopes, "Check Cashing and Payday Loan Services," IBISWorld Industry Report OD5408, February 2014, 14. December IBISWorld 2016 report predicts that payday lending market in the US is expected to slow in growth through 2021. This slower growth will not be because of improved worker outlooks or prospects. Instead the domestic market for payday lending is expected to decline because of (a) potential/likely increase in unemployment; (b) increased competition among other short-term cash advance instruments and vendors (e.g. check cashers and online payday lenders); (c) payday lender market expansion internationally. See Kelsey Oliver, "Fast cash: Consumers' recessionary struggles proved beneficial as more people sought industry services." Check Cashing & Payday Loan Services in the US. IBISWorld Industry Report OD5408, December 2016. http://clients1.ibisworld.com/ reports/us/industry/default.aspx?entid=5408.

167. Ibid., 26.

168. Ibid., 8.

169. Ibid., 26–27.

Epilogue

1. A way of complementing the measure to make college accessible would be to keep college prices under better control by, for example, also pegging college costs to the rate of inflation or median wages and perhaps to graduation rates.

2. To complement this, a tax could be imposed on federally insured banks. Funds from this levy would be used to create a nonprofit online and bricks-and-mortar, short-term lender for those engaged in market and civil labor work. Given that the rise of payday lending reflects a structural problem of the worker and wage economy, passage of the Raise the Wage Act would increase incomes for at least 30 million workers and index this wage to increase as the median wage for US workers increases. Contrary to working assumptions, research indicates that businesses aren't harmed by minimum wage increases. For more on the Raise the Wage Act, see http://www.epi .org/action/raise-the-wage-act/. For a definition of civil labor, see Roberta Rehner Iversen, "What Do You Do? Ideas about Transforming 'Work' in

the United States," in *Social Policy and Social Justice*, ed. John L. Jackson, Jr. (Philadelphia: University of Pennsylvania Press, 2017), 87–96.

3. David Frum, *How We Got Here: The 70's: The Decade that Brought You Modern Life (For Better or Worse)* (New York: Basic Books, 2008), 350.

4. David Jacobs and Jonathan C. Dirlam, "Politics and Economic Stratification: Power Resources and Income Inequality in the United States," *American Journal of Sociology* 122, no. 2 (September 2016): 469–500.

5. See, e.g., Ken-Hou Lin and Donald Tomaskovic-Devey, "Financialization and US Income Inequality, 1970–2008," *American Journal of Sociology* 118 (2013): 473; Jacobs and Dirlam, "Politics and Economic Stratification," 290.

6. Larry Bartels, *Unequal Democracy: The Political Economy of the New Gilded Age* (Princeton, NJ: Princeton University Press, 2010), 98.

7. See "Talking Points" with Larry Bartels on Princeton University Press website, http://press.princeton.edu/releases/m2_8664.html (accessed January 29, 2017).

8. Unlike the lobbying elite, nonelite lobbyists have a smaller impact on lawmakers themselves than they do directly on voters and the electorate by getting people to the polls.

9. Sean McElwee, *Whose Voice, Whose Choice: The Distorting Influence of the Political Donor Class in Our Big Money Elections* (New York: Demos, December 8, 2006), http://www.demos.org/sites/default/files/publications/Whose%20Voice%20Whose%20Choice_2.pdf.

10. Anne E. Baker, "Getting Short-Changed? The Impact of Outside money on District Representation," *Social Science Quarterly* 97 (November 2016): 1096–1107.

11. Daniel M. Butler and David E. Brockman, "Do Politicians Racially Discriminate Against Constituents? A Field Experiment on State Legislators," *American Journal of Political Science* 55, no. 3 (2011): 463–77, http://isps.yale.edu/node/19868#.V84ihzvEHdk.

12. Bartels, *Unequal Democracy*.

13. Ibid., 285.

14. Jacob Hacker and Paul Pierson, *Winner Take All Politics* (New York: Simon and Schuster, 2010), 114.

15. http://www.opensecrets.org/lobby/.

16. Ibid.

17. Butler and Brockman, "Do Politicians Racially Discriminate?"

18. Isaac Arnsdorf, "Trump Rewards Big Donors with Jobs and Access," *Politico*, December 27, 2016, http://www.politico.com/story/2016/12/donald-trump-donors-rewards-232974.

19. Betsy DeVos, "Soft Money Is Good: 'Hard-Earned American Dollars That Big Brother Has Yet to Find a Way to Control,'" *Roll Call*, September 6, 1997.

20. Martin Gilens and Benjamin I. Page, "Testing Theories of American Politics: Elites, Interest Groups, and Average Citizens," *Perspectives on*

Politics 12, no. 3 (September 2014): 565–77, https://scholar.princeton.edu/sites/default/files/mgilens/files/gilens_and_page_2014_-testing_theories_of_american_politics.doc.pdf (accessed February 22, 2017).

21. "Talking Points" with Larry Bartels.

22. Ibid.

23. Bartels, *Unequal Democracy*, 77.

24. Thomas Frank, *What's the Matter with Kansas? How Conservatives Won the Heart of America* (New York: Henry Holt, 2004).

25. Mark Lilla, "The End of Identity Liberalism," *New York Times*, November 18, 2016, https://www.nytimes.com/2016/11/20/opinion/sunday/the-end-of-identity-liberalism.html?_r=0 (accessed January 3, 2017).

26. Bartels, *Unequal Democracy*.

27. In Michael Dawson's 1994 book *Behind the Mule*, he shows that middle-class Black voters subordinated their personal economic interests out of a sense of race-based political utility and linked fate.

28. Jennifer L. Hochschild, and Vesla Weaver, "The Skin Color Paradox and the American Racial Order," *Social Forces* 86, no. 2 (2007): 643–70, http://www.jstor.org.proxy.lib.ohio-state.edu/stable/20430757.

29. Jennifer Hochschild and Vesla Weaver, "Is the Significance of Race Declining in the Political Arena? Yes, and No," *Ethnic and Racial Studies*, 38, no. 8 (2015): 1250–57; Claudine Gray, Jennifer Hochschild, and Ariel White, "Americans' Belief in Linked Fate: A Wide Reach but Limited Impact," revision of APSA 2010 Annual Meeting Paper, June 3, 2014.

30. Gray, Hochschild, and White, "Americans' Belief in Linked Fate."

31. Gabriel R. Sanchez and Natalie Masuoka, "Brown-Utility Heuristic? The Presence and Contributing Factors of Latino Linked Fate," *Hispanic Journal of Behavioral Sciences* 32, no. 4 (October 2010): 519–31.

32. Larry Bartels and Christopher Achen, *Democracy for Realists* (Princeton, NJ: Princeton University Press, 2016).

33. Ibid., esp. chap. 8.

34. Frank, *What's the Matter with Kansas?*

35. Bartels, *Unequal Democracy*.

36. Richard Alba, "The Likely Persistence of a White Majority: How Census Bureau Statistics Have Misled Thinking about the American Future," *American Prospect*, January 11, 2016, http://prospect.org/article/likely-persistence-white-majority-0. For a counterpoint to the Alba thesis, see G. Christina Mora and Michael Rodriquez- Muñiz, "A Response to Richard Alba's 'The Likely Persistence of a White Majority,'" *New Labor Forum: A Journal of Ideas, Analysis, and Debate*, April 28, 2017, http://newlaborforum.cuny.edu/2017/04/28/a-response-to-richard-albas-the-likely-persistence-of-a-white-majority/.

37. Alba, "Likely Persistence." See also Richard Alba, "The Myth of a White Minority," *New York Times*, June 11, 2015, https://www.nytimes.com/2015/06/11/opinion/the-myth-of-a-white-minority.html.

38. According to the Pew Center, 57 percent of multiracial adults identify with or lean toward the Democratic Party, while 37 percent identify with or lean toward the Republican Party. This twenty-point gap is wider than that among adults in the general public—53 percent of whom identify with or lean toward the Democratic Party, compared with 41 percent who identify with or lean toward the GOP. See Pew Research Center, "Multiracial in America: Proud, Diverse, and Growing in Numbers," http://www.pewsocialtrends.org/files/2015/06/2015-06-11_multiracial-in-america_final-updated.pdf.

39. Ibid.

40. Heather K. Gerken, "Second-Order Diversity: An Exploration of Decentralizations Egalitarian Possibilities," Public Law Research Paper No. 591, Yale Law School, https://papers.ssrn.com/sol3/papers2.cfm?abstract_id=2868032 (accessed February 5, 2017).

41. See, e.g., Bartels, *Unequal Democracy*; and Bartels and Achen, *Democracy for Realists*.

42. Emmanuel Saez and Gabriel Zucman, "Wealth Inequality in the United States since 1913: Evidence from Capitalized Income Tax Data," *Quarterly Journal of Economics* 131, no. 2 (May 2016): 519–78, https://eml.berkeley.edu/~saez/SaezZucman2016QJE.pdf.

43. For more discussion of the equity stripping of today's middle class as well as some potential pitfalls of asset building, see Robert Hiltonsmith, *The Retirement Savings Drain: The Hidden and Excessive Costs of 401(k)s* (New York: Demos, May 29, 2012), 2, http://www.demos.org/sites/default/files/publications/TheRetirementSavingsDrain-Demos_0.pdf (accessed August 16, 2016). According to Hiltonsmith, the average 401(k) accountholder loses $155,000 in fees and loss earnings over the life of the plan.

44. Sean Wilentz, *The Age of Reagan: A History, 1974–2008* (New York: HarperCollins, 2009), 194–200; for a more critical view of deregulation in nonfinancial industries, see, e.g., Phillip Longman and Lina Khan, "Terminal Sickness," *Washington Monthly*, March–April 2012; and Leah Platt, "Predatory Pricing," *American Prospect*, December 19, 2001.

45. Ron J. Feldman and Jason Schmidt, "Noninterest Income: A Potential for Profits, Risk Reduction and Some Exaggerated Claims," *Fedagazette*, October 1999, https://www.minneapolisfed.org/publications/fedgazette/noninterest-income-a-potential-for-profits-risk-reduction-and-some-exaggerated-claims; Robert DeYoung and Tara Rice, "How Do Banks Make Money? The Fallacies of Fee Income," *Economic Perspectives* 28, no. 4 (November 2004): 34–51.

46. Elizabeth Warren, "Middle Class on the Precipice," *Harvard Magazine*, January/February 2006, https://harvardmagazine.com/2006/01/the-middle-class-on-the-html.

47. Consumer Financial Protection Bureau, "CFPB Takes Action," October 9, 2014.

48. National Economic Council, "The Competition Initiative and Hidden Fees," December 2016, https://obamawhitehouse.archives.gov/sites/whitehouse.gov/files/documents/hiddenfeesreport_12282016.pdf.

49. Charlie Anderson, "White House Blog: Follow the Fees," https://obamawhitehouse.archives.gov/blog/2016/12/28/follow-fees.

INDEX